Women in the Scottish Wars of Independence 1296–1357

For the women of Scottish history. May we hear your voices.

Women in the Scottish Wars of Independence 1296–1357

Beth Reid

AN IMPRINT OF PEN & SWORD BOOKS LTD.
YORKSHIRE – PHILADELPHIA

First published in Great Britain in 2025 by
PEN AND SWORD HISTORY
An imprint of
Pen & Sword Books Ltd
Yorkshire – Philadelphia

ISBN 978 1 39904 765 4

A CIP catalogue record for this book is available from the British Library.

Typeset in Times New Roman 11.5/14.5 by
SJmagic DESIGN SERVICES, India.
Printed and bound in the UK by CPI Group (UK) Ltd, Croydon, CR0 4YY.

The Publisher's authorised representative in the EU for product safety is
Authorised Rep Compliance Ltd., Ground Floor, 71 Lower Baggot Street,
Dublin D02 P593, Ireland.
www.arccompliance.com

For a complete list of Pen & Sword titles please contact:
PEN & SWORD BOOKS LIMITED
George House, Units 12 & 13, Beevor Street, Off Pontefract Road,
Barnsley, South Yorkshire, S71 1HN, England
E-mail: enquiries@pen-and-sword.co.uk
Website: www.pen-and-sword.co.uk

or

PEN AND SWORD BOOKS
1950 Lawrence Rd, Havertown, PA 19083, USA
E-mail: uspen-and-sword@casematepublishers.com
Website: www.penandswordbooks.com

Contents

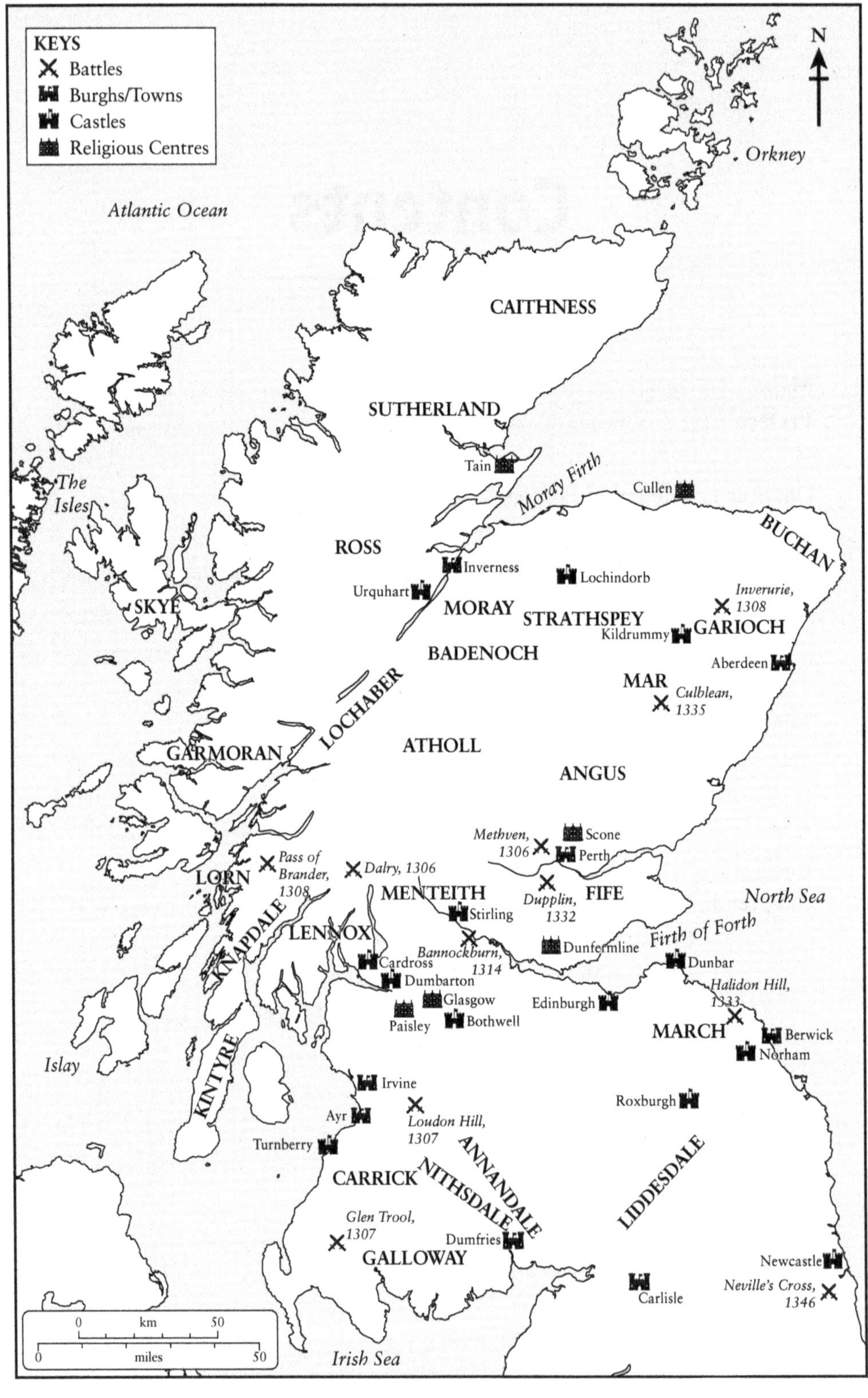
KEYS
Battles
Burghs/Towns
Castles
Religious Centres
N
Orkney
Atlantic Ocean
CAITHNESS
SUTHERLAND
Tain
Moray Firth
Cullen
The Isles
BUCHAN
ROSS
Inverness
Lochindorb
Urquhart
MORAY
STRATHSPEY
Inverurie, 1308
SKYE
Kildrummy
GARIOCH
BADENOCH
Aberdeen
LOCHABER
MAR
Culblean, 1335
GARMORAN
ATHOLL
ANGUS
Methven, 1306
Scone
Perth
Pass of Brander, 1308
Dalry, 1306
LORN
MENTEITH
Dupplin, 1332
FIFE
North Sea
Stirling
KNAPDALE
LENNOX
Bannockburn, 1314
Dunfermline
Firth of Forth
Cardross
Dunbar
Dumbarton
Halidon Hill, 1333
Glasgow
Edinburgh
Paisley
Bothwell
MARCH
Berwick
Islay
KINTYRE
Norham
Irvine
Roxburgh
Ayr
Loudon Hill, 1307
Turnberry
ANNANDALE
LIDDESDALE
CARRICK
NITHSDALE
Glen Trool, 1307
Dumfries
GALLOWAY
Newcastle
Carlisle
Neville's Cross, 1346
0 km 50
0 miles 50
Irish Sea

Preface

What were the Scottish Wars of Independence? This warfare is a dominating period in the vast scope of Scottish history, with two distinct phases. The first war began in 1296 with Edward I of England's invasion of Scotland, which was preceded by a Scottish succession crisis from 1286 upon the death of Alexander III of Scotland. This phase came to a close in 1328 at the signing of the Treaty of Edinburgh-Northampton. War quickly broke out again and the second stage of this conflict began in 1332 as Edward III of England invaded Scotland with Edward Balliol and the Disinherited. The Treaty of Berwick in 1357 concluded the second stage on the ransomed release of King David II of Scotland from English captivity.

This warfare was not the seemingly straightforward 'Scotland versus England' antagonism that it can be portrayed as. Claims to overlordship of Scotland by the Plantagenet kings of England and responding Scottish aggression to English territories did play a significant part in the conflict. However, Scotland's internal political factionalism and dynastic ambition were also major themes which influenced the course of the war and its aftermath. Succession crises, changing ruling dynasties and new royal policies in Scotland altered the landscape of Scottish politics and landholding in a kingdom ravaged by warfare. From the battlefields of Stirling Bridge and Bannockburn in the first stage of the wars, to the besieged castles and torched regions of the second, the Scottish Wars of Independence changed the path of Scottish history.

The bloody nature and political turmoil of this period of warfare saw the establishment of key male figures in leadership whose places in Scottish history would be affirmed, whether as protagonists or antagonists. Men like Robert Bruce, William Wallace and James Douglas would become heroic legends for their contributions to this warfare, while the likes of Edward I of England and John Comyn of Badenoch would be remembered as villains. While the accuracy of these popular understandings (or misunderstandings?) can and should be questioned, the dominance of male political and military figures within a medieval patriarchal society during a time of war is undoubtful. This can be compounded by the consistent male presence in various forms of evidence from this period.

However, what is equally undoubtful is that women were involved in and affected by this warfare. They did not hide away in their homes or remain locked in their towers, waiting for warfare and its political impact to pass. They were protagonists and antagonists alongside their male counterparts, victims and victors in this defining period of Scottish history. While it is absolutely necessary to acknowledge the challenges posed by sporadic evidence for this period, particularly for studying women and especially for women of lower classes, the female experience is not wholly absent from sources. Evidence can be garnered from various disciplines and sources to supply an understanding of the lives and careers of elite women in thirteenth- and fourteenth-century Scotland, including during the Scottish Wars of Independence. Nevertheless, historiographical study and popular knowledge of this period sees the sidelining of the female experience during this infamous period of warfare. This book will seek to correct this by shedding light on the women of the Scottish Wars of Independence.

I have written this book as a narrative history, focusing on the experiences and perceptions of real people and retelling the events of this iconic period in Scottish history. It is not rooted in historiographical debate or theory, and while it aims to uncover new details about women within the wars, it is ultimately a collation of original research and source-based references with a renewed focus on women. This will be done as the evidence allows. An extensive bibliography, acknowledging the invaluable contributions of others, and for further reading is included at the end of the book.

The book structure has been split into three sections: Women in Politics, Women in Captivity and Women in Warfare. Women in Politics will offer a wider focus on elite women during the Scottish Wars of Independence. This section will primarily focus on royal women, particularly highlighting the impact that queens and princesses had on a kingdom's political stability through its dynastic prospects. Beginning with Margaret Maid of Norway as the short-lived hope of Scotland's future, the experiences of Elizabeth de Burgh and Joan of the Tower as Bruce queens will also be explored, in addition to the daughters of the Bruce dynasty. Moreover, this section will examine the political influence of elite women, considering the implications that changing landholding policies had on their position. Elite women who were not within the royal party and were opposed to the kingship of Robert I of Scotland will be examined by focusing on the events of the Soules Conspiracy in 1320. Each chapter will demonstrate that women were central factors in the key issues of succession and political factionalism that ravaged the Kingdom of Scotland during the Scottish Wars of Independence. While evidence for this book cannot offer a thorough and deserving biography of the royal and elite women considered, the impact of the wars upon their position can be assessed.

Women in Captivity will focus on the suffering of a specific group of women as a result of their involvement and association with key figures in the first stage of the Scottish Wars of Independence. In 1306, five women allied to the freshly-crowned usurping Robert Bruce were captured and imprisoned in England: Elizabeth de Burgh, Marjory Bruce, Mary Bruce, Christina Bruce and Isabella MacDuff. It cannot be doubted that these women suffered immensely for their blood and political ties to Robert, with two imprisoned in a cage, two placed under religious imprisonment and one under various forms of house arrest. One of these women died in captivity, with the longest of these imprisonments lasting eight years. Moreover, the imprisonment of Elizabeth de Burgh, Robert's wife, and Marjory Bruce, his daughter and only child, placed the survival of the fledgling Bruce dynasty in an exceptionally compromising position. Despite the sacrifices of these women and the political ramifications of their captivity, their roles within the Scottish Wars of Independence remain understudied and unknown in the popular knowledge of the conflict. It is high time their names and experiences were better appreciated and remembered.

Finally, Women in Warfare will include a general overview of the conflict's military impact on women, before focusing on four key military events in which women played central roles. All four of these events occurred in the 1330s during the second stage of the wars; the implications of this concentration of events will be considered. Christian Cheyne's involvement in the failed defence of Berwick Castle in 1333 provides an insight into perceived and actual female roles in siege warfare and a lens through which to understand the rekindling of warfare in the opening stages of the second Scottish War of Independence. The victories of Christina Bruce and Agnes Randolph at their respective castles of Kildrummy and Dunbar will be explored, demonstrating the crucial military role of women in ensuring the progress of the Bruce party against their Anglo-Balliol opponents. Katherine de Beaumont's defence of Lochindorb across the winter of 1335 to 1336 is an event as worthy of fame as Randolph at Dunbar, seeing a Disinherited countess withstand military aggression of the Guardian of Scotland and invoke the involvement of the King of England himself.

This book could – and should – be longer. There are issues within this topic that would benefit from further research. How did this warfare impact women of lower classes? In what way were the experiences of female religious figures, such as abbesses and nuns, changed during this warfare? What further evidence is there to explore in relation to the lives and careers of the queens of this period? Did the Scottish Wars of Independence impact female identity? Further historiographical study could continue to answer these questions, and there is unquestionably more to be done to improve the knowledge of the female experience of this period. It is my hope that this book will offer an accessible correction to the wider understanding of thirteenth- and fourteenth-century Scottish women in warfare. I hope it inspires and contributes to conversations already underway by other historians. Above all, I hope it introduces new minds and history lovers to this topic, whilst sharing the voices of the women who lived and breathed in the Kingdom of the Scots 700 years ago.

Chapter 1

Women in Politics

In March 1296, Edward I of England invaded the Kingdom of Scotland. This was in retaliation to Scottish resistance to Plantagenet overlordship of Scotland, which Edward had exerted since the Scottish succession crisis of 1290 (see page 5 on Margaret Maid of Norway for detailed discussion). Edward's selected King of Scots in 1292 was John Balliol, who, having paid homage to Edward for Scotland at Newcastle that same year, struggled with the English king's authority over his kingdom. By 1295, efforts to resist Edward were being made by the Scots and included the signing of the Treaty of Paris in October 1295, more famously remembered as the birth of the Auld Alliance between the Kingdoms of Scotland and France. This treaty was a result of imminent war between France and England, with the Scots rebelling against their sworn fealty to provide military support to Edward and instead diplomatically aligning themselves with France. It is unclear whether such an act of rebellion was made by John Balliol's direction or that of the Council of Twelve which established itself in Scotland in July 1295. However, Edward I's unassailable fury at this treaty was perfectly clear.

The English army marched to Scotland in the spring of 1296, beginning by brutally sacking the Scottish coastal burgh of Berwick (modern day Berwick-upon-Tweed) before defeating a Scottish army at the Battle of Dunbar. The destruction of Berwick and the Scottish defeat at Dunbar was enough to establish Edward's position in Scotland, and he continued to sweep through the kingdom to secure his conquest. This culminated in the ceremonial abdication of John Balliol at Montrose in August 1296, where he was stripped of his regalia and taken prisoner to England. In the aftermath of this conquest, Edward set up an administrative government in Scotland and continued to militarily occupy the kingdom.

Edward I's conquest and occupation of Scotland also resulted in the king enacting harsh landholding policies from 1296 towards 'traitorous' Scots, with land and title forfeited by the English Crown and stripped from families who were seen to be involved in any resistance to the English administration. Historian Cynthia J. Neville has demonstrated that many of these initial 'traitors' were killed or taken captive after the disastrous Battle of Dunbar, this landholding policy immediately had a detrimental impact on the women left behind. Widows and daughters of killed men lost their inheritances and terce rights, while the female family of imprisoned men saw their lands forfeited and redistributed to landholders in Edward's favour. This placed swathes of women from various political backgrounds, social class and marital status in a vulnerable position, left to support themselves and families on very little and as prey to the ambitions of others.

Neville has also shown that the impact of this included women in cross-border marriages, who despite their own political loyalties, could be deprived of estates and inheritance in either kingdom based on the actions of their husband. In 1297, when William Douglas, Lord of Douglas, was imprisoned on account of his part in rebellions against Edward's administration in Scotland, it forced his English wife, Eleanor Ferrers, into a difficult situation. In addition to all of Douglas' lands being made forfeit, Eleanor's estates in Essex, Hertfordshire and Northumberland were all confiscated by the crown. After petitioning Edward for restoration of her estates, Eleanor was only fully restored to her lands in England in 1299 and her dower lands in Scotland in 1305. This must have been a deeply distressing period for Eleanor, having to manage the prospect of losing her estates and main income in addition to the loss of her husband after his death in 1298. Eleanor is just one example, explored by Neville, of English women who were just as drastically devastated by this Anglo-Scottish warfare as their Scottish counterparts.

Following Balliol's forced abdication, Edward held an assembly at Berwick on 28 August 1296 where the Scots were requested to pay homage to him as overlord of Scotland. Part of this sworn fealty included affixing seals to the Ragman Roll, a document which recorded the names of all the individuals who pledged their allegiance to Edward. The 1296 Ragman Roll included the names of approximately seventy women from various classes and families, demonstrating the place that women held within medieval Scottish landholding. The creation of the

Ragman Roll provided evidence for Edward and his administration's responses to petitions for restoring lands and title and allowed a system for which the decision to restore or not could be made. If men were found to be in Edward's peace prior to the Treaty of Paris in October 1295 or if they had died prior to John Balliol's abdication, then they were found not guilty of treason and lands were restored to their female family members. This is exemplified by the restoration of around thirty widows to their estates and dower lands in September 1296, in exchange for their allegiance on the Ragman Roll.

While on the surface, this system of automatic forfeiture and justified restoration seems like an unsurprising legal system from a king intent on occupying another kingdom, Neville argues that it was a method of threatening women into submission by giving them a brief taste of the punishment for participating in or being connected to rebel activity. This fact is not surprising. Neville explains that Edward's approach to war with Scotland from 1296 to 1307 – as a territorial dispute, not as against another Christian kingdom – was conducted brutally and negated chivalry. This was especially clear in the way in which he punished women through these landholding policies and in his deliberately leisurely responses to frantic petitions by destitute widows. The systematic targeting of women in warfare and captivity during this period will be discussed later in this book.

The political and personal impact of warfare on female landholding did not end with Edward I of England. After his victory at the Battle of Bannockburn in June 1314, Robert I of Scotland enacted a policy of forfeiture towards his remaining opponents at a parliament at Cambuskenneth Abbey, near the site of Bannockburn. Any Scottish or English individual with land in Scotland who continued to stand against Robert's kingship would be stripped of Scottish estates and titles. This created a group called the Disinherited who would continually appeal for restoration of their lands for the remainder of the Scottish Wars of Independence and become the primary antagonists of the second stage of the wars from 1332. For pro-Bruce supporters, this was a show of strength by Robert in eliminating his opponents. For those opposed to his kingship, this was theft of ancestral land and title that removed families from estates which they had held for generations under a policy comparable to Edward's approach to landholding after 1296. The unprecedented change that this brought to Scottish landholding again affected the heritable claims of women alongside men. A notable example of this was Alice Comyn, who should have inherited the Earldom of Buchan in Scotland's northeast after she became heiress to her uncle John Comyn, Earl of Buchan, in 1308. Alice, alongside her husband Henry de Beaumont, would relentlessly pursue her claims to her family's earldom well into the 1330s, with Henry being a primary Disinherited leader during the second stage of the wars.

The huge landholding impact that the Scottish Wars of Independence had on women cannot be understated and was an extensive political factor that this warfare brought to the women of both Scotland and England. Edward I and Robert I's landholding policies and their consequences for women demonstrate that this warfare did not just target women as victims of war or captivity, or indeed as leaders in warfare, but also caused great strain politically and financially. Oftentimes, with men absent from lands, whether due to imprisonment or death, women bore the brunt of the brutal impact of changing landholding policies.

With this context of dramatic changes to landholding and political claims to power, the Scottish Wars of Independence emphasized the central role of women in dynastic claims. Women held a unique role as transporters of blood and consequently of heritable claims to land and title. Indeed, two of the defining families of this period, the Balliols and the Bruces, pressed for their claim to the throne of Scotland via the great-granddaughters of King David I of Scotland. In a period where families were at risk of being stripped of their lands and magnates jostled for territorial expansion and claims to the throne, the significance behind family and dynasty were at an unprecedented high. This added more weight to the political symbolism and influence of an elite woman, who carried the identity and heritage of their ancestral families in addition to that of their marital. This was a heightened responsibility that would have been felt across the Scottish political class, from royal women to landholders.

The following chapters will present the roles that women held within Scotland's political landscape during the Scottish Wars of Independence, by focusing on specific individuals within certain contexts. A primary chunk of this section will focus on royal women, particularly highlighting the impact that queens and princesses had on royal dynasty, particularly during the instability of war. Beginning with Margaret Maid of Norway, the experiences of Elizabeth de Burgh and Joan of the Tower as Bruce queens will then be explored, in addition to other royal Bruce women. This section will also examine the political influence of elite women who were not within the royal party and were opposed to the kingship of Robert I of Scotland, by focusing on the events of the Soules Conspiracy in 1320. Each chapter will demonstrate that women were central factors in the key issues of succession and political factionalism that ravaged the Kingdom of Scotland during the Scottish Wars of Independence. Above all, it is my hope to emphasize that these were real women affected by a conflict that often placed them in situations of both personal and political pressure.

Margaret Maid of Norway

> 'While twice three years roll by, and moons thrice three,
> Without a prince the widow'd land shall be.'
>
> *Liber Pluscardensis*

On 19 March 1286, King Alexander III of Scotland died. He had reigned for nearly thirty-seven years, with his adult reign popularly heralded as a golden age for Scotland. Alexander's three children – Margaret, Alexander and David – had all died before their father, meaning that his death did not bring a smooth transition of power. From 1286 to 1290, his young granddaughter Margaret was accepted as Scotland's new monarch upon inauguration, but her tragic death at the age of only nine in 1290 ended this period of tentative succession. This plunged Scotland into an all-out succession crisis as various magnates laid claim to the throne, which ultimately led to the invited mediation of King Edward I of England in the selection of a new King of Scots. These are the events which set the stage for the Scottish Wars of Independence, a conflict that would last for nearly sixty years.

Alexander III's death in 1286, tossed from his horse at the cliffs of Kinghorn during a storm whilst travelling to his queen, can often be the focal point as the one disaster which triggered the conflict to come. However, the shocking death of his nine-year-old granddaughter in 1290 was in fact the catastrophic moment that pushed the Kingdom of the Scots to the brink of civil war. The short period in which Margaret was heir to her grandfather can sometimes be underestimated as a brief factor prior to the outbreak of war. This should be taken more seriously: Margaret's death not only triggered a cataclysmic succession crisis that would continue for the next sixty years, but also brought a harsh end to the royal MacMalcolm dynasty which had ruled Scotland since 1058. This little girl's death defined and changed Scottish history.

Heir Apparent

Margaret, often referred to as the Maid of Norway, was born in 1283 as the only child of King Eric II of Norway and Margaret, the daughter of Alexander III of Scotland. Eric and Margaret senior had been married in 1281, a union formed with the hope of soothing the strained relationship between the Kingdoms of Scotland and Norway after hostilities between the two earlier in Alexander's reign. Margaret died shortly after giving birth to the Maid of Norway in the spring of 1283, most likely due to complications from childbirth. Her death was one of three tragedies which struck Alexander III's reign in the early 1280s; between 1281 and 1284, all three of his children died. His youngest son, David, died in 1281 at only eight years old, while his eldest son, Alexander, died suddenly in 1284. The death of this twenty-year-old heir after the passing of his other two children was surely a painful blow to Alexander III, both politically and personally. All three of his legitimate children were dead, with the king a widower since the death of his queen, Margaret of England, in 1275. The King of Scots now turned to his infant granddaughter, Margaret Maid of Norway.

The young Margaret's place in Alexander's succession can sometimes be misunderstood as an absolutely disastrous situation that placed Scotland into turmoil. Indeed, the prospect of a child inheriting the throne, and the undoubted resulting political tension was not particularly reassuring. However, it cannot be disputed that Alexander threw himself wholeheartedly into his granddaughter's new place as his heir. On 5 February 1284, Alexander had Margaret recognized as his heir-presumptive by the political community of his kingdom; his son had died less than a month before. The earls and barons of Scotland swore to recognize Margaret in the event that Alexander did not produce other children, or that his late son's widow did not have a posthumous child. This shows that despite there being a certain level of hope that

Alexander the heir's widow, Margaret of Flanders, may have been pregnant, King Alexander was not prepared to delay his granddaughter's recognition while waiting for the result of this. Indeed, despite the personal and political weight of this time for Alexander, he expressed his positivity for his granddaughter as his heir in a letter to his brother-in-law Edward I of England in April 1284:

> 'Though death has carried off all of his blood in Scotland, one yet remains, the child of his own dearest daughter ... now under divine providence the heir apparent of Scotland. Much good may yet be in store for them.'

This letter has also been widely interpreted as indicative of Alexander's intention to see Margaret united by marriage to England. Indeed, Alexander and Edward appear to have had an amicable relationship as brothers-in-law through Alexander's marriage to Margaret of England – notwithstanding Edward's attempts to persuade Alexander into paying homage. Moreover, both kings displayed genuine affection to the other's family, with the regular exchanging of gifts and letters. Edward would have been personally vested in the calamity which struck Alexander in 1284, and a union between the Maid of Norway and the Plantagenets of England was surely seen as natural.

However, this point is perhaps negated by Alexander's decision to marry his second wife, Yolande of Dreux, in October 1285. Yolande was the daughter of Robert IV, Count of Dreux, and Beatrice de Montfort, Countess of Montfort, meaning that she was related to the powerful Capetian dynasty of France. Alexander's choice of bride was perhaps indicative of a Scottish conscious decision to strengthen ties with the Kingdom of France and not over-rely on the politics and family connections to the ambitious Edward I of England. This may also indicate that Margaret of England's death in 1275 had weakened the friendliness of Alexander and Edward's relationship. Alexander's marriage to Yolande also shows that although he displayed an acceptance and general hope for his granddaughter's new position as heir of his kingdom, the pressure to produce more heirs was still apparent.

It is impossible to assess how Margaret Maid of Norway's new role as the heir to Scotland may have impacted her life. She remained in Norway after her confirmed place in her grandfather's succession, most likely due to her age, as she was not yet a year old. Moreover, Margaret was also the only child of her father, Eric II of Norway, who was surely reluctant to see his daughter leave Norway. At only fifteen years old, Eric's reluctance was no doubt shared by the key members of his government, who he relied upon as a minor ruler and who held custody of his own daughter. Margaret had been raised in the custody of Narve, Bishop of Bergen, a key political figure in Norway who deliberately ensured that Margaret was raised in what was at that time Norway's capital. From her birth, Margaret was destined to be involved in the heart of Norwegian politics and foreign policy for her prestigious position as the daughter of the King of Norway and granddaughter of the King of Scots. Indeed, the marriage contract of Eric II and Margaret's mother in 1281 stated that any children born of their union would have a place in the Scottish line of succession.

The political communities and royalty of Scotland and Norway may have expected that Margaret would remain in Norway until she was married or succeeded her grandfather. This expectation was dramatically cut short when Alexander III of Scotland died unexpectedly on 19 March 1286. The day of his death had seen the king in Edinburgh with his royal council, before setting off on the journey to Kinghorn in Fife to be with his new wife and queen, Yolande. A great storm had swept over Scotland's east coast and Alexander was advised on several points of his journey to wait until the storm had cleared before continuing. The king was not to be deterred and his retinue pressed on before being separated in the inclement weather. It was the following morning before Alexander was found on the shores of the Firth of Forth, his neck broken, probably after being thrown from his horse or suffering a fall. With Alexander III's death, so ended the golden age of Scotland.

The King is Dead

Despite the oaths of acceptance made in 1284 for Margaret Maid of Norway as the late king's heir, this did not constitute a straightforward succession following the events at Kinghorn and Alexander's funeral at Dunfermline Abbey on 29 March 1286. Instead, the issue of succession appears to have been contested by Yolande of Dreux's possible pregnancy. This was similar to the death of Prince Alexander in 1284, in which there had been a very brief potential heir through his widow Margaret of

Flanders. However, unlike in 1284 when a lack of pregnancy seems to have been identified quickly, the confirmation of Margaret succeeding her grandfather did not occur until November 1286. This suggests that Yolande had indeed been pregnant, hence the delay to the succession, and perhaps suffered a stillbirth in November.

In the aftermath of Alexander's death and the wait to see who would succeed his throne – three-year-old Margaret Maid of Norway or a newborn – the Scottish political community sought to fulfil the void left behind by an absent monarch. Contact was quickly made with Edward I of England to seek his help, a sensible decision based on his position as the late king's amicable brother-in-law and feudal lord for any English lands held by Scots. However, Edward's own interests in issues in Gascony distracted him from any involvement in Scotland at this stage. Instead, the Scottish political community saw to the election of six guardians to head a royal government and rule the kingdom in the continuing absence of a sitting king or queen. These guardians represented the three primary components of Scotland's political class: the church, the earls and the barons. Despite the guardians and the wait for succession, tension between potential claimants to the throne of Scotland was already beginning to increase as early as April 1286. This tension was primarily between Robert Bruce of Annandale (grandfather of the future Robert I of Scotland) and John Balliol, who could both claim blood ties to the throne. Even with Yolande's unborn child and Margaret Maid of Norway, the prospect of an adult male claimant versus a royal child allowed factionalism to emerge as noble houses prepared for what could come.

The stillbirth of a royal heir in November 1286 finally confirmed what the late Alexander had set out in 1284: Margaret Maid of Norway was to succeed to her grandfather's throne. There was obviously a general lack of enthusiasm over the reality of a little girl raised in a foreign court being the new Queen of Scots, as displayed by an ill-calculated military outburst by Robert Bruce in response to the news of Margaret's succession. This was surely an attempt by Bruce to set himself up for the throne and to establish a regional dominance over his near competitor, John Balliol, in the southwest of Scotland. This, however, did not amount to any attempted coup, which may show that reluctance over Margaret's inheritance was not nearly as strong across the kingdom as anticipated. However, Bruce's actions would contribute to the increasing factionalism under the guardians' rule and would be echoed much more severely in the years to come.

It is difficult to assess what the reaction in Norway would have been to the king's daughter inheriting the throne of Scotland. While it was an occurrence that should have been expected considering Alexander's ensuring of Margaret's position as his heir, the premature dawning of such a succession for the King of Norway's three-year-old daughter must have come with mixed reactions. From a positive aspect, Eric and his advisors could delight in a Norwegian princess inheriting the throne of Scotland by her own right, but the removal of his only legitimate child – even if that child would never be his heir – also meant the removal of the king's child from court and kingdom. Margaret had been raised in Bergen in the heart of Norwegian politics; her removal to another kingdom would see Eric and his political advisors lose a key tool.

However, Eric's reluctance to see Margaret leave Norway for her new Scottish kingdom most likely arose from the sheer political instability and threat to his daughter's safety in the wake of Alexander's death. The violence displayed by Robert Bruce in response to the loss of Yolande's child and Margaret's confirmation as heir no doubt emphasized this concern to Eric. His lack of willingness to send Margaret to Scotland from November 1286 was not helped by the fact that the new guardians had failed to deliver overdue payments for his late queen's dowry. Considering that the guardians were reliant upon Eric's goodwill to receive their new queen, this error was a diplomatic blunder.

As a result, the guardians of Scotland oversaw the royal government, without Margaret being in the kingdom, from 1287 to 1290. The first two years of their continuing governance appear to have settled down in regards to claims of kingship and military threat, but by 1289 this was beginning to quickly unravel. The deaths of two guardians – the elderly Alexander Comyn of Buchan and the murder of Duncan of Fife – in this year tipped the balance of power, in addition to contributing to the growing unrest and factionalism. While the guardians of the kingdom could operate government, it was difficult for them to manage the political ambitions, rivalries and upsets that were rapidly developing in the absence of a king. In order to resolve these issues within the kingdom and to persuade Eric of Norway to send Margaret to Scotland, the guardians and the Scottish political community needed to rely on the diplomatic intervention of Edward I of England. Again, it is important to remember that Edward was no stranger to the Scots and held a reputation as a successful mediator in Europe in addition to that of a military leader. By allying with Edward, the Scots would be able to press for Margaret Maid of Norway's passage to her kingdom.

In 1289, Edward I became involved in Margaret's situation primarily through the proposition of her marriage to his son and heir, Edward Caernarfon. This was not Edward slyly taking advantage of Scotland's political state despite its advantages to him; this was a union that may have been suggested in earlier years by the Scots, Norway or perhaps even Alexander III before his death. The increased activity of envoys and embassies between Scotland, Norway and Gascony in early 1289 were topped off by Edward's request for a papal dispensation for his son's marriage to Margaret in May 1289. When Edward finally returned from Gascony to England that summer, formal discussions between the three kingdoms began. The result on 6 November 1289 was the Treaty of Salisbury, which set out the required conditions prior to any marriage taking place and Margaret's return to Scotland. Essentially, this treaty stated that Margaret would only be sent from Norway to Scotland or England once her kingdom was secure and safe for her arrival, with Eric and Edward continuing to be the primary marriage negotiators. While this does point to an element of control of Margaret's situation, the conditions of security and safety in Scotland also demonstrate the genuine concern and care for her wellbeing as a little girl soon to be queen of a foreign kingdom.

Diplomatic negotiations for Margaret's marriage continued into 1290, culminating in the Treaty of Birgham of July 1290. The conditions of this treaty are indicative of a certain level of anxiety experienced by the Scots in anticipation of Margaret's marriage to Prince Edward. The reality was that by marrying the heir to the English throne, Margaret's reign would see Scotland become a dominion of the Plantagenets. While this was not necessarily viewed as a disastrous event – indeed the Scots appear to be in sincere favour of the marriage – there were efforts made to secure recognition of various rights for the Scottish kingdom. This included a distinct separation of the realms of Scotland and England: 'Scotland shall remain separated and divided and free in itself, without subjection to the realm of England.' Other issues were also straightened out, including Scottish magnates seeking a level of minimal interference from the English Crown in the running of their estates. Another key issue was the protection of the Scottish Church as a 'special daughter' of the papacy, ensuring that Scottish clergy would be prioritized for offices and appointments in Scotland over their English counterparts. Importantly, the Treaty of Birgham not only confirmed the upcoming marriage of Margaret Maid of Norway, but also demonstrated the ability of her political community to seek the recognition of her kingdom's position and how it operated.

After ratifying the treaty in August 1290, Edward I of England quickly made his royal authority known with his own responding conditions. This included his involvement in the Western Isles and the Isle of Man, the latter of which had been held by Scotland since the 1260s, but now came under Edward's grasp. Additionally, Edward stipulated that all royal castles in Scotland had to be handed over to him in the name of Margaret and her future husband, and appointed Antony Bek, Bishop of Durham, as lieutenant for the royal couple and thus a leading figure in Scotland. These conditions, especially the appointment of the military figure of Bishop Bek, must have irked various facets of Scottish political society. However, Edward had proved his diplomatic reliability and usefulness to the Scots, as his promise that Margaret would arrive in Scotland or England by November 1290 appeared to be fulfilled. Margaret departed from Norway in September 1290 after Edward had persuaded Eric II of Norway to allow his only child to travel to either Scotland or England. Aged only seven, it is difficult to imagine how this situation must have been for Margaret, a little girl who was to leave her home in Bergen to journey across the North Sea to a foreign kingdom, made her own by a grandfather she never met. Perhaps she was old enough to realize that she was leaving her home for somewhere completely new. Perhaps she was too young to fully understand the magnitude of what was occurring.

The Queen That Never Was

The careful plans of Scotland's guardians and magnates, and Edward's steady installation of his authority in Scotland, would all be in dreadful vain. In October 1290, a gathering of Scottish and English nobles at Perth received word that their queen, Margaret Maid of Norway, was dead. The chaos that followed this news speaks to the ongoing political tension in Scotland despite her impending arrival, but also to the confusion that this unofficial news brought. Margaret departed Norway in September with a Norwegian retinue that included Narve, Bishop of Bergen, whose custody she had been raised in. The group arrived in Orkney that same month, shortly after which Margaret died. Different suggestions for the seven-year-old girl's untimely death range from severe motion sickness to food poisoning, but the definitive reason will ultimately remain a mystery. It may have also been a mystery to Margaret's contemporaries, who had been waiting expectedly for her arrival in Scotland, with Bishop Bek travelling north to meet her. Indeed, in the wake of news of Margaret's death there were rumours of her recovery from illness, creating confusion amongst the Scottish political community. The gathering at Perth may even suggest that plans were in motion to see to the young queen's quick inauguration at Scone, before she inevitably continued south to England to her future husband.

The impact of Margaret's tragic death was significant. Almost immediately the competition for claiming the throne of Scotland renewed. The factions which had been developing since Alexander III's death in 1286 assembled to support the claims of two primary rivals: Robert Bruce, Lord of Annandale; and John Balliol, Lord of Galloway. Both men had the strongest claims to the Scottish Crown through their descendancy from David, Earl of Huntingdon, a grandson of King David I of Scotland. Their place at the heads of the extreme political tension in the wake of Margaret's death had been culminating for years, and at this stage drove the Scottish kingdom to the brink of civil war. Alexander's death in 1286 introduced a period of political tension and instability; Margaret's death in 1290 was a succession crisis on a disastrous scale. Margaret Maid of Norway was the final living heir of the MacMalcolm dynasty and the last gasp of a house which had ruled Scotland since 1058. Her death brought the end of this powerful royal line, the impact of which would be felt sorely by Scots and English alike for the next sixty years.

In October 1290, William Fraser, Bishop of St Andrews, wrote to Edward I of England informing him of the rumours of Margaret's death and the threat of civil war which loomed over the kingdom. While Fraser's letter indicates that at this stage Margaret's death was a rumour and with hope for her recovery still existing, it also tells us of the reactions of the Scottish political community to these rumours: 'There sounded through the people a sorrowful rumour that our said Lady should be dead, on which account the Kingdom of Scotland is disturbed and the community distracted. And the said rumour being heard and published, Sir Robert of Brus who before did not intend to come to the foresaid meeting, came with a great power to confer with some who were there. But what he intends to do or how to act, as yet we know not. But the Earls of Mar and Athol are collecting their army; And some other nobles of the land are drawing to their party and on that account there is fear of a general war and a great slaughter of men, unless the Highest, by means of your industry and good service, apply a speedy remedy.'

It is within this context of confusion and the threat of civil war that Bishop Fraser finished his letter by asking Edward to intervene in the situation that had gripped Scotland: 'If it turn out that our foresaid Lady has departed this life, and may it not be so, let your excellency deign if you please to approach towards the March, for the consolation of the Scotch people and for saving the shedding of blood.'

In hindsight, Bishop Fraser and his contemporaries may have come to regret his letter requesting Edward's help in managing the reactions of the magnates to Margaret Maid of Norway's death. However, it is key to understand that this request was made on the basis of Edward's already existing involvement in Scotland's succession, in ensuring the delivery and arranging the betrothal of Margaret to his own son. Edward's own hopes for what this betrothal would result in for the Plantagenet dynasty would not have been lost on the Scots, as demonstrated by the Treaty of Birgham, but he remained a powerful neighbour on whom the guardians hoped they could rely to choose between Bruce and Balliol as the new King of Scots and avoid a civil war.

Instead, at Norham in May 1291, Edward agreed to judge Scotland's succession solution only as the superior lord of the kingdom. This ambition was no longer hidden or tamed by the marriage of Scotland's queen to his son, a patient and long game by the King of England. This was Edward's opportunity to progress his claims of overlordship over Scotland. Edward was initially rejected by the likes of Robert Wishart, Bishop of Glasgow, with the Scots responding that only Scotland's king could answer Edward's claim to homage. Edward agreed to this, but before mediating the selection of a new king declared that any claimants to the throne must first pay homage to him. The military and political might of Edward I of England was no match for the personal ambitions or desire for peace from the Scots and such homage was made, giving Edward feudal authority over the Kingdom of the Scots. Over the next year and a half, Edward would sit as a feudal judge – not an external mediator – over the Great Cause, a lengthy legal process which considered the claims of thirteen competitors to the Scottish throne. In November 1292, Edward selected John Balliol to be King of Scots.

Conclusion

These events set the stage for the Scottish Wars of Independence, which would erupt in 1296 when attempted resistance to Edward's authority resulted in his military conquest of Scotland and removal of Balliol as Scotland's king. The ultimate catalyst was not the death of Alexander III of Scotland, but that of Margaret Maid of Norway, Scotland's queen that never was. Had Margaret lived and married Edward Caernarfon, how would Scotland's history have played out? Indeed, what would Britain look like today? Children produced from this union would have gone on to inherit the thrones of both England and Scotland. Would the Union of the Crowns in 1603, when James VI of Scotland inherited the English throne from his heirless cousin, Elizabeth I of England, have happened centuries earlier from the heirs of Margaret and Edward?

Margaret's inheritance of Scotland and subsequent betrothal to Edward was arguably one of the most important potential marriages that would have occurred in Scottish and English history. Instead, the tragic and premature death of Margaret, hundreds of miles from home, would plunge Scotland into a state of political unrest and violence for the next sixty years. The events of the Scottish Wars of Independence and the resultant altered relationship between Scotland and England would be felt for centuries to come, the effect of which can arguably still be identified today. This would be a conflict remembered as one dominated by famous and infamous male leaders, but the central involvement of women can be symbolized by the seven-year-old girl whose death triggered the beginnings of war: Margaret Maid of Norway.

Royal Bruce Women

'For scho wes swete, and debonare,
Curtas, hamely, plesande, and faire'

Andrew of Wyntoun,
Orygynale Cronykil of Scotland

Elizabeth de Burgh was twelve or thirteen years old when she married Robert Bruce, Earl of Carrick, in 1302. Her new husband was fifteen years her senior, an ambitious twenty-eight-year-old earl who had recently defected from the Scottish resistance against Edward I's occupation of Scotland to support the English king. Robert and Edward were already known to one another based on the Bruce family ties to the English Crown through landholding, homage and politics, with Robert even spending his bachelor years at Edward's court in London. Similarly, Robert would not have been a stranger to Elizabeth. He was the Earl of Carrick, lord of a coastal earldom in the southwest of Scotland. Indeed, the seat of the Earldom of Carrick was Turnberry Castle, a fortress situated on a small peninsula that gazed out across the Irish Sea to the Carrick connections in Ireland.

The Bruce connections to Ireland ran deep through their regional authority in Carrick and through Robert's mother. Marjory, Countess of Carrick, was the daughter of Níall of Carrick and Margaret Stewart. She became countess to the earldom in her own right in 1256 when her male cousin, who was her father's heir, unexpectedly died. Marjory's heritage through her father included lands and family connections in Ireland, particularly to Irish kings. This Irish connection would be evident in her eldest son's marriage to Elizabeth de Burgh in 1302, as she was the daughter of Richard de Burgh, Earl of Ulster. Robert would later call on these Irish connections in 1315 as part of a Bruce military campaign to Ireland. He was also known to have spoken fluent Gaelic, as many lords of Scotland would have done in the late thirteenth and early fourteenth centuries, and was possibly fostered in Ireland as a child, as per Gaelic tradition.

Richard de Burgh, whose family had been present in Ireland since the twelfth century as part of English colonial activity, was very well connected to the Bruces. In 1286, Robert's grandfather, Robert Bruce the

Competitor, formed the Turnberry Bond with Richard de Burgh and other Irish and Scottish west coast figures in anticipation of competition for the throne of Scotland. The contextual political and blood relationships between the Bruces and major families in Ireland should demonstrate that Elizabeth de Burgh likely did not marry a complete stranger in 1302.

Whatever Elizabeth expected of her marriage, it probably was not what it turned out to be. After only four years of marriage, Robert would seize the throne of Scotland in March 1306 after murdering his rival, John Comyn of Badenoch, the month before. Elizabeth was inaugurated as Robert's queen, apparently sarcastically commenting that they would only be king and queen of the May, casting her doubt over the reality of Robert's intentions for kingship. Elizabeth was not wrong: the pair were separated by warfare in the summer of 1306 and Elizabeth was captured by the English in autumn. She would spend the following eight years in English captivity, being regularly moved around from different imprisonment locations (more on this in Women in Captivity). Elizabeth would finally be released in late 1314 in a prisoner exchange after Robert's victory at the Battle of Bannockburn in June 1314 and return to Scotland. This Queen of Scots was only seventeen when she was separated from her thirty-two-year-old husband and sentenced to perpetual captivity. Her return in 1314, now a twenty-five-year-old woman to a husband who she did not, by all intents and purposes, have a positive or familiar relationship with, must have been incredibly challenging. Especially so, considering Robert was under intense pressure for an heir.

A Bruce Dynasty

Robert's victory at Bannockburn in June 1314 is often popularly misrepresented as the concluding factor of the Scottish Wars of Independence. This could not be farther from the truth, with Robert not achieving recognition of his kingship or Scotland's sovereignty for another fourteen years through the Treaty of Edinburgh-Northampton in 1328. Even after that, warfare erupted with the second stage of the Scottish Wars of Independence in 1332, which would not tentatively close until October 1357.

Bannockburn was a watershed moment for Robert's kingship in defeating Edward II of England's army and setting a precedent for forfeiting any continuing opposition to him in Scotland, but it was not the delivery of unquestionable royal claims that it can be misunderstood as. Indeed, major political opposition to Robert's position was uncovered as late as 1320 as an assassination plot against the king and a resettlement of Scotland was thwarted by Robert's regime. This shows that despite the progress he had made by 1314, Robert was not fully accepted as a royal figure, but still viewed as a magnate who had usurped the throne. Robert was clearly all too aware of his continuing political and military challenges after 1314, utilizing symbols of legitimacy and authority where possible.

One theme that continued to undermine his position as the head of a new royal dynasty and dog his grasps at legitimacy was his succession. Without a strong heir – particularly a male heir – Robert was just another magnate who seized the throne, but could not keep it. Pressure over his succession was recurrent through his reign and was especially disadvantaged by the fact that his queen, Elizabeth de Burgh, was held in English captivity for the first eight years of Bruce kingship. Additionally, Elizabeth was captive alongside Robert's only legitimate child, a daughter by his first marriage, Marjory Bruce. Elizabeth and Marjory were the strongest keys to unlocking the Bruce royal dynasty, but were kept away from 1306 to 1314. In that sense, Robert's victory at Bannockburn was more than just a battle for his kingship, but was a battle for the very future of his claims to the throne of Scotland.

Medieval women have traditionally been relegated to the roles of wife and mother, with their contributions restrained privately to their marriage and household. However, historians have challenged this notion of private versus public roles and the gendered differences between the two, instead presenting a much more fluid system in which men and women operated. Katrin E. Sjursen's exploration of the roles of noblewomen in the fourteenth-century Breton Civil War is particularly useful in this, highlighting that marriage was a political partnership in which elite women continued to be political assets as well as wives, mothers, and widows. She demonstrates that marriage and producing children did not necessarily equate to a lack of female political importance. Indeed, the birth of a child was as much a political and public event as it was personal, particularly in the context of dynasty. Cynthia J. Neville's work on the presence of women in Scottish charters from the twelfth to fourteenth centuries helps us understand this better. In marrying and having children, medieval women were enacting their unique role in continuing bloodlines and claims to title and property. Essentially, women were at the heart of the success of a dynasty and claims to power. In a time such as the Scottish Wars of Independence, when familial claims to earldoms, lordships and even the throne were under scrutiny, the elite female role in the continuing of a dynasty had arguably never been so public or important.

The pressure of this was probably at the forefront of Elizabeth de Burgh and Marjory Bruce's minds when they were released from English captivity in the months after October 1314. For Elizabeth, the prospect of returning to a husband that she had not seen for eight years was surely worsened by the length of time she had spent in England and by the fact that her father was her husband's enemy. Richard de Burgh, Earl of Ulster, remained an adherent to Edward II of England, despite his brief influence in easing the harshness of Elizabeth's imprisonment. She may have been considerably apprehensive about returning to Scotland, and indeed, to Robert. Would she be welcomed as the queen who scorned Robert's seizing of the throne in March 1306?

The anxieties felt by Robert in the hope and need for a male heir are reflected at the Ayr parliament on 26 April 1315. This parliament, called in anticipation of the Bruce military aggression in Ireland which would begin in a month's time under Edward Bruce, notably saw to the consent of an act of succession, or a tailzie. This tailzie very much laid out a contingency plan in regards to the succession of the Bruce dynasty. With this occurring in advance of Edward Bruce's Irish Campaign and within months of Elizabeth de Burgh and Marjory Bruce's return to Scotland, Robert appears to be silencing any questions over his succession, which indicates his forward planning, but may also betray his anxieties over producing a male heir himself. This act, 'by the consent of the said lord king and Marjory, his daughter', decreed that Robert's last surviving brother, Edward Bruce, would be his heir apparent over Marjory. Additionally, Edward's legitimate children – which in the end he did not produce – would succeed to the throne in the event of Robert and Edward's death, before Marjory and her children. The decision to make Edward the heir apparent of the Bruce dynasty in 1315 made sense. Marjory was nineteen years old and only recently freed from an eight-year captivity in England, while Edward was 'a vigorous man and tested on many occasions in acts of war for the defence of the right and liberty of the kingdom of Scotland.' Robert's decision to make Edward his heir, confirmed by parliament, was an effort to avoid any vulnerabilities for a kingdom at war under a young female ruler, as evident by the events concerning Margaret Maid of Norway from 1286 to 1290.

However, this act did not rule out female succession in its entirety, with Marjory set as Robert's heir in the event that Edward Bruce did die without any legitimate children, and Robert without any male heirs. Moreover, in acknowledging Marjory's continuing, albeit relegated, place in the Bruce succession, the 1315 tailzie also stated that 'the succession of the aforesaid kingdom of Scotland should revert to the aforesaid Marjory or failing her to the nearest heir of the body of the lord king Robert, descending lineally without any contradiction.' This failsafe may have been included to keep the opportunity open to bring Robert's sisters into the line of Bruce succession. Robert's other captive sisters, Christina and Mary, had also been released by October 1314. Although Christina would not remarry until 1326, possibly in grief for the execution of her first husband Christopher Seton in 1306, Mary may have been key to this line in the 1315 act of succession. Mary married Robert's ally Neil Campbell of Lochawe on an unknown date, but likely shortly after her release from captivity in 1313 or 1314. By Neil, Mary had a son, John Campbell, who must have been born before 1317 with Neil's death occurring in 1316. She may have been expecting or have already delivered her son by the time of the 1315 act of succession. Indeed, Robert's confirmation of Mary's son John as Earl of Atholl in 1320 was perhaps indicative of the king's possible intentions for this particular nephew.

Robert had another sister, Matilda Bruce, who appears to have evaded capture in 1306, but married Hugh, son of William, Earl of Ross. Again, we have no confirmed date for Hugh and Matilda's marriage, with peerage records having shakily dated this marriage to around 1308, but it is possible that they married as early as 1306 which may explain Matilda avoiding capture with her other sisters (more discussed on this in Women in Captivity). Robert's considerable gifts to Hugh through the 1310s may indicate that he was already a brother-in-law of the king before the first charter which was jointly directed to the couple in 1323. Moreover, the coming-of-age of Hugh and Matilda's son in 1336 suggests that he was born sometime between 1316 and 1318. With two daughters also produced from the marriage, perhaps in the early 1310s, it could act as an indication of the marriage of Hugh and Matilda occurring earlier. Although it is difficult to pinpoint a date for Matilda's marriage to Hugh, the patterns of marriage and births by Marjory Bruce, Elizabeth de Burgh and Mary Bruce after 1314 suggest that the king would have wasted no time in also securing Matilda's marriage to Hugh, if it had not already occurred by this stage. Therefore, the 1315 tailzie's reference to 'the nearest heir of the body of the lord king Robert' may have been made with Matilda and Hugh of Ross in mind, as well as Mary and Neil Campbell.

Utilising the children of royal sisters was a method explored by David II in his reign, during the second stage of the Scottish Wars of Independence. Similarly to his father, David would spend much of his reign dogged by the pressure of succession. Married in 1328 to Joan of the Tower, a daughter of Edward II of England, no children came of this thirty-four-year-long marriage, which ended with Joan's death in 1362. Indeed, despite two marriages and various mistresses, David never did produce a child, which certainly suggests that the king struggled with infertility. This infertility probably became evident to David as he grew older, and intent on refusing the succession of his nephew, Robert Stewart, Marjory Bruce's son, he turned to the children of his other sisters. David may have even regarded Marjory Bruce as not being a true sister in an attempt to undermine Robert Stewart's claims to succession; they did not share a mother and Marjory had died seven or eight years before David was even born. In contrast, David had two full sisters, Margaret and Matilda Bruce, and sought to use their offspring in his succession plans. The primary target of this was Margaret Bruce's son, John of Sutherland, by her husband, William, Earl of Sutherland. From Margaret and William's marriage in 1342, David sought to elevate the political position of this couple, not just in an act of brotherly affection, but also to prepare for a potential son who he could claim as his heir by his elder sister. Margaret gave birth to her son John in 1346 and died shortly thereafter, most likely as a result of complications in childbirth. This again highlights the danger of medieval pregnancies and childbirth, and the personal sacrifices made by women across the centuries in the continuation of their family blood. John's own death on 8 September 1361 of plague, whilst acting as a hostage in London for David, brought an end to David's plans of a Bruce dynastic succession via his sister's son.

There was one condition to Marjory Bruce's place in the Bruce succession in 1315: 'provided, nevertheless, that the said Marjory is joined in marriage by the consent of the said lord king, failing whom, which God forbid, by the consent of the greater part of the community of the kingdom.' The king's daughter was to be married, and the inclusion of 'the consent of the greater part of the community of the kingdom' in the 1326 act of succession suggests that her betrothal was discussed and finalized at this same parliament. Robert's choice, which was obviously supported by the majority of his political community at Ayr, was Walter Stewart, the hereditary High Steward of Scotland. Stewart, who was a similar age to Marjory, was already a loyal Bruce adherent, having fought at Bannockburn in 1314 in support of his king. The reasons behind the selection of Walter as Marjory's husband ran deeper. His father, James Stewart, had been a close ally of the Bruces and connected to the family in support of their claims of the Scottish throne. In 1297, James had taken up arms with Robert at Irvine in rebellion against Edward I of England, although the two were quickly pressured to submit. Moreover, the Steward had taken as his third wife Egidia de Burgh, a sister of Richard de Burgh of Ulster and therefore an aunt of Robert's queen, Elizabeth de Burgh.

Further de Burgh connections can be identified in Richard de Burgh and the Steward's presence in Carrick in 1286 at the Turnberry Bond, a precursor to Robert Bruce the Competitor's claims to the Scottish throne. In the 1310s, Walter Stewart's allegiance to Robert I was a natural result of family and regional history. This contributed to his new position as Marjory Bruce's betrothed in April 1315, in addition to de Burgh connections that may speak to Elizabeth's influence in her and Robert's selection of a husband for Marjory. The timing of this prior to Edward Bruce's invasion of Ireland, which specifically targeted Richard de Burgh, Earl of Ulster and Elizabeth's father, may also indicate that Elizabeth had a far greater hand in influencing her husband's political planning than she has been given credit. Such an influence would also suggest that Elizabeth's return to Scotland in October 1314 was certainly willing and that her role in Irish affairs was a vengeful product of her father's minimal attempts to secure her release from captivity, despite being an ally of Edward II of England.

While there is no date for Marjory's marriage to Walter, it probably occurred shortly after the April 1315 parliament. An undated wedding gift to Walter and Marjory of the baronies of Ratho and Bathgate in Lothian had an extensive witness list of various bishops, earls and barons, which suggests that the betrothal or nuptials took place around the same time as the parliament. Edward Bruce's departure to Ireland on 26 May and Walter Stewart's accompaniment of King Robert to Tarbert around that same date likely occurred after wedding celebrations were over. Moreover, the birth of Marjory and Walter's son, Robert, on 2 March 1316 is solid evidence that the couple were at least married by June 1315.

It was this son, Robert Stewart, who would be a leading magnatial figure of the second stage of the Scottish Wars of Independence from 1332 to 1357. Robert would also become the first King of Scots of the royal Stewart dynasty in 1371, which would rule both the Kingdoms of Scotland and England from 1603 until 1714. Marjory Bruce, therefore, was not just a daughter of Robert I and a Bruce princess, held captive before being married off to quickly produce an heir; she was the mother of one of the longest reigning royal houses in the history of the British Isles, founded in the heart of the Scottish Wars of Independence. Her premature death in 1316 or 1317 in unknown circumstances – although local Renfrewshire history speaks of an accident after she fell off her horse near Paisley – was a great loss to the royal Bruces and later the Stewarts. This was a woman who died at only twenty years of age and had suffered immensely in her life as an English captive, and yet changed the course of Scottish and British history. She was interred at Paisley Abbey, where a memorial to her still exists today.

Marjory's pregnancy in 1315 and the birth of Robert Stewart in March 1316 may have eased the pressure on Elizabeth, as Robert could now count on Edward Bruce and his baby grandson in his succession. We know that Robert and Elizabeth had four children, including two daughters that were likely born prior to 1324, but unfortunately their dates of birth are not recorded. The historian Michael Penman has attempted to narrow down on potential dates for these daughters, utilising the dates and locations of royal business conducted by Robert in addition to the king's acts of piety. In the autumn of 1315, royal acts suggest that Robert spent several months near Dunfermline where Elizabeth may have been prior to or following the birth of their eldest daughter, Margaret. Dunfermline, the resting place of Scotland's only royal saint, St Margaret, was not an unusual choice of location for Elizabeth to give birth. St Margaret of Scotland was associated with childbirth, particularly so in the context of delivering the future of the royal dynasty and as such was especially venerated by Scottish queens during labour. The naming of Elizabeth de Burgh and Robert I's eldest child and daughter as Margaret certainly indicates their gratitude to this royal saint after a safe delivery, possibly in autumn 1315. In the early sixteenth century, Margaret Tudor, queen consort of James IV of Scotland, paid to have St Margaret's 'sark' brought to her, which was probably a birthing shirt worn by the saint for her own labours. Margaret Tudor and the Scottish queens before her, possibly including Elizabeth de Burgh, may have worn or held St Margaret's shirt during the delivery of their royal children. In June 1566, Mary Queen of Scots requested that the relic of St Margaret's head be brought to her delivery room. This rather gruesome event is symbolic of the genuine faith and reliance medieval queens placed on this Scottish saint as they entered the dangerous battlefield of childbirth.

If Elizabeth did give birth to Margaret Bruce in the autumn of 1315, around a year after her release from captivity, the pressure to produce an heir may have reduced, timed with Marjory Bruce's delivery of Robert Stewart in March 1316. However, the strains of succession which plagued Robert's kingship had returned by the late autumn of 1318, when news reached Robert of his heir apparent's death at the Battle of Dundalk on 14 October that year. Edward Bruce's death not only signalled the end of Bruce military aggression in Ireland, but also removed an adult male heir from the Bruce succession so carefully laid out in April 1315. Robert's heir was now his grandson by Marjory Bruce, a toddler aged about two-and-a-half. The reality of Robert's heir, in the event that something should happen to the king, did not strike confidence among the Scottish political community. This is obvious in legislation introduced by the king at a parliament on 8 December 1318, which prohibited 'anyone [from being] a conspirator or an inventor of tales or rumours by which a source of discord shall be able to arise between the lord king and his people'. That Robert felt the need to curb such rumours demonstrates the political instability of his regime in the light of his succession issues.

This parliament also saw an update to the 1315 act of succession: 'It was ordained and assented by the unanimous consent of all and singular of the aforesaid people that if it should happen, which God forbid, that the aforesaid lord king reaches the day of his death without a surviving and enduring heir male legitimately begotten of his body, Robert [*Stewart*], the son of the lady Marjory of honourable memory, daughter of the said lord king, legitimately begotten from her marriage to the noble man Sir Walter the steward of Scotland, should succeed in every way the same lord king in his kingdom as his nearest and legitimate heir, whom all the abovesaid people of the kingdom will obey and faithfully assist in all things, just as was expressed above concerning the person of the lord king.'

Clearly, the death of Marjory Bruce in 1316 or 1317 and of Edward Bruce in October 1318 had triggered the need for the Bruce succession to be re-emphasized. However, this time it was minus two key names, and the continuation of Robert's dynasty, which he desperately needed to legitimize as far as possible, rested with his young grandson. If the December 1318 parliament betrays any political angst in Robert's regime, then this certainly informs us that Elizabeth de Burgh and her husband faced increased pressure over producing a male heir.

It may be possible that Elizabeth delivered another daughter, Matilda, before this event in 1318, or that she had suffered miscarriages or stillbirths in the three years since Margaret's potential birth in autumn 1315. However, Michael Penman again attempts to narrow in a date for Matilda's birth a little later, in the autumn of 1321. Several acts of piety by Robert indicate that Elizabeth was expecting a child in 1321: a grant made to Dunfermline Abbey on 8 July for candlelight before the tomb of St Margaret and in honour of the Virgin; a visit in early August to one of Elizabeth's preferred pilgrimage locations at Cullen; and a grant to Arbroath Abbey in October 1321. This final grant was in honour of God, the Virgin and Thomas Becket, the latter of which was a saint personally venerated by Robert throughout his life, and thus possibly indicative of a major life event for the king. Recurring peace talks with England through 1321 have also been suggested by Penman as evidence of the birth of another Bruce child. These talks, originally set for the beginning of the year, but only properly getting underway in April 1321, allegedly saw the Scots propose a long truce of twenty-six years, according to reports by English envoys to Edward II. This may seem like a random number for an awfully long ceasefire, but Penman suggests that this number might have been calculated based on Elizabeth being pregnant. If a truce of twenty-six years was agreed, then the potential son born to Elizabeth would have been bought time to enter his majority as king before renewed warfare. Talks were delayed, with a new date for envoys chosen as 1 September 1321, a date which again may have been chosen deliberately as a point by which the Scots would know if Elizabeth delivered a son or a daughter. In the end, a son was not born, and the autumn of 1321 may have seen Elizabeth and Robert welcome their daughter, Matilda, or an unrecorded stillborn baby.

It would not be until March 1324 that Elizabeth and Robert celebrated the long-awaited birth of a male heir to the Bruce dynasty. On 5 March 1324 Elizabeth gave birth to twin boys, John and David. The survival of both babies and their mother is quite incredible when we consider the higher risks involved with a twin pregnancy, let alone labour and delivery. This must have been a truly momentous occasion for the Bruce dynasty and a symbolic event, with two sons for the king born in a leap year and a decade on from Robert's victory at Bannockburn and Elizabeth's release from captivity. On a personal note, the safe delivery of John and David must have been an immense relief for Elizabeth de Burgh after ten years of pressure for a male Bruce heir.

The Bruce Family

As will be pointed out throughout this book, there is unfortunately very little evidence to grant us expansive insight into the everyday responsibilities of royal women of the Scottish Wars of Independence. Glimpses of Elizabeth de Burgh's influence on events during her husband's reign are evident, such as the Bruce campaigns in Ireland which targeted her father, Richard de Burgh, Earl of Ulster. Robert's establishment of a family manor at Cardross from 1325 likely reflects elements important to himself and Elizabeth. A jetty was included in construction plans for ships belonging to Robert and key Bruce figures which would allow quick access onto the Clyde and out to the Irish Sea and beyond. Moreover, the construction of chambers for a king and a queen at Cardross is also evident that the manor was intended to be a family home. Robert was fifty when building works began on Cardross, so it may be that he intended this to be a home for Elizabeth, fourteen years his junior, to last beyond his death.

Cardross Manor may have been a primary residence for Elizabeth and Robert's children Margaret, Matilda and David when it became habitable from 1327. After Prince David's marriage to Joan of the Tower in 1328, only four and seven years old respectively, they were brought to Cardross to visit Robert by Thomas Randolph and James Douglas, as the ailing king had been too ill to attend the wedding at Berwick. While David and Joan were soon moved to Turnberry Castle, it is possible that Margaret and Matilda remained at Cardross, or that it continued to be a primary family residence in the years following their father's death in 1329. This is supported by records from the Exchequer Rolls of Scotland which note that repairs were carried out on Margaret and Matilda's bedchamber at Cardross Manor in 1331.

The same issue regarding evidence exists for better understanding the lives of these two Bruce sisters. Above, evidence for their childhood at Cardross has been outlined until 1331, and this may have continued until their likely move to the safety of Dumbarton Castle in 1332 with the invasion of the Disinherited. In 1331, the sisters attended David's coronation at Scone in November, as the chamberlain accounts note the preparation of chambers for them, their royal brother and Joan of the Tower, in addition to their aunt Christina Bruce. These accounts also note royal expenses for the girls from 1330 to 1331, including new girdles for both sisters, a new bed and headdresses for Margaret and coloured fabric for Matilda that would likely be made into clothing. Payment for Margaret's headdresses in 1330 may help us in narrowing down what age she might have been. If she was indeed born in late 1315 then she would have been aged fourteen or fifteen in 1330 and thus legally viewed as an adult and introduced to wearing the hair coverings that were the standard of the day for teenage girls and young women. Although we do not have records of expenses for the Bruce sisters upon their flight to France from the Anglo-Balliol invasion of

Scotland in 1334, we can imagine how these princesses would have continued to be looked after at David's court in France where they would spend the next seven years of their lives with their brother.

It is possible to understand Margaret and Matilda's significance as active political assets by examining their marriages, which contrasted quite considerably. The elder of the two sisters, Margaret Bruce, married William, Earl of Sutherland, in the 1340s. If Margaret was born in late 1315 and thus twenty-seven, she was a little older than royal daughters were stereotypically married. This delay was a result of the seven years spent in exile in France at her brother's court. David and his advisors perhaps sought to prevent Margaret from marrying until returning to Scotland, in order to best use her political importance as the king's sister to their advantage. For a king returning to his kingdom after a seven-year absence in which magnates had little royal interference in their expansion, David's ability to bind nobles to his circle via a marriage to his sister would have been crucial.

On returning to Scotland, this was an advantage on which David was able to capitalize. The king received a papal dispensation for Margaret's marriage to Earl William in December 1342, but it is possible they were married before this after the royal return from France in June 1341. David made a grant to the couple of land in Forfarshire and Kincardineshire, in addition to free regality for the Earldom of Sutherland, in an act that looks like a wedding gift, but the grant's date of 28 September 1345 does not correlate with the dispensation date. However, it is likely that this grant was indeed for a celebration: Margaret was pregnant. The birth of her son, John, in 1346 confirms this grant from the king as one of a brother delighted for his sister's pregnancy. As discussed earlier, this grant was also indicative of David's favour for Margaret, her husband and later her son as key individuals in his succession planning. However, the birth of John of Sutherland in 1346 came at a great price. Margaret Bruce died close to her son's birth, most likely as a result of complications of childbirth. Again, this serves as a devastating reminder of the understood risks taken by medieval women in producing children.

Margaret's marriage to an earl and the treatment of her son as a potential heir to the throne indicates her importance as a royal woman in the Bruce dynastic plan, and in her brother's bolstering of allies upon his return to Scotland in 1341. David's other sister, however, is a different story. Matilda Bruce, possibly born to Elizabeth and Robert in 1321 or at another time from 1315 to 1327, was married to a man named Thomas Isaac, described in Walter Bower's *Scotichronicon* as 'a certain man-at-arms'. Therefore, it appears that a daughter of Robert I of Scotland and his queen, Elizabeth de Burgh, married a soldier who may not have even been of a knightly status. This is quite a contrast to Margaret's marriage to Earl William in 1342 and might speak to this as a love-match rather than a politically approved marriage. Matilda probably married Thomas after her return to Scotland from France in 1341, as he is not mentioned in any account of the royal party's journeys to and from France. Moreover, Thomas Isaac was not included in David's grant to Margaret Bruce and Earl William in 1345, which stipulated that if the couple did not produce any male heirs, half of this would be inherited by Matilda, 'his sister'. This may suggest that Matilda's marriage to Thomas did not take place until after 1345. Matilda and her soldier-husband had two daughters, Joanna and Katherine, before her death on 20 July 1353.

This marriage of a high-status woman to a man of a lower status was not a sole occurrence during this period. In the early 1330s, Isabella, Countess of the much-coveted Earldom of Fife, married her ward, Sir William Felton of Northumberland. This was a union which dashed the plans of various Scottish magnates, including Robert Stewart, with their eyes on Isabella's prestigious earldom. A similar reaction was surely had at the news of the marriage of one of Robert I's daughters to an unknown soldier or knight. However, that Matilda was able to marry a lesser man, possibly as a love match, perhaps speaks to her positive relationship with her brother. The three surviving Bruce siblings may have been close, having together fled Anglo-Balliol danger in Scotland and endured journeys to and from France and exile at Chateau Gaillard for seven years. David's personal affection for his sisters is possibly demonstrated on 6 November 1343 when he sought papal permission to choose confessors for himself, his queen, Malcolm Fleming and both of his sisters. With Fleming as David's principal guardian from their departure to France in 1334 and viewed as the king's foster-father, his name alongside David's wife and sisters indicates that this was a petition reserved for the king's close family members. We should also consider that David sought this permission after Margaret's marriage to William,

Earl of Sutherland, which again could speak to his continuing firm bonds with his sister. These sibling dynamics were possibly representative of the Bruce family unit – or the Thomas Randolph influence – that the siblings were exposed to in the 1320s and early 1330s.

Conclusion

Elizabeth de Burgh, the key to the Bruce dynasty and the queen of Robert I of Scotland, died on 26 October 1327 aged only thirty-eight. The circumstances of her death are unclear, with traditional tales stating that a fall from her horse led to her passing. We should also consider the physical toll that the births of her two daughters and twin sons may have had, especially if she had experienced any other pregnancies or stillbirths that are unknown to us.

While the cause of her death is not a surety, the reaction to it certainly speaks of a much-loved queen and wife. Elizabeth died at Cullen; a location also visited by her husband that suggests it was a personal favourite residence for the royal couple. Her death in northern Scotland away from her family suggests that it was unexpected; unsurprising for a woman of thirty-eight. Preparations for her funeral would have begun quickly, with her interment to be at the royal mausoleum of Dunfermline Abbey. The abbey was already the burial place of various kings and queens of Scotland prior to the end of the MacMalcolm dynasty in 1290, and Robert had been consciously building a royal relationship with Dunfermline to align himself with previous Scottish royalty. His own burial would take place here in 1329, as would those of many members of his family and key supporters of the Bruce crown.

Elizabeth's body would have to make the long journey from Cullen to Dunfermline, a distance of approximately 180 miles. In order to ensure her safe and intact arrival, her body was prepared at Cullen through an embalming process and the removal of her internal organs. These organs were then buried at Cullen at a religious site that may have been of significance to her in a practice that was common during the fourteenth century. Indeed, on his death in July 1329, Robert's entrails would be buried near his place of death at Cardross and his heart buried at Melrose Abbey, while his body was interred at Dunfermline Abbey. In an act of both thanks to the community of Cullen for so diligently caring for his queen's body and in memory of his wife, Robert founded a chaplainry at Cullen in 1328, dedicated to St Mary. The widowed king also made a perpetual endowment of five Scottish pounds to this chaplainry for prayers to be said for Elizabeth's soul. Incredibly, this is a payment still made today to the Auld Kirk at Cullen, confirmed and amended by Mary Queen of Scots in the sixteenth century and by Moray Council in 1975. This payment, now at £2.10 per year, is twinned with an annual memorial service for any losses in the local community held by the Auld Kirk in Elizabeth's honour. Nearly seven centuries have passed since Elizabeth de Burgh died, but her legacy is still felt in a place that was important to her during her lifetime.

Key evidence for understanding the financial and estate-related responsibilities held by medieval elite women can often be found in their surviving wills. Again, the sporadic nature of evidence from medieval Scotland drastically negates this, while studies of elite women of medieval England can often – but not always – make use of this important source. It is not surprising that Elizabeth de Burgh's will has not survived alongside the many missing written records of this period. However, chamberlain accounts from 1328 include lists of bequests made by Elizabeth from her will, particularly to her servants. Examples of this include forty shillings to Ada, keeper of Elizabeth's money, and twenty shillings each to Gilbert, William and Andrew, who cared for the queen's horses. Elizabeth also left bequests to servants involved in various duties from baking to managing her wardrobe, alongside a generous gift to her lady-in-waiting, Elizabeth Denton, who must have been her friend as well as her assistant. The chamberlain accounts also include a final act of piety from Elizabeth's will, in which she paid for a new frontal for the altar of St Mary at Dunfermline Abbey. Such evidence is crucial for providing us with glimpses into the pious life of this fourteenth-century queen and of the people who were part of her everyday life.

On Elizabeth's death, her husband's acts of piety in remembrance of his late wife surely demonstrates that she was a deeply respected queen. The care for her body by the people of Cullen and the dignified funeral procession and interment at Dunfermline Abbey would have been deserving of a woman who sacrificed much for her position as queen and her marriage to Robert I of Scotland. Robert needed a great deal to secure the legitimacy of his kingship and the continuation of his authority through the Bruce dynasty; this chapter has attempted to emphasize that Elizabeth de Burgh was the most crucial factor in this. Elizabeth was the very key to the Bruce dynasty, with her daughters continuing that importance into the reign of her son, David II. Without her return from captivity in 1314, Robert I of Scotland's kingship would certainly have concluded very differently and the remaining path of the Scottish Wars of Independence dramatically altered. In recognising and celebrating such a giant of Scottish history, we must also recognize his queen: Elizabeth de Burgh.

The Soules Conspiracy

> '… where the countess of Strathem and the lord of Soulis were found guilty of the crime of high treason'
>
> *Liber Pluscardensis*

In April 1320, three letters were sent to Pope John XXII from the Kingdom of Scotland: one from King Robert I, one from the Scottish Church and one from the barons. Of these three letters, only the latter has survived and has become famously known as the Declaration of Arbroath. This letter, representative of the political community of Scotland, stated Scotland's position as a sovereign kingdom and Robert's position as that kingdom's lawful king. It is popularly interpreted and celebrated as the first written record of a Scottish national identity, and as one of the great successes of Robert I's reign. With the seals of eight earls and around forty barons appended to a document supporting Robert as king and declaring Scotland's right to sovereignty, how else could this famous document possibly be interpreted?

This written symbol of Scottish political unity behind Robert was completely contradicted by another major event which occurred in 1320: the uncovering of an assassination plot against the king. The intentions and aftermath of this plot arguably placed a considerable stain on Robert's kingship, with its very existence demonstrating that even six years after Bannockburn and the forfeiture of his opponents, his position as king was contested and insecure. Importantly for us, one of the key instigators and possible informants of this plot was a woman.

Context

The Declaration of Arbroath, dated 6 April 1320, was no random outburst of Scottish pride or support of Robert I as king. Instead, this document was the result of several years of diplomatic pressure as Scotland and England sought papal support against the other. Robert's relationship with the papacy had been strained since his resultant excommunication in 1306 for the murder of John Comyn at the altar in the Church of the Greyfriars in Dumfries. While this excommunication was absolved from around 1308 to 1310, the years following his victory at the Battle of Bannockburn saw renewed tension with Avignon. From 1315, the Scots began a three-year military campaign in Ireland, headed by Robert's only surviving brother, Edward Bruce. While this campaign was ultimately a failure, ending in Edward's death at the Battle of Faughart in October 1318, these three years of battling inclement weather conditions and famine, as well as the English administration in Ireland, put extended pressure upon Edward II's government. Moreover, whilst Edward led the Irish Campaign, crowned High King of Ireland in June 1315, Robert simultaneously conducted a series of brutal raids of northern England. By opening the Bruce war with England on two fronts, Robert sought to drain English resources and strain an English Crown already struggling with internal political crises. The outbreak of the Bruce campaign in Ireland had an immediate consequence: Robert's second excommunication.

Edward Bruce's death in Ireland in 1318 brought another damning consequence to Robert's position as king. In April 1315, prior to his departure to Ireland, Edward Bruce was named Robert's legal heir at a parliament assembled in Ayr. At this stage, Robert had no male heir – he would not until the birth of the future David II in 1324 – and had only recently been reunited with his queen, Elizabeth de Burgh, and his only legitimate child, Marjory Bruce, who had been captive in England since 1306. For Robert, now in his early forties and having faced serious health issues, the need for an unquestionable male heir was a pressure that would recur through this reign as a means for establishing the Bruce dynasty. Edward Bruce was a man in his thirties who had proven his military capabilities alongside his brother, and thus was a more secure candidate than Robert's recently returned teenage daughter Marjory. The naming of Edward as Robert's heir in

April 1315 was an act to secure the Bruce dynasty, but also betrayed the anxieties that Robert had and the concerns that he faced from Scotland's political community. This is a theme that would remain worrisome for Robert.

In the wake of Edward Bruce's death in October 1318, a parliament in December named Robert's grandson by Marjory Bruce, Robert Stewart, as heir to the throne. However, Marjory's son was an infant, thereby returning the Bruce king to the succession anxieties he faced before 1315. Indeed, the prospect of baby Robert as the Bruce successor versus the presence of Edward Balliol at the English court from 1318 would have been a point of severe concern. Edward was the son of John Balliol, King of Scots from 1292 until his forced abdication in 1296 at Edward I of England's invasion of Scotland. By contrast to the infant Robert Stewart, Edward Balliol was in his thirties and surely appealed to those Scots and English who had been disinherited by Robert after the Battle of Bannockburn in November 1314. Again, the severity of these concerns was betrayed at the same parliament in which Robert Stewart was named heir, in which a law was enacted to stop rumours being spread about the Bruce government.

The political pressure and unrest which Robert was facing, even before Edward Bruce's death, may have been a key factor in his decision to attack Berwick in April 1318. Berwick, a significant Scottish coastal burgh for trade, had been hammered by Anglo-Scottish warfare since 1296, and had been in English hands since that date. By assaulting Berwick, Robert was making a statement of his authority and re-establishing his capabilities as king. While the town fell to James Douglas and Patrick of Dunbar in April 1318, Robert arrived to personally lead an eleven-week siege on Berwick's castle, which fell to the Bruce Scots in the summer of 1318. This was a monumental moment, considering that the burgh had been held by the English since the sack of Berwick over twenty years before. However, Robert's assault on Berwick renewed open warfare with England, and again triggered papal reaction.

As a result of particularly challenging weather and subsequent famines, in addition to diseases which wiped out sheep and cattle populations, the years following Bannockburn had seen a military stalemate between England and Scotland. Moreover, in 1317, the papacy under Pope John XXII had brokered a truce between the Scots and the English in the efforts to achieve peace and reroute military attention to a crusade. By attacking Berwick in 1318, Robert not only ended the stalemate between Scotland and England, but additionally broke the truce established by the papacy. This affront to the papacy was worsened by the Battle of Myton in September 1319, in which James Douglas and Thomas Randolph soundly defeated an English army led by William Melton, Archbishop of York, in Yorkshire. This Scottish victory on English soil is often referred to as the Chapter of Myton or the White Battle, due to the sheer number of clergymen who were killed in battle. The combinations of the military events of 1318 and 1319 surely enraged Pope John XXII.

Numerous Papal Bulls were dispatched to Scotland, which summoned Robert and three of his Scottish bishops to an audience with the Pope in Avignon on 1 May 1320. These bulls also renewed Robert's excommunication for John Comyn's murder, meaning that he was a king who was thrice excommunicated. Importantly, the papal sanctions of excommunicating a monarch meant that the ties of loyalty and allegiance between subject and monarch were dissolved. As has been established, this placed Robert in an even more precarious situation than before. A firm response was required to defend his actions and his position as King of Scots. The result was the Declaration of Arbroath.

Within this context, it is important to understand that the Declaration of Arbroath was not a popular outpouring of support for the King of Scots in the wake of these papal sanctions, but rather a document orchestrated and engineered by the Bruce regime. It would have taken weeks to gather the signatories and seals from the Scottish political community, with questions over the authenticity of these seals often being asked. This is particularly so when we consider that four of the nobles whose names appear on the declaration would be involved in an assassination plot against Robert that same year. While the declaration did have an immediate impact on Pope John XXII's attitude towards the Scots, seeing him pressure Edward II of England for peace and for the first time referring to Robert as King of Scots, peace would not be secured between the two kingdoms for another eight years. Moreover, the Bruce regime's concentrated efforts at displaying a unifying front would be upturned within months.

Women of the Soules Conspiracy

The political tension and unrest of Robert's reign in the years following Bannockburn has been demonstrated. If the Declaration of Arbroath had not occurred in April 1320, then the sudden eruption of the Soules Conspiracy later that year would probably not appear all that surprising, especially when we consider the succession crisis that Robert faced in addition to the December 1318 law forbidding rumours against the king and his government. Within this context, it is probably unlikely that the uncovered assassination plot against Robert was a surprise. Robert had proved himself a shrewd politician, as well as an exceptional military leader; he was no fool to think that such a conspiracy did not exist in the context of Edward Balliol's presence in England and his own domestic pressures.

The Soules Conspiracy points to a political conspiracy which sought to remove Robert from the throne and install William Soules as King of Scots. William, Lord of Liddesdale and Butler of Scotland, was a close relative to the Comyns who had been in English service, but defected to the Scots following the Battle of Bannockburn in 1314. Soules was rewarded for his changed loyalties to Robert with the appointment as Butler of Scotland in 1318, with his name present on the Declaration of Arbroath. However, William Soules was a relatively low-key political figure in Scotland, and it is far more probable that he was involved in a plot to place Edward Balliol on the throne, rather than himself. While his own ambitions for the throne cannot be directly eliminated, the active presence of Edward Balliol in the English court from 1318, coinciding with Bruce royal anxieties of rumours against the king, was surely no accident. Soules' relation to the Comyns, staunch supporters of John Balliol's kingship and stauncher opponents to Robert, surely meant that his involvement in a plot to reinstate the Balliol dynasty was a naturally occurring alliance. The infamous naming of the Soules Conspiracy, rather than the Balliol Conspiracy, may have even been consciously done by the Bruce regime and later royal governments to downplay the very real dynastic threat faced by Robert from 1318 to 1320.

How did this conspiracy come to light? Chronicle coverage of the event varies in who the informant of the plot was. Sir Thomas Gray in his *Scalachronica* names Murdoch of Menteith as the one who exposed the plot to Robert. The grant of forfeited lands to Murdoch in the aftermath of this even may have been a reward for his role in uncovering this conspiracy. It has also been suggested that Patrick, Earl of Dunbar, was a key informant of the plot. He had quickly abandoned a diplomatic mission to Avignon to return to Scotland, and was not long after married to Agnes Randolph, the daughter of one of Robert's key lieutenants Thomas Randolph, Earl of Moray. However, Archdeacon John Barbour's *The Bruce* provides us with another informant: 'But all of them were exposed by a lady, as I heard, before they could carry out their intentions. For she told everything to the king, their aims and their plans, how he would have been dead and how Soulis would reign in his place, and told him the exact evidence that this intention was a matter of truth.'

Barbour does not name the lady who ultimately saved Robert's life and prevented the premature downfall of the Bruce dynasty. There is, however, another woman who is named as being one of the ringleaders of the plot: Agnes Comyn, Countess of Strathearn.

Agnes was the daughter of Alexander Comyn, Earl of Buchan, and Elizabeth de Quincy of Winchester. This made her part of one of the most powerful noble families of medieval Scotland, who were struck down by Robert Bruce in his efforts to seize power in Scotland. Her brother was John Comyn, Earl of Buchan as inherited by their father, who was married to Isabella MacDuff, the woman who defected from the Comyns to participate in Robert's inauguration in 1306. Agnes was also the aunt of Alice Comyn, who by the 1330s was one of the last remaining Comyn heiresses to relentlessly claim back her disinherited land and title during the second Scottish Wars of Independence. Her cousin was John Comyn of Badenoch, the man who Robert murdered at the altar of the Church of the Greyfriars in Dumfries in 1306. Clearly, Agnes Comyn was a woman of powerful heritage that had been all but destroyed by Robert. It is therefore unsurprising that multiple chronicle accounts of the 1320 plot place her, 'the Countess of Stratherne', as one of the ringleaders.

Agnes' position as Countess of Strathearn came through her marriage to Malise, Earl of Strathearn, probably occurring sometime in the 1280s to 1290s. This could be estimated by Agnes' activities in 1306, when her husband was captured and imprisoned in England for allegedly supporting Robert's usurpation of the throne. Agnes petitioned for Malise's release, citing that he had been wrongfully imprisoned, alongside their son, who entered the written record for the first time at this point. This suggests that Agnes and Malise's son was relatively young to be first recorded at this stage in partnership with his mother, and only in the absence and imprisonment of his father. Despite Agnes' furious petitions to Edward I for her husband's innocence and release, and the English king's order of an inquiry into Malise's captivity, nothing came of these interventions. When Malise was finally released from captivity in 1310, he lost the Earldom of Strathearn when his defence of Perth against Robert fell in 1313. In the aftermath of this, he and Agnes' eldest son, Malise, took control of Strathearn as a staunchly loyal supporter of Robert's kingship. This was surely salt in the wound for Agnes, who had watched her natal family fall to the Bruces and who had been separated from her husband for four years on account of Robert's usurpation and Malise's alleged wrong conviction for supporting this.

Agnes was named as a ringleader of this plot in a parliament called in August 1320 that would see the trial and conviction of those involved in the Soules Conspiracy. This parliament has been dubbed the Black Parliament, on account of its grim nature and the brutal punishments for treason that were its result. This parliament is recorded only in chronicle accounts, with John of Fordun dating the parliament to the beginning of August 1320 at Scone. Fordun begins by convicting his ringleaders: 'There, the lord William of Sowlis and the Countess of Stratherne were convicted of the crime of high treason, by conspiring against the aforesaid king; and sentence of perpetual punishment was passed upon them. The lords David of Brechin, Gilbert of Merlb, John of Logie, knights, and Richard Broune, esquire, having been convicted of the aforesaid conspiracy, were first drawn by horses, and, in the end, underwent capital punishment.'

Agnes' sentencing of life imprisonment alongside William Soules as the primary leaders of the plot seems relatively merciful compared to the fate that befell the other conspirators who were found guilty. Barbour provides us with more detail as to 'Sir Gilbert Malherbe, Logy and Richard Brown', who were drawn, hanged and beheaded. Barbour also writes that 'good Sir David Brechin' was also drawn and hanged, not for participating in the plot, but for being aware of it and failing to inform the king. Brechin's 'disgraceful death', alongside the bizarre guilty conviction of Sir Roger Moubray's corpse, only saved from a post-mortem execution by Robert's mercy, are the particularly grisly and harsh punishments which lend to the Black Parliament's name. For a king who had been magnanimous towards his former opponents until this point, the savage punishments of this episode were quite a display of brutality from Robert. This surely indicates to us the severity of this conspiracy and the genuine threat and instability that had been occurring under his reign.

It is not known where Agnes was imprisoned, but William Soules' perpetual imprisonment in Dumbarton Castle may indicate that she was similarly placed here. Indeed, she does not appear again in record and presumably died in imprisonment. However, it could be possible that Agnes was afforded a less harsh form of imprisonment, placed under house arrest in a similar way to that experienced by Elizabeth de Burgh in England. Indeed, the experience of Elizabeth, Robert's own wife, may have moved the king to prevent Agnes being imprisoned in as harsh a condition as Soules. It could even be considered that Elizabeth may have intervened on this, a role often undertaken by medieval queens in interceding for a doomed receiver of the king's wrath and pleading mercy from the king on their behalf. It isn't so far removed to wonder that Elizabeth may have done so, especially in the context of her eight years of imprisonment in England under house arrest.

It has been suggested that Agnes Comyn, Countess of Strathearn, was the same woman that Barbour describes as being the one to reveal the plot to Robert. Why Agnes would do this, considering the certain hostility she must have felt towards Robert in the context of his relationship with her natal family and husband, is unclear. She would surely – and perhaps understandably – have celebrated the downfall and assassination of a man who had decimated her family and inheritance. However, the very magnanimity with which Robert approached his previous opponents, in addition to his policies of landholding and title as reward, may have been enough to convince Agnes to back out of the plot. Moreover, she may have been concerned about her son's position with the king and over Strathearn, should she be caught in the group behind the conspiracy. Nevertheless, Agnes was still sentenced to life imprisonment and named as a key leader in the plot. This perhaps contradicts the possibility of her being the lady who revealed the Soules Conspiracy to Robert.

Who could this other woman have been to save the life of the king and continuing existence of the Bruce dynasty? In order for her to have been made aware of, approached about or involved in the plot, she must have been connected by a shared interest in placing Edward Balliol, or possibly William Soules, on the throne. A key candidate could be Isabella Strathbogie, daughter of the Earl of Atholl, brutally executed in 1306 for supporting Robert's seizing of the throne, and sister to David Strathbogie, the disinherited Earl of Atholl. In addition to Isabella's family being ousted from Atholl by Robert in favour of Neil Campbell of Lochawe, she may have felt a personal resentment towards Robert for the death of her father in 1306. John Strathbogie had been captured after the Battle of Methven and was hanged in London in November 1306. His hanging took place on gallows that were specially constructed to be thirty feet higher than usual, to signify the monumental nature of his execution; John was the first earl to be executed in England in 230 years. The humiliation and personal devastation of this event would not have been quickly forgotten by his children, including Isabella.

However, Isabella was likely further resentful of the Bruce king due to the actions of his brother, Edward Bruce. By 1312, Isabella's brother David had resubmitted to Robert after defecting to the English in 1307. In reward for this return to Robert, David was named Constable of Scotland and Isabella was betrothed to Edward Bruce, the king's only surviving brother. This was a significant betrothal which brought the Strathbogie Earls of Atholl close to the king's inner circle, with Isabella set to become the king's sister-in-law. However, according to Barbour's *The Bruce*, Edward 'held … Dame Isabel, in great distaste,' instead favouring another Isabella, who was daughter of the Earl of Ross. When we consider that Edward Bruce had an illegitimate son, Alexander, by Isabella Strathbogie of Atholl, this appears to be quite an unpleasant situation in which Isabella was placed as a mistress rather than as a wife, replaced by another woman. Barbour claims that this situation was what caused Isabella's brother to defect to the English on the eve of Bannockburn in 1314.

This situation, in addition to previous points, may have been enough to sour Isabella's relationship to Robert's kingship to the extent that she was involved in the Soules Conspiracy. However, despite the rather unclear circumstances of her relationship with Edward Bruce, Isabella chose to remain in Scotland while her brother went to England. Moreover, her son, Alexander Bruce, would become one of his royal uncle's favourites, while Isabella was referred to by Robert as the Countess of Atholl. This continuing and seemingly positive relationship between Isabella and the Bruce king may have neutralized her interest in a plot to remove him and been enough for her to warn him of this threat.

Conclusion

The Soules Conspiracy of 1320 is one the most significant moments of Robert I's reign, but it is largely unknown. This is partly due to being overshadowed by the famous Declaration of Arbroath occurring in the same year, but also as a result of a concentrated effort by the Bruce dynasty and later regimes to downplay this event as a brief issue, rather than the genuine dynastic threat that it posed. Importantly, women are at the centre of what was arguably the biggest disaster of Robert's reign that may have transformed Scotland's history.

Barbour's claim that the conspiracy was exposed to Robert by a lady is crucial, as he chooses to credit the plot's downfall to a woman rather than to Murdoch of Menteith or Patrick of Dunbar, as other chronicles have done. It could be that none or all of these individuals were involved, but Barbour's inclusion of a lady as Robert's saviour is noteworthy.

However, what is undisputed is that one of the primary instigators of this plot, and therefore one of the greatest opponents of Robert I of Scotland was Agnes Comyn, Countess of Strathearn. Whether Agnes changed her mind and decided to inform the king, thus being Barbour's lady, cannot be known, but her involvement in the plot is firm. With women as both the informant and the ringleader of a plot to assassinate Robert, this demonstrates the political power and presence of elite women during the Scottish Wars of Independence. Ultimately, this shows that women were certainly involved in and affected by this conflict, so much so that Agnes Comyn plotted the killing of a king and downfall of a dynasty. To underestimate or ignore women in the Scottish Wars of Independence, is to ignore key historical figures who nearly changed the course of history.

Joan of the Tower

> 'And off Dame Jhone als off the Tour,
> That syne wes of full gret valour'
>
> John Barbour, *The Bruce*

The second stage of the Scottish Wars of Independence has been somewhat overshadowed by the first stage in popular understanding of this warfare. Dramatic tales of heroism (or villainy?) committed by iconic figures like William Wallace and Robert Bruce are well known, and watershed events such as the Battle of Bannockburn and the Declaration of Arbroath are etched into Scotland's national consciousness and education. By comparison, the military and political achievements of leaders from the 1330s to 1350s are not so well known.

This could be for a number of reasons. The reign of Robert Bruce's successor, David II, is often portrayed as that of a man who did not quite fill the boots left behind by his father, although this has been contested by historians. Moreover, David was absent from Scotland for two lengthy periods, first for seven years in France and later for eleven years in English captivity. What use are tales of heroism and patriotism if there is not a present and inspiring king at their forefront?

Another explanation might be that this period saw an extreme hardship that would shape the future of the medieval and early modern European world: the Black Death. This plague arrived in Europe in 1348, spreading to Scotland in 1349, and killed approximately one third of Europe's population. The plague did not discriminate between social classes, and the socio-economic implications of its devastation would change medieval society.

Finally, the second stage of the Scottish Wars of Independence could arguably be viewed as far less straightforward than the first. This was a period of consequence and retaliation over landholding and title, in addition to grappling for control over a kingdom. Moreover, Edward III of England's focus on France with the outbreak of the Hundred Years War in 1337 prevented Scottish leaders from facing one primary antagonist. With a regularly absent David II of Scotland and a distracted Edward III of England, it is trickier to portray this period as 'Scotland versus England'.

The overshadowing of this stage and the lesser-known reign of David II have contributed to the greater misunderstanding of the life and reign of his queen, Joan of the Tower. It is particularly important for this to be corrected, especially when we consider that Joan was queen of a kingdom with a captive king for eleven years. Moreover, she was a queen caught between two kingdoms: that of her husband and that of her natal family. This chapter will attempt to shed light on this queen consort within the context of the second Scottish Wars of Independence.

Childhood

Understanding the early years of medieval women – even those of the noble and royal classes – is a difficult task to undertake. The ramifications of sparse evidence for medieval Scotland have made this particularly challenging for studying the women of fourteenth-century Scotland. Much of this is the same for Joan, but it is possible for us to glean a greater understanding of her childhood, thanks to her position as a daughter of the King of England.

Joan was born on 5 July 1321, the youngest daughter and final child of Edward II of England and Isabella of France. Her birth in the Tower of London lent her the name she would be known by: Joan of the Tower. The first two weeks of Joan's life were spent with her parents in the Tower, as her father was in London at the time of her birth and quickly joined her mother for nearly a week after her delivery. From records of Edward's finances, we know that he gifted eighty pounds to the messenger who travelled across London to inform him of Joan's birth, which surely speaks to his joy at this event.

Joan's birth made her one of four royal siblings: the eldest, Edward of Windsor, was born in 1312; John of Eltham was born in 1316; and Eleanor of Woodstock in 1318. Joan and her siblings would be raised in a reign fraught with bouts of political tension and upheaval, due to her father's controversial political 'favourites' and military failures. In the midst of this increasing tension in 1324, Joan and her older sister, Eleanor, were entrusted to the guardianship of Ralph de Monthermer and Isabella Hastings.

Monthermer was Joan's uncle through his marriage to Edward II's sister, the late Joan of Acre, a strong family connection which explains his role as guardian for the two princesses. Isabella Hastings was a daughter of Hugh Despenser the Elder, the father of Edward's favourite, Hugh Despenser the Younger, and thus a beneficiary of the king's favouritism. As such, Isabella's role in the guardianship of the king's daughters surely contributed to the increasing resentment of the Despensers among the English nobility. This guardianship likely contributed to Edward's souring relationship with his queen, Isabella of France, who despised the Despensers and their influence over her husband.

Joan's childhood was also notably marked by the marriages which were sought for her by her father before his deposition, and her mother in its aftermath. Initial marital talks resulted in Joan's betrothal in 1325 to Pedro, the eldest son of Alphonso, who was heir to the kingdom of Aragon. As Pedro was only born in 1319 and Joan in 1321, this betrothal would not have been expected to come to immediate fruition, but is evidence for the careful future planning of Aragon and England's relationship. This betrothal also reflected Edward's consistent interests in marrying his children into the kingdoms of Aragon and Castile. In the same year of Joan's betrothal to Pedro of Aragon, her older sister, Eleanor, was betrothed to King Alphonso XI of Castile. Additionally, Edward actively pursued a marriage for his son and heir, Edward of Windsor, to Alphonso's sister, Leonor. Edward's desire to see his children united within these kingdoms, particularly Castile, stemmed from his need for more political allies amidst tension with France, but also from his own personal connection as the half-Castilian son of Eleanor of Castile.

Queen Isabella departed England for France in March 1325, commissioned by Edward to pursue a peace treaty with her brother, Charles IV of France, and was later joined by her and Edward's eldest son and heir, Edward of Windsor. However, by December 1325 she refused to return to England and was effectively holding her eldest son hostage to apply political pressure upon her husband and against the Despensers. When Isabella did return in September 1326, it was at the head of an army and alongside her political ally (and lover?) Roger Mortimer, with the intention to remove the Despensers from power. Her daughters, Joan and Eleanor, had been moved to Bristol to be placed under the guardianship of Hugh Despenser the Elder, and Isabella's personal participation in the leadership of the Siege of Bristol speaks to her disapproval of Despenser's care of her daughters. Isabella and

Mortimer's invasion was successful in destroying the Despensers and resulted in Edward II's deposition and Edward of Windsor's instating as King Edward III of England.

The explosive events of 1326, in which her father was deposed and imprisoned by an invading army headed by Queen Isabella and Roger Mortimer, brought Joan and her sister's potential marriages to Aragon and Castile to a close. Edward II's best laid plans to see his son and heir married to Alphonso of Castile's sister were dashed by his queen's betrothal of their son to Philippa of Hainault in 1326, in order to secure military support for the invasion of England. While the political chaos in the aftermath of these events no doubt placed the marriages of children on the backburner, the cancellation of the Castilian betrothal may have offended Alphonso and his regents enough to cancel the second betrothal to Eleanor of Woodstock. This additionally would have had a clear effect on Joan of the Tower's intended marriage to the future Pedro of Aragon. Joan's mother, Isabella, had a crucial purpose for Joan's hand much closer to home.

Marriage

Isabella and Mortimer's deposition of Edward II and removal of the Despensers was intended to oust a regime made unpopular by favouritism. However, continuing favouritism and Isabella's dubious financial activity resulted in their own unpopular ruling of England on behalf of the fourteen-year-old Edward III, who was crowned on 5 February 1327. The result was continuing political chaos, with several attempts being made to free the imprisoned former Edward II from his captivity in Berkeley Castle.

It was in this chaos that Robert I of Scotland made the decision to intensify Scottish aggression against England. For the Scots, the 1320s had included applying diplomatic pressure on England, with Robert acting with greater royal confidence after rooting out his key opposition in the Soules Conspiracy of 1320. While the Declaration of Arbroath in 1320 had not resolved Anglo-Scottish warfare – nor indeed Scotland's internal political instability – it had resulted in the softening of papal attitudes towards the Scots and pleas to Edward II of England to push for peace with his northern neighbour. This change was more a result of the papal agenda of promoting a united Christian crusade, but the outward desire for peace between Scotland and England was a factor of which the Scots sought to take advantage. A thirteen-year truce was struck between the two kingdoms in May 1323, before Scottish embassies departed to Avignon and Paris in 1325 and 1326. The former resulted in papal recognition of Robert Bruce as King of Scots in exchange for the Scots pushing for peace with England to allow a crusade. The latter resulted in the Treaty of Corbeil, signed on 26 April 1326. This treaty between the Scots and Charles IV of France was signed in the context of burgeoning Anglo-French warfare and applied further diplomatic pressure to Edward II.

Robert's regime had also been humiliating Edward II in military terms with relentless raids of northern England and defeats on English soil. The Scots waded into the long-awaited civil war that erupted in England in 1321 after years of increasing friction between Edward and his magnates by flirting with a potential alliance with Thomas of Lancaster's rebels. After defeating these rebels at Boroughbridge in March 1322, a victorious Edward marched north to Scotland that same year, but was forced to retreat after the Scots employed a scorched-earth tactic across the Lothians, depriving Edward's army of supplies. Robert and his lieutenants followed this by again harrying the north of England in Edward's wake, before defeating Edward on 14 October at Old Byland in Yorkshire, nearly capturing the English king and queen on their home turf.

The collapse of Edward II's government, Isabella and Mortimer's invasion in 1326 and the crowning of the minor Edward III on 1 February 1327 presented an opportune moment for Robert to increase pressure for a settlement. Robert sought to provoke instability in England by ramping up the severity of the brutal Scottish raids on northern England and dabbling with involvement in rebellions against Isabella and Mortimer's regency. This triggered a response from Edward III's new council, who mustered troops to march north and prove themselves with a military victory against the Scots. This was to be a disaster for Edward III's fledgling regime. In June 1327, Scottish forces under Thomas Randolph, Donald of Mar and James 'the Black' Douglas conducted a series of raids known as the Weardale Campaign, delivering immense damage across northern England before confronting Edward III's army at Stanhope Park, near Durham. After weeks of raiding and evading the English, the Scots attacked the English camp in a terrifying night attack, cutting the guy ropes of tents to create disorder and panic across the sleeping English army. Edward III himself was trapped inside his own collapsed tent. The Scots managed to outwit the English and fled unscathed, leaving a fourteen-year-old Edward III in tears.

While the psychological, physical and financial damage of the Weardale Campaign and Stanhope Park cannot be understated, the impact was doubled by the news that Robert I of Scotland had crossed to Ulster. Robert's father-in-law, Richard de Burgh, had died the previous year, and during his four-month stay in Ulster in 1327, Robert sought to bolster Scottish claims to the earldom whilst threatening Edward III's regime with his mere presence there. The events of 1327 at the hands of the Scots had created a cacophony of disaster for Isabella and Mortimer's regency: the Weardale Campaign had been catastrophic on numerous levels, revolt was imminent in Wales and Ireland and criticism of their regency was rampant.

In October 1327, the English government presented terms to Scotland for peace, which were accepted. The result of this was the Treaty of Edinburgh-Northampton, ratified in the spring of 1328. The treaty had several crucial terms: Edward III renounced all claims of Plantagenet overlordship of Scotland, Robert Bruce and his heirs were recognized as King of Scots, Scotland's territories were to revert to their state at the time of Alexander III's reign and the Scots would pay around £20,000 in reparations to England. Importantly, the Treaty of Edinburgh-Northampton did contain another term that would alter Joan of the Tower's future: 'and for the security and permanence of that peace it is settled and agreed that a marriage take place ... between David the son and heir of the King of Scotland and Joan, the sister of the King of England, who as yet are of so tender an age that they cannot make contract of matrimony.'

To reaffirm this treaty and the new peace between kingdoms, Joan of the Tower was to wed Robert I of Scotland's four-year-old son, Prince David. Joan's proxy marriage to David – neither bride nor groom were old enough for the fulfilment of the marriage – took place at Berwick on 17 July 1328. This was a lavish celebration and according to Walter Bower, 'an occasion of unutterable joy for among all the people of both kingdoms'. Tellingly, neither Robert I of Scotland nor Edward III of

England were present at the event, with Joan's mother Queen Isabella accompanying the bride to her wedding celebrations. Barbour tells us of this seven-year-old English princess and her first moments in Scotland following her proxy marriage to David: 'the queen left her daughter there with great riches and royal ceremony. I'm sure that for a long time no lady was conducted home so richly. The earl [Randolph] and the lord Douglas received her honourably as was certainly appropriate, for she was afterwards the best and fairest lady you needed to see ... with all their company went speedily toward the king, taking with them the young David and also the young lady, Dame Joan.'

Joan's arrival in Scotland as the spouse of the future King of Scots was the product of a peace treaty after decades of Anglo-Scottish warfare. The Scots apparently nicknamed her Joan 'make-peace', whether affectionately or in mockery of what was to come, we cannot be certain. However, the child-couple David and Joan heralded hope for the kingdom's future in the twilight years of Robert I's reign and signalled the peace settlement and royal dynastic future of the Bruces. However, their union cemented a treaty which – while ultimately resulting in Robert's long-sought security of his dynasty and territorial ambitions – was achieved under an increasingly unpopular government and during the minority of a teenage king. It was therefore unstable and viewed by the young Edward III as an embarrassment. Joan of the Tower's new life in Scotland in 1328 symbolized a peace that she and her new husband may have been too young to understand and brought an end to the first stage of the Scottish Wars of Independence. But it was not a peace that would last.

Warfare Renewed

Again, the sparse nature of evidence for medieval Scotland and the study of women prevents us from fully understanding Joan's life following her arrival in Scotland. Therefore, we must rely on the wider context to form ideas of what her life looked like in the six years she spent in Scotland before fleeing to France.

The death of Robert I of Scotland on 7 June 1329 heralded a change in the Bruce dynasty: Joan's five-year-old husband, David, would be King of Scots. However, unlike previous instances of a minor inheriting the throne, David and Joan were not quickly whisked from their residence at Turnberry Castle to Scone for a transition of power. Instead, their coronation as king and queen would not occur until November 1331, leaving a gap of around two-and-a-half years where Scotland did not have an inaugurated monarch. The rapid transition of power between king and heir was a necessity in similar instances: in 1249 upon the unexpected death of Alexander II of Scotland, his queen Marie de Coucy ensured the quick inauguration of their only son at Scone within days of his death.

The gap to David's ascension to the throne could be compared to the four years between Alexander III's death in 1286 and Margaret Maid of Norway's planned arrival in Scotland in 1290, when a group of guardians ruled in her stead in the interim. Similarly, Robert I's death in June 1329 saw power transition to a regency under a key military and political lieutenant of the Bruce regime: Thomas Randolph. Randolph's new role as regent occurred without resistance, as this was planned well in advance of Robert's death with the knowledge of a boy-king inheriting his throne. However, the key difference between David and Margaret's respective delays of ceremonies was that Margaret was in Norway under the authority of her royal father and his advisors. David was very much in Scotland in 1329, based at Turnberry Castle as the seat of the Bruce Earldom of Carrick. It may have been that there was no pressing need to see David and Joan's quick coronation in 1329 under the smooth transition of power to Randolph's guardianship, and that the Scots were content to wait until the new king was older. This does seem strange when we consider the lengths that the late Robert I went to in establishing the legitimacy of his dynasty.

David was eventually crowned king on 24 November 1331 at Scone, with Joan of the Tower crowned queen on the same day. This event was monumental as a continuation of the Bruce dynasty, but also as the first official coronation in Scotland rather than an inauguration. A coronation involved the anointing of the king with holy oil as a symbol of sacred authority, thus signifying God's blessing and creating a powerful act of legitimacy for a new regime. The full rites of a coronation had been pursued by the Scots for over a century to bring Scottish royalty and sovereignty equal to that of England and other kingdoms. David and Joan would be the first beneficiaries of papal granting of these rites in the weeks following Robert I's death.

Despite their coronation, David and Joan were still minors and governance continued under Thomas Randolph. That the years of 1329 to 1331 appear rather uneventful compared to the decades of the first Scottish War of Independence is testament to Randolph's capability as a level-headed and respected regent. There is no doubt that there were the usual resurgences of political rivalries in a kingdom without a king, particularly following the deaths of other key Bruce figures – William Lamberton, Bishop of St Andrews and James 'the Black' Douglas in 1328 and 1330 respectively. Nevertheless, Randolph held the reins of governance effectively and was no doubt an influential figure to the young and impressionable royal couple, David and Joan.

Further evidence of Randolph's strength as Scotland's regent can be seen in what occurred only a month after his unexpected death at Musselburgh in July 1332: the outbreak of the second stage of the Scottish Wars of Independence. Although this had been inevitable, with Randolph travelling to Musselburgh with the purpose of monitoring imminent military activity from the south, the quick trigger of warfare immediately after his death surely indicates his role as the last bastion of Bruce strength under a child-king.

The new opponents of the Bruce regime were the Disinherited, the men and women who had been stripped of their Scottish lands and titles in Scotland by Robert I. By 1332, their persistent mission to return north and claim back that which was taken from them had formed under the leadership of Edward Balliol, the son of John Balliol who was forcibly abdicated by Edward I of England in 1296. For the Disinherited, Edward Balliol was an adult male claimant to the throne of Scotland, currently held by an eight-year-old David Bruce and his eleven-year-old queen, Joan of the Tower. In the face of a royal child-couple and the death of Thomas Randolph, this was the moment that Balliol and his Disinherited forces decided to strike back.

Edward Balliol's Disinherited army landed in Scotland within weeks of Thomas Randolph's death, making quick progress across Fife to meet the Bruce Scots at the Battle of Dupplin Moor on 11 August 1332. The Disinherited annihilated the Bruce Scots, who had been struggling under unclear leadership in the wake of Randolph's death and the resurgence of factionalism. This battle was a brutal defeat which saw the deaths of many key Bruce Scots, including

Randolph's heir, who had only been Earl of Moray for a month. With many submissions to Edward Balliol in the aftermath of the battle, Balliol was crowned king at Scone on 24 September 1332. David and Joan were most likely kept in the west for their own safety, perhaps moving from Turnberry Castle to the solid fortification and safety of Dumbarton Rock.

On paper, this certainly appears to be an absolute disaster for the Bruce regime. However, within weeks of his coronation, Edward Balliol was on the backfoot as his party grappled for power with Bruce Scots, who pushed back against his and the Disinheriteds' claims in Scotland. Balliol's struggles resulted in him seeking and accepting the aid of his powerful neighbour south of the border. On 23 November 1332, the Kingdom of Scotland was once again submitted by a Balliol king to a Plantagenet: Edward III of England.

Edward III had been waiting for this moment, having overthrown the government of his mother, Isabella, and her ally, Roger Mortimer, in 1330 and denouncing the Treaty of Edinburgh-Northampton as a shameful falsehood. In December 1332, Edward revived Plantagenet claims to Scotland by formally declaring the treaty as illegal in anticipation of an Anglo-Balliol invasion of Scotland the following year.

It was within this context that Edward Balliol proposed to marry Joan of the Tower in February 1333. This union would cement the new submission of Scotland to England, an antidote to the symbolism of David and Joan's proxy marriage. As a further carrot, Balliol promised to increase Joan's jointure and 'to provide for' the young David Bruce himself, which would likely have been safe passage away from Scotland. Under her older brother's declaration, Joan's marriage to David was no longer a legal requirement and could have been annulled on the basis of the marriage being unconsummated as they were both still minors. It is unclear whether Edward III accepted or confirmed the betrothal of an almost fifty-year-old Edward Balliol to his eleven-year-old sister. Again, the young Joan of the Tower was placed at the centre of the future of the Kingdom of Scotland and its relationship with her home the Kingdom of England.

In the summer of 1333, Edward III of England marched north in support of Edward Balliol and the Disinherited. His invasion began by taking over the siege of the coastal burgh of Berwick, already a victim to the Anglo-Scottish warfare of the thirteenth and fourteenth centuries many times over, which had been ongoing since March under Balliol. Berwick surrendered on 20 July 1333 after the Battle of Halidon Hill, which could be argued as the most disastrous battle for the Bruce Scots on Scottish soil. This utter destruction of the Scots in Edward III's first battle resulted in the deaths of several senior Bruce Scots, including the regent, Archibald Douglas, and was a devastating blow to the Bruce regime in Scotland and a major boost to the Balliols and the Disinherited. The Scots' defeat was so severe that Edward III viewed that the war was already over, with Balliol's position as a vassal king under England secure.

We also know that the defeat at Halidon Hill was a grim severity for the Bruces as it was the final factor which led to the decision to evacuate David and Joan from Scotland. In May 1334, they set sail, probably from Dumbarton, supervised by Malcolm Fleming of Dumbarton. The royal couple did not go alone with Fleming, but with other young members of their court: David's sisters, Margaret and Matilda Bruce; the sons of the late guardian, William and John Douglas; and the illegitimate son of James 'the Black' Douglas, Archibald. This group, the next generation of the Bruce regime of the 1310s and 1320s, fled to France from the rapid military progress of Edward Balliol and his all-important ally, Edward III of England.

Exile in France

In late May 1334, an exiled child-king and his other young companions arrived on the shores of Normandy. Bower tells us that they were 'honourably received by the king and people of France,' spending time with Philip VI of France near Paris before being transferred to their own residence at Château-Gaillard. Overlooking the River Seine, this mighty hilltop fortress was constructed in the late twelfth century under Richard the Lionheart and was once a coveted military fortification that had become a royal prison in the fourteenth century. In 1334, Château-Gaillard became the home of the exiled court of David II of Scotland and is where he and Joan would spend the next seven years.

Unfortunately, little evidence survives to provide details about David and Joan's time at Château-Gaillard. The royal couple would have been kept under the watchful guardianship of David's 'foster-father', Malcolm Fleming, continuing any tutelage that they had been receiving in Scotland. They were also in the company of other young Bruce Scots who had travelled with them in May 1334, including David's two sisters, Margaret and Matilda. This was not how Robert I of Scotland would have hoped that his three surviving children and his son's queen would spend seven of their teenage years, and as David grew older, he must have been very aware of his isolation from his war-ravaged kingdom. For Joan, this would be the third kingdom in which she spent her formative years: England from her birth to the age of seven, Scotland from seven until thirteen and now France where she would remain until she was about twenty years old. It is easy to imagine that Joan may have entered adulthood with a conflicting sense of identity and loyalties, although her presence amongst a Brucean court from 1328 must have formalized her own political ties.

In David and Joan's absence from Scotland, the 1330s saw warfare rage across Scotland between the Bruce Scots and the Anglo-Disinherited who sought to regain what they had lost under Robert I. In addition to spectacular military events which centred around women in this period (see Chapter 3: Women in Warfare), this period also saw conflicting political leadership under changing guardians, in addition to the ambitious rise to power of David's nephew, Robert Stewart. By the time that David and Joan returned to Scotland in 1341, they returned to a kingdom which had scarcely emerged from Anglo-Scottish and internal warfare, with new political figures at play who would either support or problematize the remainder of David's reign.

One of these men was Robert Stewart. As the grandson of Robert I of Scotland by his eldest child from his first marriage, Marjory Bruce, Robert was directly in line for the throne of Scotland should David die without an heir. Robert would hold the position of guardian twice in the period from 1334 to 1341 and displayed himself as a lord seeking to take advantage of dubious financial situations and self-serving landholding policies. Essentially, this young lord sought to elevate his position in Scotland against other magnates in the absence of a royal figurehead. This period would set Stewart up for leadership in another decade where David II would be absent from Scotland, and clearly marked his early ambitions as a candidate for Scotland's crown.

In 1336, as had occurred in the 1310s and 1320s, the papacy attempted to intervene in the renewed Anglo-Scottish conflict. As with previous attempts, this was done to divert attention to the goal of a united crusade; war between Scotland and England and increasing Anglo-French tensions hampered such a goal. An offer was tabled to the young David II's court at Château-Gaillard over the winter of 1335 to 1336, proposed by the papacy: David would relinquish his title to Edward Balliol and become his heir, and Balliol would marry Joan of the Tower. Joan's central involvement in such an offer demonstrates that Balliol's offer to marry Joan in 1334 was taken seriously by both Edward III and the papacy, and that even with Joan in France this was still a possibility. David's resignation of the throne to become Balliol's heir was not necessarily as ridiculous a suggestion as it looked. With a childless Edward Balliol now in his early fifties, David would inevitably inherit. This would, however, be a considerable gamble and the outright rejection of this settlement by David's party is not surprising.

While other activity from David and Joan is difficult to identify during their period in exile in France, towards 1340 it is clear that David was beginning to attempt to exercise a level of diplomatic and military presence. In 1339 and 1340, David was present in military campaigns by Philip VI of France against Edward III, as the Hundred Years' War raged in its opening years. While the fifteen-year-old king did not gain any battle experience as these campaigns amounted to very little, they act as evidence of him cultivating a royal presence in public. Around this time, David also began to participate in tourneys and issue royal acts, and while it cannot be evidenced, it is likely that Joan also began to exercise her position as his queen. This demonstrates the couple's burgeoning roles as king and queen in anticipation of a return to Scotland.

Return of the King and Queen

By 1341, David's lieutenants in Scotland had achieved a position against Balliol and his English support that was strong enough to ensure that the seventeen-year-old king could return to his kingdom. This was a result of war efforts by Bruce captains such as Andrew Murray of Bothwell and Avoch, Alexander Ramsay of Dalhousie, William Douglas of Liddesdale and even Robert Stewart. However, their success was possible due to English failures to establish long-term authority in Scotland, or to consistently deliver campaigns against the Scots that were brutal enough to stamp out opposition. Moreover, Edward III's attentions were turned from the mid-1330s by the outbreak of the Hundred Years' War; it was this focus on France that would change the nature of Anglo-Scottish warfare over the coming decades.

David, Joan and their courtly retinue departed Boulogne in late May of 1341, arriving in Scotland in Inverkeithing in June. This must have been a monumental journey for David, who was finally returning to claim his authority in his kingdom after seven years of absence. For Joan, this may have been a far more complex moment for her. Aged twenty and most likely officially married to her husband, she was returning to a kingdom in which she had lived in for a short period as a child, and of which she had only been queen from afar. Additionally, this was a kingdom still at war with her brother, although limited to cross-border raiding rather than all-out invasions. Moreover, David's awareness that he must establish a personal authority and control over his competitive nobles after his lengthy absence must have also been held by Joan. She was surely apprehensive of the allies she might have in Scotland and of the work she would have to do to establish her own position as queen in a kingdom that had been ruled by nobility for seven years.

The opening years of David's personal rule can be defined as a test of his ability to rule a realm, particularly including the management of his ambitious magnates who had grown accustomed to a kingdom without a king. From 1341 to 1343, David appeared to struggle with this; vicious feuding between his magnates and competition for lordship dogged his efforts, with rivalry with his nephew and heir-apparent, Robert Stewart, remaining strong. Similarly to his father, David employed a tactic of reward and resources to cultivate a circle of support, from those who had already supported him long-term and from new allies. David's employment of this may have extended to Joan, who no doubt picked from the families of David's loyal adherents and new favourites to bolster her royal household, including ladies-in-waiting, and form her own allies. The limited evidence for Joan's role in the establishment of her husband's new regime is frustrating.

By 1346 David appeared to have gained a semblance of control over his nobility, but a further test of his authority and his ability as a military leader was to come. From David's return to Scotland, Scottish military aggression had been based on cross-border raids, which David had begun to participate in from 1345. Any Anglo-Scottish warfare was very much dependent on Edward III's focus on the Hundred Years' War with France, and this would be put to the test in 1346. The English king's victory over the French at the Battle of Crécy and the Siege of Calais which followed it were devastating blows to the French. As a result, Philip VI of France called upon the Scots for military support. David was a receptive listener, and already insistent upon (or pressured to) providing Scottish military aid to the kingdom which had sheltered him from 1334 to 1341. This also offered the young King of Scots the opportunity to flex his authority and test the waters with his military ability, as the son of Robert I.

After assembling an impressive army which featured many key Scottish magnates and noble figures, the Scots invaded England. However, this was not a united front, as feuding between Scottish leaders destabilized tactics and routes into and through England. The severity of this is best summarized by William, Earl of Ross, taking advantage of the assemblage of nobility by murdering his opponent Ranald MacRuari before returning home – the Scots had not even departed Perth. Once in England, David's force confronted an army led by Ralph Neville and William de la Zouche, Archbishop of York, near Durham in the disastrous Battle of Neville's Cross. Swathes of Scottish barons were killed or captured in this battle, including key military figures such as Robert Keith and John Randolph, the last surviving son of David's regent. David himself was taken captive and badly wounded. The King of Scots would remain in English captivity for the next eleven years. This was a captivity that would define the final decade of the Scottish Wars of Independence and the relationship between king and nobility in Scotland.

Kingless Queen

The disastrous result of Neville's Cross undoubtedly placed Joan in a difficult position. While queens consort could retain a level of power in the absence of a king or in the rule of a minor, Joan was not the mother of an heir or a queen managing the kingdom during a king's illness or military expedition. Her husband was the captive of her brother, and although Joan had not lived in England for nearly twenty years, this fact surely made it increasingly difficult for her to represent David's authority. The capture of the king and the brutal loss of around fifty Scottish barons left the door open to David's nephew, Robert Stewart, to once again take the reins of power. This time, however, David was not operating or represented from a court in France; the king was in an English prison. There was little that Joan or the sparse remnants of David's supporters could do to withstand Stewart's windfall of advantages in the wake of Neville's Cross.

The eleven-year period of David's captivity in England can be best summarized by the increasing power of Scottish magnates and the desperate attempts by the Bruce party to free their king. This should also be viewed in the context of wider European events, including ongoing Anglo-French warfare and the outbreak of the Black Death, which spread to England in 1348 and Scotland in 1349. Such context surely contributed to the length of David's captivity, in addition to Edward III being content to wait for a release deal that would best benefit his own plans for Anglo-Scottish relations.

It is possible that by the time David was captured in 1346, the relationship between him and Joan was already strained. They had been married for nearly twenty years and probably able to produce an heir for several years – especially with David's assumption of power in 1341 – and so by 1346 the pressure of a lack of heir may have been affecting the royal couple. David would have two wives, marrying Margaret Drummond in 1363 following Joan's death, and publicly had mistresses. However, he never did produce an heir despite his many known relationships, and so it is likely that it was David who was unable to produce children – not his wives or mistresses. In 1346, the reality of David's infertility may not have been apparent, but he and Joan's struggle to produce a child was surely an immense political and personal weight on both king and queen. This would have been felt all the more strongly as David's rivals became the fathers of multiple children: by 1346 Robert Stewart already had four legitimate sons while Edward III of England had a large family with his queen, Philippa of Hainault.

However, Joan's activity in the years immediately following Neville's Cross indicate that she and David still had an effective working relationship. By 1347 or 1348, Edward III's attitude towards the future of Scottish kingship appeared to have changed, with a brief reattempt at a coup by Edward Balliol limited to Galloway and largely unsupported by English troops. Balliol was now in his mid-sixties and childless, while Edward held a Bruce King of Scots who was in his early twenties and married to his English sister. It was clear that the English king now looked to David as an opportunity rather than a hindrance. The two kings began to develop a relatively positive relationship, despite the circumstances, with David participating in a tournament in April 1348 to celebrate the birth of Edward's sixth son, and possibly being present at the initiation of the Order of the Garter in August of that same year. Although Edward and David's newfound respect was no doubt an element of common sense and opportunity for the ambitious Edward, it could be suggested that Joan played a role in his changing attitude to David. On 10 October 1348 Joan received an indefinite safe conduct to England, which may have followed personal petitions to her brother after David's capture two years previously. Her personal intercessory role for her husband may have contributed to the increasingly positive relationship between the two brothers-in-law.

Joan was surely apprehensive about this return to England; she may have been born in the Tower of London and raised for seven years as a daughter of Edward II and Isabella of France, but she left this kingdom at a young age and had not returned for twenty years. She can hardly have viewed England as home and more likely saw Scotland and France in that light. This perhaps explains why she chose to go between Scotland and England from 1348, only taking up a longer-term residence in England from 1353. She may have been the sister of David's captor and subsequently viewed in a suspicious light by some Scots, but it is unlikely that Joan would have gone to England in 1348 in triumph and ease. Joan was seven and Edward was sixteen when they were last together; now at twenty-seven and thirty-six and with one holding the other's husband captive, this must have been a peculiar return for Joan to her natal family kingdom.

Joan's safe conduct from 1348 also demonstrates that she chose to remain in Scotland for the first two years of David's absence, suggesting that she was attempting to act as a continuing symbol of her husband's royal presence. Indeed, 1348 saw David and Joan conducting business together, sending joint papal petitions in pursuit of beneficiaries for Scottish clergy. This is a role that Joan would remain involved in for the remainder of her queenship, either in partnership with David or solely on her own authority. Cultivating allies and authority for herself – or for both she and David – within the Scottish Church may have been an important responsibility that Joan undertook both during and after David's captivity, with the significance of this most strongly felt while David was absent from a Stewart-run Scotland. Her petitions in 1348 to the papacy, completed in both she and David's names, demonstrate that the royal couple were continuing to work together on business from afar or together from Joan's safe conduct in October 1348.

There is one instance in 1348 that provides a very illuminating insight into Joan's activities and motivations in the years directly following Neville's Cross. In December 1348, the young heiress to the Earldom of Menteith, Margaret Graham, received a papal dispensation to wed John Murray of Bothwell, the Pantler of Scotland. Importantly, permission for this marriage to proceed was granted 'at the request of the Queen of Scotland'. The Graham-Murray marriage in 1348 has been interpreted by historians as an action ushered in by Robert Stewart, who at this time held the reins of government in David's absence. By marrying John Murray to Margaret Graham, this placed a loyal Stewart adherent in an earldom that was coveted by the Stewarts, thus further extending Stewart regional authority in Scotland. However, the Murrays did not come into the Stewart nexus of followers until the late 1350s, when Thomas Murray of Bothwell headed the kindred after his brother John's death. In 1348, the Murrays under John Murray appear to be firmly in the Bruce camp, holding the office of Pantler and clearly being connected to Queen Joan. John Murray was also either the son or stepson of Christina Bruce, the king's aunt, which again highlights the Murray-Bruce adherence in 1348. Joan's orchestrating of this marriage was the opposite of Robert Stewart's intentions, and instead placed a Bruce adherent in an earldom in central Scotland that would challenge Stewart interests in Perthshire. This is evidence of Joan's role in being an active symbol of royal authority and representative of her captive husband's efforts to hold out against the free-for-all in landholding enjoyed by the likes of Robert Stewart after Neville's Cross.

Joan perhaps felt responsible for Margaret Graham, who was another female victim of the disastrous ramifications of Neville's Cross. Margaret's father, John Graham, Earl of Menteith, was one of the many barons captured in the battle and faced charges of treason. Having previously sworn fealty to the English crown, John was found guilty and was hanged, drawn and quartered in London in 1347. The personal and political impact that this had on the young Margaret Graham and her mother, Mary of Menteith, would have been detrimental. Margaret had lost her father, but his death also left her mother's Earldom of Menteith open to being taken advantage of as a teenage Margaret now became its vulnerable heiress. The Scottish historian, Sir William Fraser, lamented in 1880 that Graham's death left Margaret susceptible to the 'schemes of intriguers when so great an earldom was to be acquired by marriage'. Fraser was surely correct, and Joan's intervention in the situation of a young heiress whose life had been dramatically affected by Neville's Cross – just as Joan's was – is testament to her responsibility as queen in influencing the prospects of younger elite women in her kingdom, particularly those connected to the Bruce party. By marrying Margaret to John Murray, Joan ensured that the future Countess of Menteith was firmly within the Bruce following, influenced by her queenly patron and her new mother-in-law, Christina Bruce. This event is also surely indicative of which elite women were in the queen's party prior to and after Neville's Cross.

Whether Joan's influence and personal presence in England helped in softening her brother's attitudes to her captive husband or not, the first terms of David's release were presented by Edward in 1349. Alongside other conditions, this included David's homage to Edward III and the restoration of the Disinherited. David refused these terms. However, this did not repel Edward, and negotiations continued into 1351. It is important to consider that in addition to Joan's visits to England – the 1348 conduct may have been used for further visits – these four years also saw the ravages of the Black Death rip across Europe, killing up to one third of the population and impacting all levels of feudal society. Indeed, Edward III's own daughter, Joan – perhaps named after her aunt – died in September 1348 of plague, demonstrating the wide societal impact of the plague. These must have been grim years indeed for David, captive in the Tower of London, and Joan, who may have travelled less between Scotland and England due to the dangers of the Black Death. It should also be noted that the outbreak of the plague probably contributed to the delays in securing a release deal for the King of Scots.

The year 1350 saw changes to David's potential release. He and Edward were discussing new conditions, and Robert Stewart was removed from his role as lieutenant. Stewart was replaced by William,

Earl of Ross, Thomas of Mar and William Douglas of Liddesdale. All three of these men represented a government in Scotland that leant more to the Bruce party, and thus indicated a greater chance of David's release with his rival-nephew no longer in power. In 1351, David was permitted to travel to Scotland to personally present the new negotiated conditions for his release at parliament, which both he and Edward III had agreed to. It is possible that Joan either travelled with him or was already in Scotland to welcome David's return after five years – albeit temporarily. These new terms included David's release for a ransom of £40 000, the restoration of the Disinherited and a Scottish alliance with England (that did not include any mention of David paying homage). However, this also included the nomination of Edward III's son, John of Gaunt, as heir to Scotland for as long as David remained childless. As David was only in his late twenties, this final condition indicates that he viewed this as a worthwhile gamble to take and had hope for producing an heir with Joan. This also suggests that they were not estranged by 1351.

A second parliament at Dundee in March 1352 delivered a sore blow to David: the terms were rejected by the Scottish estates. This may have been out of genuine concern for English overlordship, a burgeoning desire for the continuation of Anglo-Scottish warfare from David's border lords or a reflection of Robert Stewart's continuing influence in Scotland despite not being the lieutenant. It was impossible that Robert and his adherents would ever support a release deal that would remove him from the line of succession. David returned to his captivity in England, no doubt with his tail between his legs over his nobility's refusal of terms he must have felt confident they would accept. This left Scotland in the continuing hands of magnates and barons who were growing increasingly used to a system with minimal royal interference that allowed them to expand their territorial and political interests. This would escalate for the next four years, with David left to his captivity in England.

The rejection of David's release in the spring of 1352 may have contributed to Joan's decision to withdraw from Scotland on a long-term basis from 1353. A safe conduct issued to her initially covered a five-month period from July to Christmas of 1353, but Joan's intention and request to remain in England evidently became clear as her brother ordered the preparation of her residence at Hertford Castle. Joan and David were not permitted to reside together during his ongoing confinement, but by this stage their relationship may have been beginning to falter under the weight of David's imprisonment and their continuing lack of heirs. Indeed, David's removal from London to Odiham Castle in Hampshire in 1355 quite obviously placed him on the opposite side of London from his queen. The Scottish king's eye for mistresses may have become more evident by this point. The chroniclers Sir Thomas Gray and Walter Bower claim that David's future mistress, Katherine Mortimer, came into the king's life during his imprisonment, with Gray stating that she was from London and Bower claiming she had Welsh heritage. However, David and Katherine's relationship only certainly became public from 1359, so it is possible that he and Joan's separate residences were possibly just another caveat of his captivity.

Release and the End

On 19 September 1356, King John II of France was captured by English forces at the disastrous Battle of Poitiers. England now held two kings captive: John II of France, and David II of Scotland. This was a monumental victory for Edward III in the ongoing Anglo-French conflict of the Hundred Years' War, but it also presented David with an opportunity to finally secure his release.

By late 1356, political and military themes that had dominated the Scottish Wars of Independence were changing. Edward of England no longer viewed the Bruce kings as outlaws, demonstrated by David's royal imprisonment rather than the punishment of a traitor. Edward Balliol resigned his title and claims over Scotland to Edward in January 1356, heralding the end of the Balliol-Bruce competition for the Scottish throne. Anglo-Scottish warfare had changed, partly due to Edward III's focus on French military activity and also his willingness to achieve a settlement with David. The English king had made his final personal military expedition to Scotland in January 1356, a consequence of French involvement in encouraging Scottish aggression against England and the escalating Scottish raids of northern England and seizing of the burgh of Berwick in November 1355. Although Edward's military response resulted in the brutal raiding and destruction of Edinburgh and the Lothians, an event known as the Burnt Candlemas, it was ultimately a failed invasion. Poor weather and supply issues forced Edward to retreat, harried by the Scots as his army returned to England. This expedition was the nail in the coffin for Edward III of England in regards to war with Scotland, and he never did lead an army into the kingdom again. Instead, his efforts remained against France. Anglo-Scottish warfare and political rivalry for the Scottish throne was changing from the mould which had fitted Scotland since the 1290s.

This context led to a climate in 1356 in which David and Edward could make stronger attempts for the Scottish king's release. While negotiations would continue for another year, terms were finally agreed on 3 October 1357 for securing David's release and return to Scotland. A ransom of 100,000 merks would be paid over ten years with Scottish nobles used as hostages for this payment and a ten-year truce was agreed. There were no conditions regarding an English succession to Scotland or homage, nor the guaranteed restoration of the Disinherited. Edward was clearly ready for settlement over the dynastic claims and warfare that had been so relentlessly pursued by his Plantagenet forbears since the death of Alexander III in 1286 and Margaret Maid of Norway in 1290.

It is important to note that the Treaty of Berwick in 1357 did not permanently end Anglo-Scottish warfare or recurring claims of English authority in Scotland. Indeed, the Anglo-Scottish warfare of the thirteenth and fourteenth centuries influenced a precedent set between the two kingdoms which would continue for centuries. It did, however, bring a conclusion to the Scottish Wars of Independence, the violent and politically unstable warfare which had rocked the Kingdom of Scotland for sixty years. The second stage of the Scottish Wars of Independence had come to a slightly underwhelming close.

In November 1357, David II of Scotland returned to his kingdom after eleven years of captivity, with Queen Joan by his side. Joan's willingness to return to Scotland after living in England since 1353 signifies her readiness to return to the queenly role that she had fought so hard to maintain from 1346 to 1353 in David's absence. It may also indicate that their relationship had not been as strained during his captivity as has been suggested, or that the pair were willing to reattempt their partnership under the continuing pressure of producing a Bruce heir. Joan was now thirty-seven and David thirty-three. Although producing a child was by no means out of the question at this stage, years of captivity and potential relationship struggles surely meant that

Joan returned to Scotland in 1357 under immense pressure politically and personally. David may have been released from England, but he returned to a kingdom of magnates that had grown used to a lack of royal authority and desperately needed a Bruce heir to reinforce his family's royal dynasty and legitimacy.

This had obviously all gone very wrong when Joan returned to England within months of her and David's triumphant return in November 1357. On 9 May 1358 Joan received a safe conduct for an indefinite period of time for an unstated reason, although it has been suggested that she returned to England under the pretence of diplomacy between her husband and her brother. The safe conduct's inclusion of Joan coming into 'the special defence and protection of the king' is interesting and may allude to her intention to remain permanently in her brother's kingdom.

Just what happened to push Joan to make a very final decision to leave Scotland for England? This cannot have been a decision made lightly when we consider the context of Joan's choice to remain in Scotland from 1346 to 1353 in David's absence and continue her role as queen. From 1359, David's relationship with his mistress, Katherine Mortimer, became publicly known in Scotland, but it could be suggested that this relationship was quickly evident in the months following his and Joan's return in late 1357. David's infidelity could certainly explain why Joan left him in May 1358, but it is possible that the king's plans to annul his marriage to Joan were also in motion. The pressure to produce an heir must be the cause behind any consideration of annulment, and David was surely becoming all too aware of the need for a Bruce heir. His return to Scotland would have brought home once again the hopes of his nephew and closest male heir, Robert Stewart, particularly when Stewart had been left to his own ambitious devices in David's absence for eleven years. Although issues of fertility clearly lay with David, by 1358 this would not necessarily have been obvious, and he may have thought it prudent to annul his marriage to Joan in favour of another for any hopes of a Bruce heir. Whether it was the discovery of a mistress or plans for an annulment that spurred Joan into making this major decision for herself, her departure for England in May 1358 must have been humiliating for David. His queen had left him and any hope for a legitimate Bruce heir at this stage was dashed. Although the two were in contact again in 1359 while applying for joint beneficiaries for Scottish clergy again, this appears to be the last of their business or personal connection.

On her return to England, Joan was again accommodated by Edward III to reside at Hertford Castle. The choice of Hertford as her residence, both in 1353 and in 1358, provides an excellent insight into Joan's personal life and what her final years spent in England looked like. Hertford Castle had been granted to her mother, Isabella of France, in 1327 in the aftermath of her father's deposition, and Isabella and Mortimer's regency. Although Isabella had all her lands confiscated in 1330 following Edward III's coup against Mortimer, she was gradually welcomed back into her son's family fold and reinstated to an influential position. From this time, Isabella's own favoured residence was Castle Riding in Norfolk, but Joan's arrival first in 1353 and then in 1358 saw the queen mother spending more time at Hertford Castle with her daughter. Joan and Isabella had presumably not seen one another since the former's proxy marriage celebrations at Berwick in 1328, when she was just seven years old. The two probably reunited on Joan's first visit to her captive husband in 1348, twenty years after their marriage. Although there is little evidence from Joan's visits to England from 1348 to 1353 of any shared activity with her mother, Isabella surely sought to be with her youngest child. Joan's residence at Hertford Castle from 1353 certainly suggests that she and her mother were choosing to be near one another.

From 1358, Joan likely retired from any primary position at court, and so we could imagine that the last years of her life may have been the most peaceful and personal for Joan. She did not have to adjust to life in a new kingdom or court. She did not have to compete with Scottish magnates for influence or fight to represent her husband's authority in his absence. She did not have to go between England and Scotland, worrying for her husband's situation or under the immense political and personal pressure of producing a royal heir. Instead, Joan spent her final four years in England from 1358 to 1362 in the company of her mother and wider family.

After her arrival in May 1358 and taking up residence at Hertford Castle, Edward III provided a household for Joan whilst her mother paid for her food and clothing. Both Isabella and Edward's queen, Philippa of Hainault, were regular visitors to Hertford Castle which again demonstrates the female family members that Joan was surrounded by on return to England. Indeed, from 1353 Joan was visited regularly by Isabella and Philippa, and these three queens were only split by Joan's temporary return to Scotland in 1357, quickly taking up their courtly companionship on her return in May 1358. In June 1358, Joan accompanied her mother on her final pilgrimage to Canterbury Cathedral, a location which both Isabella and her late husband, Edward II, had venerated during their marriage. Shortly after their pilgrimage, the two queens resided at Leeds Castle in Kent from 13 June to 2 July, indicating that Isabella had taken unwell. The sixty-three-year-old queen mother had been suffering from ill health, and her pilgrimage to Canterbury with her daughter was surely done with her mortality in mind.

The two women were back at Hertford Castle by 12 August, when messages were dispatched to London for medicine, again demonstrating that Isabella had taken unwell. Joan's mother was probably dying when physicians were quickly summoned eight days later. The great Isabella of France passed away on 22 August 1358, with Joan by her side. This must have been immensely difficult for Joan, who had clearly established a new bond with her mother after decades apart. It could be that Isabella's poor health was another factor which pushed Joan to leave Scotland for England in May 1358, a decision which allowed her to attend to her in those final months. The close relationship between Joan and her mother is evidenced by Isabella's will, in which she left her Bible, Apocalypse and Psalter to her youngest daughter. Joan would have attended Isabella's lavish funeral on 27 November of that year, where she was interred at the Church of the Greyfriars in London. It was on this date that Joan perhaps made the decision to request that when she died, she would also be buried in the same location as her mother.

Joan remained in England after Isabella's death, continuing to reside at Hertford Castle. She may have met with her estranged husband when he came to London in early 1359 on a diplomatic visit to Edward III. Papal confirmation in August 1359 of their joint petitions on behalf of clerical beneficiaries in Scotland may have been originally sent at this instance when the king and queen were together for the first time in nearly a year. Whether David attempted to persuade Joan to return with him to

Scotland is unclear, but her intentions to not return were made evident only months later when Edward began a £200 yearly allowance for Joan, on the condition that she remained in England. Joan's commitment to this demonstrates that her estrangement from her husband would remain. David may have been in pursuit of an annulment by this time, or Joan may have considered joining a religious order. The fifteenth-century chronicler Walter Bower did write that Joan spent 'a little time there [England] as a pilgrim' from 1357, but Bower was most likely referring to her pilgrimage to Canterbury with her mother in 1358.

The years 1359 to 1362 may have been busy ones for Joan, with four of her brother's children marrying in England and two unexpectedly passing away. Joan possibly attended the marriages of her nephew John of Gaunt to Blanche of Lancaster and her niece Margaret of Windsor to John Hastings, Earl of Pembroke, held only one week apart in 1359. In the autumn of 1361. Joan was likely very present with her natal family for tragedy and celebration: her nephew and the heir to England, the Black Prince, married Joan of Kent at Windsor on 10 October, while her two nieces, Margaret of Windsor and Mary of Waltham, died in September and October respectively. Joan was a retiree from court life, but she was the King of England's last remaining sibling under his protection and thus an important female Plantagenet figure. These personal family events in the wake of her mother's death in 1358 must have affected her.

Joan died on 7 September 1362 at Hertford Castle. It is unclear what her cause of death was at the age of only forty-one, with plague being suggested by some historians. Her funeral took place shortly after her death, seeing her interred in the same location as her mother at the Church of the Greyfriars in London. Just over a year later in December 1363, David II of Scotland would visit London with his new wife, Margaret Drummond, when Edward III would pay £24 for Joan's exequies. The payment of these funeral rites indicate that the two royal brothers-in-law held a belated funeral or remembrance ceremony for the late Queen of Scots, now laid to rest near her mother.

Conclusion

Joan of the Tower can be portrayed as a tragic princess of England, condemned to a life in foreign kingdoms and to a loveless marriage.

She was so much more than that. This was a queen who faced uprooting from her home on multiple occasions and weathered the resultant storms of change. Joan was queen for over thirty years and displayed an impressive ability to adapt to and refamiliarize with new political environments, as demonstrated by her decision to remain in Scotland for seven years in the absence of her captive King of Scots. Her life and career are undermined by the sparse evidence that would otherwise provide an insight into the vibrant court and activities of a medieval queen whose upbringing fused together the Kingdoms of Scotland, England, and France.

Joan's place as a Bruce queen within the Scottish Wars of Independence has been overshadowed by the inconsistent placement of she and her husband, first with exile as children to France and then with David's eleven-year captivity. Had David had a longer-term royal presence in Scotland – essentially, had he not been captured – her contribution to Scottish society and royalty would be easier to identify. Moreover, Joan and David's inability to produce any children has also resulted in her being overlooked during this period, despite this being a result of David's infertility.

Joan of the Tower was no tragedy. She was a Plantagenet princess and a Queen of Scots, who held firm in the face of exile, captivity and marital estrangement, to survive the political minefield of the Scottish Wars of Independence.

Chapter 2

Women in Captivity

On 10 February 1306 at the Church of the Greyfriars in Dumfries, Robert Bruce, Earl of Carrick, murdered his political rival, John Comyn of Badenoch. Whether it was Robert or his loyal followers who dealt the killing blow has long been the subject of debate, as has the argument of whether this was a premeditated act of violence or a crime of passion. In a kingdom without a king, governed by the overlordship of Edward I of England, Robert and John were the two strongest remaining claimants to any revival of the Scottish kingship. Both were ambitious young men from powerful families who had already come to blows while acting as joint guardians in 1300. It could be argued that the murder of one at the hands of the other was an inevitable event, and it remains one of the most impactful political events in Scottish history as well as a mystery.

Regardless of his motivations or intentions, Robert's actions had forced him into a precarious position. No doubt aware of the imminent wrath of the powerful Comyn family and their extensive network, Robert seized his opportunity. By 25 March 1306 – only six weeks later – Robert had been inaugurated as King of Scots, defying both the mighty Edward I of England and the Comyns and their allies. Robert had essentially usurped the throne of Scotland.

The consequences of these major decisions made by Robert in February and March 1306 would have a devastating impact upon him. June and July would see him defeated twice in battle, first at Methven and second at Dalry, losing significant political supporters to battle or by execution. By the final days of summer, the new King of Scots and his rapidly decreasing number of followers would flee west to the Isles, not returning to the Scottish mainland until early 1307. Over the course of 1306 and 1307, Robert would lose three of his four brothers to execution, in addition to close friends and allies. The cost of his actions was high, with personal and political damage causing an almost unimaginable struggle for the King of Scots. While the punishment suffered by Robert's allies and the adversity faced by the king over the winter of 1306-07 are not to be understated, this chapter will seek to focus on the immense hardship endured by Robert's female family members and political allies: Elizabeth de Burgh, his wife and queen; Marjory, his daughter by his first marriage; Mary and Christina, his sisters; and Isabella MacDuff, Countess of Buchan. All five of these women were captured in 1306 and would suffer eight years of imprisonment, some more severely than others, for their relation and political connection to Robert.

In *The Bruce*, the fourteenth-century epic of the life of Robert the Bruce, Archdeacon John Barbour writes of an event in early 1307 in which Robert is told the news of the varying forms of punishment his friends and allies have received over the past months. Having just returned to the mainland in early 1307 and beginning a campaign in the southwest, Robert and his followers are provided for by a female family member named Christina. While Christina's exact relationship to Robert is unknown – she may have been his illegitimate daughter later referred to in royal grants – she is the one to deliver the unfortunate tidings of the executions of the outlaw king's close supporters: John, Earl of Atholl; Sir Christopher Seton, Robert's brother-in-law through marriage to Christina Bruce; and Neil Bruce, Robert's brother. Christina also informs Robert of 'how the queen and various others who had supported his cause, had been taken, led into England and put in dreadful imprisonment.' Robert's reaction to this news clearly portrays his understandable grief for the loss of his male friends and allies, but there is no described acknowledgement of the imprisonment and suffering of his wife, nor any mention of his daughter, sisters and ally, Isabella MacDuff.

'Alas!' he said, 'because of their great love for me and great loyalty these noble and worthy men have been vilely destroyed.'

Barbour's poem certainly aimed to promote the chivalric values of the reign of Robert I, hence the grieving for his loyal knights and friends. However, the lack of thought given to the suffering of Robert's female family members represents the importance of the aim of this chapter and indeed this book in focusing on the female experience of punishment resulting from the decisions and actions of Robert Bruce.

The Consequences of an Inauguration

The speed of the timeline from Robert's murder of Comyn to his inauguration six weeks later on 25 March highlights what could be interpreted as sheer panic from Robert. In the days following Comyn's murder, Robert made his way to Glasgow to seek absolution from his actions and gain political support from Robert Wishart, Bishop of Glasgow. For a man who had just committed murder on holy ground – and would be excommunicated for such actions – gaining the support of the Scottish Church was crucial if he were to attempt to usurp the throne of Scotland; excommunicated individuals would not be supported as king. Wishart both absolved Robert and campaigned for the Scottish Church to throw support behind the would-be King of Scots, and attended the inauguration alongside William Lamberton, Bishop of St Andrews, and David de Moravia, Bishop of Moray. The political support of these three major figures of the Scottish Church would remain crucial for Robert in the years to come.

While Robert enjoyed the attendance of these three bishops at his inauguration at Scone, alongside the Bishops of Dunkeld and Brechin, the representation from the highest noble class of Scotland was indicative of the immense opposition he would face in his kingdom: John Strathbogie, Earl of Atholl; Alan, Earl of Menteith; Malcolm, Earl of Lennox; and the infant Donald, Earl of Mar. English records of the arrests, forfeitures and executions from 1306-07 suggest that there were a substantial number of knights and esquires in attendance, despite the poorer numbers of elite nobility.

A critically important attendee and participant in the inauguration ceremony was Isabella MacDuff, Countess of Buchan. In the face of great criticism and opposition, Robert needed to take advantage of every symbol of legitimacy that he possibly could in his inauguration ceremony. This can be seen in the ceremony's location being at Scone, probably on Moot Hill, the traditional inauguration location for Kings of Scots. Various ceremonial rituals were probably included: the Gaelic reciting of the king's royal genealogy, thus justifying his blood claim to the throne; oaths taken by Robert as to his duties as king; and items such as a sceptre, orb and coronet. Isabella's active participation in the ceremony fulfilled a traditional role held by her natal family, the Earls of Fife, in placing the new king on the Stone of Scone, the historic seat of Scottish kings. This was an integral symbol of legitimacy in the inauguration process.

Isabella's presence and actions at the inauguration are not to be understated. As the daughter of the previous Earl of Fife and sister (or perhaps aunt?) of the current earl, a minor in English captivity, Isabella was the only direct relation able to fulfil the symbolic role of the Fife earls in the inauguration ceremony. Moreover, Isabella was married to John Comyn, Earl of Buchan, a close kinsman to the same John Comyn of Badenoch murdered by Robert in Dumfries only a month prior. This event was therefore a spectacular display of an elite woman abandoning her marital family to follow the duties of her natal family and enact her own political values. Isabella essentially defied her husband to participate in the inauguration of her marital family's great enemy, Robert Bruce. This is an act of personal and political rebellion which speaks volumes for the character and importance of Isabella MacDuff, Countess of Buchan.

Robert's inauguration was followed by two months of aiming to establish a functioning royal government under his kingship. This would have seen Robert – supported by his allies and now government officials – begin to make land grants, attempt to raise revenue and military service and continue the effort to improve the relationship between the crown and the Church. It may have been difficult for Robert to see progress in these efforts, as he still faced enormous opposition in Scotland and the imminent threat of the return of an English army to his border. According to English chroniclers, Elizabeth de Burgh – Robert's wife and now queen – reacted to this period by saying, 'Alas, we are but king and queen of the May', or by describing Robert as, 'King Hobbe of summer'.

Elizabeth's predictions were soon to be realized. On 19 June 1306, Robert's forces were resoundingly defeated at the Battle of Methven, near Perth, in a surprise attack by the army of Aymer de Valence, Earl of Pembroke. In reaction to the news of Robert's usurping of the throne, Edward I of England had named Valence as his Lieutenant of Scotland and ordered a merciless approach to tackling yet another act of resistance to Plantagenet overlordship. The timeline of Valence's appointment probably correlated with the famous Feast of the Swans, a chivalric celebration at Westminster on 22 May 1306 in which nearly 300 esquires were knighted by Edward and his son, the Prince of Wales. At this celebration, Edward swore to pursue two crusades: one to the Holy Land; and the other to Scotland to avenge the murder of Comyn and fight Robert Bruce and his supporters.

The zeal of Edward's anger and determination to stop Robert saw Valence arrive at Perth in June 1306 before his victory over Robert on 19 June. Methven was a disaster for the Bruce party. It saw the new King of Scots nearly captured twice before being forced to flee with a small group of followers, leaving many political allies behind to face death in battle or to suffer executions, due to Edward's merciless approach to any supporters of Robert.

Robert's ill luck went from bad to worse when within a month of Methven, he was again defeated in battle at Dalry, in Argyll. Robert and the remnants of his army were likely fleeing west from Valence, but were attacked by the powerful MacDougalls, who were close allies to the Comyn-Balliol faction in Scotland. Unable to return east due to Valence's presence at Perth, Robert was forced to engage in what may have been a very unexpected battle. The king came so close to defeat that the brooch of his cloak was allegedly snatched from him by a MacDougall, becoming an heirloom known as the 'Brooch of Lorn' and passed down between the Campbells and the MacDougalls.

Where were the women?

The disastrous defeats of Methven and Dalry exposed the military weakness of Robert's forces, in addition to the extreme political opposition he faced both from England and within Scotland. But where exactly were Robert's close female relatives and allies during this month of sheer peril for the King of Scots and his followers?

When we turn to chronicle accounts of this period, there does seem to be confusion over the timeline specifically regarding the Bruce women. In *The Bruce*, Barbour places Robert's queen, Elizabeth de Burgh, and 'other fair and comely ladies' as being in Aberdeen in the early summer, where they were visited by a morose Robert and his followers after their first defeat at Methven. As has been pointed out by historians, this timeline between Methven and Dalry does not make sense. Robert took Aberdeen in April or May of 1306, making it a newly-established Bruce location, but it was quickly in English hands when Valence seized the area in August of that year. For Robert, being hotly pursued by Valence's forces in the aftermath of Methven surely negated any opportunity to first make a journey northeast to Aberdeen, before cutting west across the country to Dalry. To flee west from Aberdeen, while avoiding Valence's reach from Perth, would mean a tricky route across the southern Cairngorms before tackling the Grampian Mountains west of the Drumochter Pass. Considering both the potential threat from the Comyn heartlands north of the Cairngorms in addition to the very real threat of the MacDougalls – which would indeed affect Robert's fortunes within the month – this would not be a wise or straightforward journey to make. It is far more likely that Barbour's account of a visit to Aberdeen to Elizabeth and her female companions occurred before Methven, if it happened at all. The purpose of Barbour including this event could be to emphasize the romantic appeal of his epic or to refer to a brief teaching on the roles of wives and husbands: 'The queen with other fair and comely ladies [came to the Bruce men], each for love of their husbands, a true love and loyalty, wanting to share their sufferings. They choose rather to take suffering and pain with them, rather than to be away from them.'

While Robert's visit to Aberdeen in the aftermath of Methven is doubtful, the presence of Elizabeth and the other Bruce women in the Aberdeenshire region is likely. Neil Bruce, Robert's brother, defended Kildrummy Castle, Aberdeenshire, against the besieging forces of Prince Edward of England in August 1306, having been positioned there as a guardian for Robert's queen, daughter, sisters and female political allies. Kildrummy Castle was the administrative centre of the Earldom of Mar and an architecturally stalwart fortress, in addition to being connected to the Bruces by Robert's previous marriage to a daughter of Gartnait, Earl of Mar. This certainly would be the ideal location for a contingent of the Bruce family to base themselves as a safehouse in May 1306 while facing an imminent English invasion and increased hostilities. Again, Barbour provides a dubious note that the Bruce women were only sent to Kildrummy with Neil Bruce and the Earl of Atholl after the Battle of Dalry. This would mean that Robert's queen, daughter and sisters, alongside Isabella MacDuff, managed to evade capture or peril during two significant Bruce defeats which saw the deaths and capture of many of Robert's supporters. It is far more likely that Robert's close female family and allies were sent to the safety of Kildrummy with Neil before Valence's arrival in Scotland. This would also correlate with Robert's visit to Aberdeen (perhaps Barbour meant Aberdeenshire?) occurring before Methven.

Regardless of locations, it would be after Robert's defeat at the Battle of Dalry at the hands of the MacDougalls that his path as king would diverge from the paths of his queen, daughter (and, importantly, heiress), sisters and MacDuff ally. Barbour's account of the Bruce women being sent to Kildrummy after Dalry with Neil and Atholl, while Robert fled west, represents the division of the two parties for the foreseeable future: one to escape, another to imprisonment and execution. In the late summer of 1306, Neil Bruce's defence of Kildrummy Castle against the Prince of Wales ended in disaster when he was allegedly betrayed by the castle blacksmith, who set sections of the castle alight. The castle fell on 13 September and Neil Bruce and various other loyal supporters of Robert's claim to the throne were captured and sent south to England, where they were executed in Carlisle.

The Bruce women had already moved on from Kildrummy prior to the arrival of the Prince of Wales, probably in anticipation of an attack. Accompanied by John, Earl of Atholl, this group fled north from the invading forces of Prince Edward and Valence. It is likely that their plan – perhaps at the behest of Robert after Dalry's defeat – was to flee to Orkney, or even to Norway, where Robert's sister, Isabel, held the powerful position of queen dowager. While Isabel might not have wielded the influence to encourage the Norwegian kingdom to go to war for her brother, offering shelter to her two sisters, niece and sister-in-law was not unthinkable. This band of fleeing women may have been small, but they were incredibly significant and held a unique hope for the fledgling Bruce dynasty as conduits of this royal blood. Elizabeth de Burgh was Robert's queen, with whom he did not yet have children. His daughter from his earlier marriage to Isabel of Mar, Marjory, was the king's only legitimate child and thus the very future of his claim to the throne. Christina and Mary, his sisters, similarly carried the weight of this dynasty as Bruce women. Isabella MacDuff, Countess of Buchan, may not have held the pressure of continuing a royal line as her fellow companions, but her political influence and direct rebellion of her marital family and English governance made her a key Bruce political figure. It could be argued that so far, Robert's success and his very hopes for the crown rested with this group of elite women.

Capture

It was probably September 1306 when the women and Atholl sought sanctuary at the shrine of St Duthac in Tain. Tain's location in the Earldom of Ross, which stretched across the Scottish northwestern mainland from the North Sea to the Western Isles, confirms the group's intention of journeying to Orkney and perhaps beyond to Norway. They were entirely separate from the men of the Bruce party, who by this point had fled well and truly west.

As a site of religious sanctuary, the group would have expected to be able to seek genuine shelter at St Duthac's during their difficult journey north. These expectations were to be dashed. A small force either instructed or led by William, Earl of Ross, breached the shrine's safety and seized the Bruce women and Atholl. Ross' violation may seem a damning act against a group of unarmed women, especially when we consider his obvious loyalties to Edward I of England, who had showered this northern earl with gifts and appointments as recently as 1304. However, Ross had already endured the wrath of this King of England; after fighting at the disastrous Battle of Dunbar in 1296 against Edward, Ross was captured and imprisoned in the Tower of London until 1303. His return south to meet with Edward at Perth in 1304 can certainly be interpreted as the actions of a reprimanded earl desperate to retain his land and title. If Ross were to be found or suspected of harbouring the wife and queen of Robert Bruce alongside his heir, sisters and the noblewoman who participated in his inauguration ceremony, then he would be placed in an increasingly precarious political position.

After their capture at Tain, the Bruce women were subsequently handed over to the English to enter a period of gruelling imprisonment. There are inconsistencies in the primary evidence at this stage as to who was captured and where. John of Fordun's *Chronicle of the Scottish Nation* sees Elizabeth flee alone to Tain directly after the Battle of Dalry while Neil Bruce escorted the rest of the ladies to Kildrummy Castle, suggesting that the women were all present at both the disastrous battles at Methven and Dalry. Barbour accounts for only Elizabeth and Marjory being captured at Tain, not including Robert's sisters, Isabella MacDuff, or Atholl in the altercation. Two English chroniclers, Walter of Guisborough and Sir Thomas Gray, respectively separate Christina Bruce from the capture of Elizabeth de Burgh. Guisborough describes Christina's capture alongside her husband, Sir Christopher Seton, at Loch Doon in the southwest of Scotland, while Gray places Christina's capture at Kildrummy and Elizabeth's at Kintyre Castle on the west coast of Scotland. This separation of the Bruce women and their subsequent captures is not impossible, but the failure to account for the other captured women casts an uncertain light on this. Moreover, English governmental records stating the offences and punishments for these captives are dated together on 7 November 1306. It is therefore unlikely that the women were separated and captured; the story of their capture at the violated sanctuary of St Duthac in Tain is the most plausible event. The presence of Atholl at this capture is also supported by a later punishment inflicted upon the Earl of Ross by Robert Bruce to pay annually for prayers to be said at Tain for the soul of John, Earl of Atholl.

Atholl was hanged in London from gallows structured 30 feet higher than other prisoners to acknowledge his aristocratic status and his shocking position as the first earl in 230 years to be executed in the Kingdom of England.

In addition to confusion in chronicle sources over the location and timing of the capture of the Bruce women, there are also inconsistencies in evidence and historical interpretation as to how many sisters of Robert I were captured and imprisoned in 1306. While English governmental records refer to only two sisters being imprisoned in England – Christina and Mary – later evidence from the *Acts of Robert I* suggests that the king had another two sisters: Margaret and Matilda, whose existence is evident in their respective marriages to William Carlisle and Hugh, Earl of Ross, but there is no mention of either of these Bruce sisters before 1315. Their absence from the record is particularly stark in the event of the brutal capture and imprisonment of Christina and Mary Bruce.

Why were two of Robert's sisters treated so harshly, while two were seemingly left free? If the *Acts of Robert I* correctly records the marriages of two of his sisters, then this is an important aspect to analyse. Margaret Bruce is recorded to have been married to William

Carlisle before 1306. As a knight of Annandale, the lordship held by the Bruces, then it is plausible that this was a marriage that occurred beyond the context of politics and dynasty, but as a natural occurrence between the daughter of a lord and one of his military followers. If this is the case, then Margaret already being married to a seemingly lesser-known knight perhaps made her less of a political threat to the English claims for governance of Scotland. Moreover, William Carlisle appears to have served Edward II of England until 1316, meaning that he opposed the kingship of his brother-in-law for a decade. Even if Robert graciously welcomed Margaret and William as his kin, his treatment of Margaret is markedly different to that of his other three sisters. Swathes of lands and grants are not placed upon Margaret by her royal brother, as enjoyed by Christina, Mary and Matilda. However, it should also be considered that rather than political differences producing a difference in attitude to Margaret by both Scottish and English governments, she may have been an illegitimate daughter of the Bruce family as she is never directly described as 'Margaret de Brus' in documents, unlike her other sisters.

Matilda's absence from captivity is not as clear as Margaret's. Matilda married Hugh, the son of William, Earl of Ross, who saw to the capture of the Bruce women at St Duthac's in Tain in 1306. Such a marriage was significant in that it bound the Earldom of Ross in loyalty to the Bruce kingship, despite the sins committed by the Earl of Ross against Robert's family. The welcome that Robert extended to the Earl of Ross in 1308 is quite extraordinary when we consider just how detrimental his actions were to the safety and security of Robert's female allies, particularly his queen and heir. The marriage of his sister to the earl's son pulled Ross into the Bruce fold in a major political move. However, Robert seems to go above and beyond for Matilda and Hugh, bestowing significant swathes of land and title upon the couple. This may have been a purely political move, or an act out of genuine affection for a sister and her husband. Regardless, it points to the significance of Matilda as a woman of the royal Bruce dynasty. Which begs the question: where was she in 1306, and how does she appear to avoid capture and imprisonment?

It could be possible that Matilda was the only one of the small party of fleeing Bruce women that successfully evaded English capture, perhaps reaching Orkney or joining her sister, Isabel, in Norway. However, it would seem unlikely that only one woman of Robert's female circle escaped unscathed and with no record of her escape or who joined her on her flight north. It also shouldn't be ruled out that Matilda was captured, but the similar issue of there being no record of her capture – unlike the detailed accounts existing for Elizabeth, Marjory, Christina, Mary and Isabella – makes this a doubtful possibility. Another reason for Matilda's evasion of capture could be that by 1306 she was already married to Hugh Ross, the son and heir of William, Earl of Ross. William's opposition to Robert in 1306 perhaps secured Matilda's safety as an extended member of the Ross kindred, saving her from imprisonment for her connection to Robert Bruce through the political loyalties of her marital family. While we have no date for Hugh and Matilda's marriage, Robert's considerable gifts to Hugh through the 1310s may indicate that he was already a brother-in-law of the king before the first charter which was jointly directed to the couple in 1323. Moreover, the coming-of-age of Hugh and Matilda's son in 1336 suggests that he was born sometime between 1316 and 1318. With two daughters also produced from the marriage, perhaps in the early 1310s, it could act as an indication of the marriage of Hugh and Matilda occurring earlier. Peerage records have shakily dated this marriage to about 1308, but it could be possible that the original date was actually closer to 1306, bringing Matilda safely outside the window of capture and imprisonment in the wake of Robert's usurping of the throne. It is a difficult and near impossible task to locate Matilda Bruce based upon the sporadic evidence, but her absence from records of imprisonment is notable.

Imprisonment

On 7 November 1306, orders were given for the custody of captured Bruce women: 'The countesses of Carrick [Elizabeth] and Buchan [Isabella], Marie and Christine the sisters, and Margerie the daughter, of Robert de Brus'. While all five of the women were likely captured together and sentenced to imprisonment at a similar time, the punishment issued to them varied considerably. Orders for their imprisonment initially given in 1306 would change throughout the course of their imprisonment, a period which would last around eight long years. The women were moved locations, placed into the custody of different men and forced to endure changing forms of punishment depending on their situation.

Their captivity in England means that there is a considerably stronger trail of evidence for understanding where these women were, what they suffered and with whom they kept company. Such evidence provides a crucial and unique insight into the state of imprisonment for female Scottish captives during the Scottish Wars of Independence, shining further light onto the general suffering of female prisoners during the early fourteenth century.

Isabella and Mary: The Women in the Cages

> 'Because she has not struck with the sword, she shall not die by the sword ... let her be closely confined in an abode of stone and iron, made in the shape of a crown, and let her be hung up out of doors in the open air … that both in her life and after her death she may be a spectacle and eternal reproach to travellers.'
>
> Speech by Edward I of England,
> *Flores Historiarum*

Of the five women, the sentencing of Mary Bruce and Isabella MacDuff, Countess of Buchan, was the most severe. Orders issued for Isabella saw her placed into the custody of John de Sandale, the Chamberlain of Scotland, a key figure within the royal English administration. Sandale held this office from 1304-05 until the death of Edward I of England in July 1307, after which he went on to serve in government under Edward II. His orders for Isabella's imprisonment were clear: she was to be kept in a cage.

Within one of the towers of the castle at Berwick (the modern-day town of Berwick-upon-Tweed), Sandale was instructed to oversee the construction of a cage made of strong slats and bars which could be closed and locked. In this cage, he was to imprison Isabella and ensure that she was meticulously watched at all times. It is crucial to note that these instructions repeated the phrase, 'in which she could not get out', a chilling reminder of the harshness of her imprisonment. Isabella's placement within this cage has been previously misinterpreted as seeing her placed in a cage which hung outside the castle of Berwick-upon-

Tweed. In reality, the orders for this cage's construction included that it was to be inside the tower and large enough to act as a bedchamber for the countess. Therefore, it is likely that Isabella had such amenities as a bed and was protected from the elements to which a castle positioned on the North Sea would be exposed. The misunderstanding of the extreme brutality of her imprisonment possibly comes from an account by Sir Thomas Gray of Isabella's condition: 'The countess was taken by the English … and brought to Berwick ... she was put in a wooden hut, in one of the towers of Berwick Castle, with criss-crossed walls so that all could watch her for a spectacle.'

Although Gray does note that Isabella's cage was to be inside the tower of Berwick Castle, his inclusion of being watched by all as 'a spectacle' has perhaps lent to the imagery of the caged countess being outdoors or at the view of all. Gray's spectators probably correlated with the orders for her imprisonment, in that she was to be guarded at all times.

Moreover, a speech by Edward I in the *Flores Historiarum*, a fourteenth-century chronicle, also describes his desire to see her placed in a cage to be hung 'in the open air' in order to make a spectacle of her suffering. However, as with all chronicles, we should consider this with caution as Edward's savage speech may be a product of the chronicle author's own exaggeration of events and intentions for Isabella to be caged outdoors may never have existed. Nevertheless, the indoor nature of her captivity does not negate the sheer cruelty of placing her within a cage and with little privacy from her captors.

Isabella was assigned one or two women to be her attendants to provide any necessary care for her, such as bringing her food or drink or any other requirements of that nature. It is interesting to see that Sandale was instructed to pick these women from the town of Berwick and to ensure that they were English. Isabella was also forbidden to speak to anyone except these two women and those who guarded her, with an especial reminder included in her orders that she could not converse with anyone from Scotland. This indicates a deliberate intention of completely isolating the countess from anyone she may have known and managing a strict monitoring of her contact to prevent any communication with individuals in Scotland. While this could be simply viewed as a standard practice of her imprisonment, it should be noted that other female prisoners, such as Elizabeth de Burgh and Christina Bruce, did not receive such details in their custody orders. Moreover, prisoners across the period of the Scottish Wars of Independence were allowed to temporarily return to Scotland on a case-by-case basis. A key example of this is William Lamberton, Bishop of St Andrews, who regularly travelled between Scotland and England by order of Edward II during his period as a captive. The clear instructions for Isabella's prevention of communicating with anyone from Scotland again emphasizes a particularly harsh approach taken to her captivity.

The brutal approach taken to Isabella's captivity surely demonstrates two key points: she was being deliberately and specifically punished, and that she was viewed as a politically important figure during this period. Unlike her fellow captives, her crime was not being a blood relation of Robert Bruce. Nor was her role as a prisoner one of withholding a valuable family member from Robert – such as a queen or an heir – that could potentially be used in future prisoner exchanges or negotiations. Isabella was a rebel who independently chose to participate in the inauguration of a new Scottish king, a direct act of subversion of the royal authority of Edward I of England. Her choice to abandon her marital family and politically align herself with the man who murdered one of her marital kin further damned her position to that of a captured rebel. Isabella's choices in the spring of 1306 were clearly viewed by Edward's administration as deliberate, calculated and treasonous.

The total ban placed upon Isabella's communication with the world beyond Berwick Castle, particularly with anyone from Scotland, indicates both the severity of her imprisonment and her significance as a political figure. Clearly, it was seen that any conversation between Isabella and Scotland would act as a disadvantage for the English administration; if she were viewed as an uninfluential figure in Scottish politics, the emphasis on such a ban surely would not be so intense. This prohibition on Scottish communication may also have included her marital family, and it appears that her husband and his kin made no effort to secure Isabella's release or the relaxing of her imprisonment orders. Her husband's death in December 1308 may have further sealed Isabella's fate.

Indeed, Isabella would remain in her cage in Berwick with no recorded improvement to her condition until April 1313 – a period of nearly seven years. On 28 April that year, orders from Edward II of England were made to the warden of Berwick regarding Isabella, who had been 'a prisoner there since the late King's time'. She was to be delivered to her nephew-in-law by marriage, Henry de Beaumont, an ambitious political figure of early fourteenth-century England who had married the niece of Isabella's late husband, Alice Comyn. Alice's position as the late Earl of Buchan's niece and heiress meant that Henry held the title of Earl of Buchan through marriage. Isabella's delivery to Henry, and presumably Alice, demonstrates the marital link to the Comyns and Buchan which Isabella retained, although not necessarily at her advantage. While we know that Isabella was able to leave her surely hated prison at Berwick behind her, it is at this stage that we completely lose track of what happened next.

The orders for Isabella's moving from Berwick in April 1313 are the final record in history of Isabella MacDuff, Countess of Buchan. When a prisoner exchange in the aftermath of the Battle of Bannockburn in 1314 secured the release of Scottish prisoners in England, Isabella's name was not among those who received their freedom. It is very likely, therefore, that the countess had died only a year before she was able to be released from imprisonment. Indeed, it could be suggested that her removal from Berwick into the custody of her marital family was potentially a result of Isabella's declining health, perhaps from illness or her worsening physical condition after experiencing such a terrible imprisonment for an extended period of time. Her story is one of tragedy and suffering, but is also testament and evidence of the independent political opinions and decisions made by elite women of the fourteenth century. Isabella was no wallflower or unimportant figure in the annals of Scottish history; she was unexceptionally and unequivocally influential and significant.

The harsh conditions of imprisonment inflicted upon Isabella were also ordered for another of the captive Bruce women: Mary Bruce, the sister of Robert Bruce. On 7 November 1306 orders for Mary's custody included that she was to be sent to Roxburgh Castle to be kept in a cage. When we consider the detail included in Isabella MacDuff's custody orders, we know comparatively little of what Mary's captivity was to look like. However, the entry for Mary's custody directly follows Isabella's, so it could be suggested that the instruction to imprison Mary in a cage was similar to the earlier detail given for Isabella.

The reasons for Isabella's extreme imprisonment conditions are somewhat clear, having considered her role as an active political ally to Robert Bruce and a traitor to both her marital family and Edward I of England. However, the case of Mary Bruce's imprisonment in a cage is a little perplexing. Of the Bruce women related to Robert who were captured – Elizabeth, Marjory, Christina and Mary – she is the only one to be sentenced to long-term imprisonment in a cage (Marjory Bruce's initial custody orders regarding a cage will be discussed later in this chapter). While Robert's other female family members were issued a punishment resembling house arrest, Mary received the brutal treatment given to a recognized rebel. This may suggest that, like Isabella MacDuff, she had similarly committed a specific action subversive of Edward I of England, of which no record survives.

However, when taking the location of Mary's imprisonment into consideration, it could be possible that she was selected of the women to tempt, or perhaps humiliate, Robert into action. During the medieval period, Roxburgh was one of the more significant burghs in the borderlands with a position close to the border with the Kingdom of England, some 20 miles west of Berwick. The English administration successfully capturing and imprisoning two women close to Robert within the border of Scotland (disputed border, in Berwick's case) was surely a humiliating defeat against the new King of Scots. Moreover, one of these women being the king's sister may have been utilized as a way of tempting Robert into trying to rescue Mary in an area firmly held by the English. Such a location for the more politically important prisoners Elizabeth de Burgh and Marjory Bruce would not be considered, but using one of Robert's sisters may have been viewed as less of a loss in the event that she was successfully rescued.

While Mary's rescue did not come to pass – and with no record of any rescue attempt made – her imprisonment in a cage at Roxburgh in what we can only assume to be similar conditions to Isabella MacDuff did not last nearly as long as the former's captivity. By 1310, efforts were being made by the English government to release Mary in exchange for English prisoners in Scotland. On 30 March 1310, Henry de Beaumont – at this time constable of Roxburgh and thus Mary's captor – was commanded by Edward II to exchange Mary for Walter Comyn, 'a prisoner among the Scots'. Edward was clearly under pressure to see to Walter's release who, despite being a relatively junior member of the Comyn kindred, had allies petitioning the king on his behalf for his release. Henry obviously failed in this attempt at a prisoner exchange, as by 15 October 1311 a list of expenses due to prisoners in Newcastle included Mary Bruce, 'sister of Robert de Brus'. These expenses for Mary were backdated to 29 January 1311, meaning that she was likely imprisoned in Newcastle around this date. This provides a period of around nine months from March 1310 to December 1310 when Mary was potentially in a different location from both Roxburgh and Newcastle during negotiations for a prisoner exchange involving her.

Mary's transfer to Newcastle from Roxburgh over the winter of 1310-11, after the aborted prisoner exchange, is not surprising. Her brother's political and military momentum was growing exponentially. In February 1307, Robert and his allies returned to the Scottish mainland after spending the winter of 1306-07 hiding and preparing in the Western Isles. From this point, Robert's forces made concentrated efforts to tackle the English administration in Scotland through methods of guerilla warfare, which included the taking back of castles and harrying of English opposition. A succession of victories in battle against the English, such as Glen Trool and Loudon Hill, timed well with the death of Edward I of England in July 1307 while en route to Scotland to see to Robert's defeat himself. His successor, Edward II, did not continue his father's invasion, returning south for his coronation and to tackle the political and economic mess that his father's military legacy had left to him. Edward's distractions were increased with his own creation of political issues, and a concentrated English military return to Scotland did not occur until 1310, and ultimately collapsed. This meant that from mid-1307 to 1310, Robert turned his focus to tackling his opponents in Scotland.

From 1307 to 1308, Robert operated a ruthless guerilla warfare campaign against his Scottish enemies, namely the Comyns and the MacDougalls. His ability to seize and destroy castles across the Comyn heartlands in northern Scotland weakened his opponents, with his victory at the Battle of Inverurie in May 1308 effectively dismantling the power of the once mighty Comyns in Scotland. The Herschip of Buchan – the utter destruction of the core of Comyn lands – which followed tore out any remaining opposition to Robert in Scotland's northeast. Robert then crossed west to defeat the MacDougalls at the Battle of the Pass of Brander, overrunning the lands and power of the MacDougalls. These intense guerilla efforts meant that by early 1309, Robert controlled Scotland north of the River Tay, an immense achievement for a man who three years earlier had been forced to flee from the mainland. That same year, Robert was politically strong enough to call his first Parliament and was formally recognized by the Scottish Church as King of Scots.

The capture of Linlithgow in 1310 saw Robert's military successes creep further south and heralded a renewed focus on challenging any remaining English presence in Scotland. Therefore, the removal of his captive sister, Mary, from Roxburgh was timely. As Robert's successes and authority increased, so did the potential of more strongholds falling to the Bruce Scots. Indeed, Robert's lieutenant James Douglas would capture Roxburgh Castle in a daring attack in March 1314, highlighting the gradually increasing vulnerability that the garrisons stationed at locations such as Roxburgh were surely feeling as early as 1310.

Mary's removal from Roxburgh to Newcastle heralded a change in her imprisonment. While her initial four years of dreadful captivity in a cage in Roxburgh can be interpreted as a symbolic warning to any opposition to the English Crown, from 1310 her status became that of a valuable political prisoner. This is demonstrated by the move from Roxburgh occurring at the same time that Mary began to be used as a bargaining chip between the Scots and the English. Moreover, her changing value was reflected in the improved conditions of her imprisonment; her captors would need her alive if they wished to use her in negotiations. Indeed, Mary's new living quarters in Newcastle were vastly different to the cage that was her home for four years in Roxburgh. Newcastle Castle's high-status prisoner cell can still be visited today and provides illuminating insight into Mary's experience. The cell is small, but comparable to the other private rooms in the castle, complete with its own private garderobe and an aumbry for storage of personal items. Moreover, the cell also has a window which could be a luxury for a prisoner. However, the window also indicates the use of this room as a prisoner cell, as it is a narrow slit to prevent occupants from escaping. Overall, Mary's captivity in Newcastle was not in a grim dungeon or cage, but in relative comfort and privacy. From 1310,

A stained-glass window depicting Margaret Maid of Norway in Lerwick Town Hall, Shetland. (Photograph by Laurie Goodlad)

Matthew Paris' Map of Britain, c.1250. The top section of the map is Paris' interesting depiction of Scotland, with the bridge crossing over the River Forth in Stirling as the most important feature. (© Picryl)

Left: Moot Hill, the inauguration site for kings of Scots. (Photograph by Graeme Johncock)

Below left: St Duthus Collegiate Church in Tain, founded by William, Earl of Ross, as penance for his capture of the Bruce women in 1306. The ruins beside the collegiate church may be those of the chapel where the Bruce women sought refuge.

Below right: A cell for political prisoners in Newcastle Castle, thought to be the very cell in which Mary Bruce was held captive.

Right: Newcastle Castle, where Mary Bruce was imprisoned c.1310 to 1313/4.

Below: The memorial park at the Battle of Bannockburn Visitor Centre. This battle was fought over Robert I's queen, Elizabeth de Burgh, as well as his kingship.

Above left: A fifteenth-century manuscript of Walter Bower's *Scotichronicon* depicts day one of the Battle of Bannockburn, 23 June 1314. (© Picryl)

Above right: Robert I of Scotland and Elizabeth de Burgh, from the sixteenth-century Seton Armorial. (© Picryl)

Left: Dunfermline Abbey, one of the most important religious institutions of medieval Scotland and the Bruce dynasty. Robert I, Elizabeth de Burgh and many of their Bruce family and allies were interred here.

Right: St Margaret of Scotland's feretory remains at Dunfermline Abbey. Many Scottish royal women, including Elizabeth de Burgh would have closely venerated this royal saint.

Below: Cullen Auld Kirk, where Elizabeth de Burgh's remains were interred following her death nearby on 27 October 1327.

Above left: David II of Scotland and Joan of the Tower are welcomed in France by King Philip VI of France. (© Picryl)

Above right and below: Kildrummy Castle, defended by Christina Bruce in 1335 against the forces of David Strathbogie. Note the stout towers and walls, which Christina's garrison would have used defending of the castle.

Above and right: The island castle of Lochindorb, held by Katherine de Beaumont against Andrew Murray, Guardian of Scotland, for nine long months from December 1335 to July 1336.

Above left and above right: The surviving ruins of Dunbar Castle, where Agnes Randolph's iconic standoff with William Montagu took place in 1338. (Photographs by Graeme Johncock)

Left: A depiction of Agnes Randolph on the ramparts of Dunbar Castle from H.E. Marshall's *Scotland's Story: A History of Scotland for Boys and Girls*.

Mary was clearly being viewed as a high-status prisoner intended for negotiations with the Scots.

On 18 February 1312, Mary was once again presented as a negotiating factor in an attempted prisoner exchange. Orders issued to the Sheriff of Northumberland outlined that Mary be delivered from her imprisonment in Newcastle to Philip de Moubray, who was then instructed to exchange Mary for his brother, Richard, another 'prisoner with the Scots'. Indeed, Moubray's instruction indicates a concentrated and deliberate attempt to exchange Mary, as in the event of his failure to swap her for his brother, Moubray was to 'get what ransom he can for her, and apply towards his pay in Scotland'. This 'get-what-you-can' attitude is a little perplexing. Why was Edward II's government so nonchalant in retaining Mary as a prisoner, particularly following the severity of her initial imprisonment? Why was this attitude not additionally directed to any of the other imprisoned Bruce women, such as Mary's sister, Christina?

As the changing perception of Mary's status as a prisoner has been noted, Edward was perhaps attempting to walk the line with the imprisoned Bruce women by preparing one of them to be used in negotiations, whilst retaining the others for greater leverage. Elizabeth de Burgh and Marjory Bruce were very unlikely to be presented for a prisoner exchange unless in dire circumstances; their importance for Robert politically and dynastically cannot be understated, thus emphasising the usefulness of their continued captivity for Edward. Robert's sister, Christina, may have been considered for similar uses as Mary, but her consistent captivity in Lincolnshire compared to Mary's continued position on the Anglo-Scottish border contrasts with this. Isabella MacDuff had clearly been resigned to imprisonment as a punishment rather than a political decision. Therefore, Mary appears to be the primary Scottish female prisoner who would realistically be used in a prisoner exchange of a minor nature.

While the benefits for the English of using Mary as a bartering tool can be understood – financially and in the return of English prisoners – the political context in which Edward was operating and making decisions in 1312 must be noted. The closing months of 1311 had seen political disaster for Edward as he was now restrained by the Ordinances, published in October of 1311. The result of four years of political pressure under Edward's reign, the Ordinances expressed concern and solutions for the primary issues identified in Edward's kingship. This included the dire financial circumstances of the kingdom which Edward had inherited; the lack of action or success with the war in Scotland; and the brink of civil war of which England was ultimately on the verge. Specifically, the Ordinances sought to challenge Edward's 'evil councillors', namely Piers Gaveston.

Gaveston, a favourite since Edward's succession in 1307 and who had already been exiled, was to be exiled once more. Gaveston left the Kingdom of England in November 1307 in line with the Ordinances, but Edward was clearly intent on repealing this direct punishment of his political and personal favourite. Indeed, Gaveston had returned to England by the end of 1311, and on 18 January 1312 Edward restored him to his position and estates and declared that the Ordainers' decision to exile Gaveston had been fundamentally unlawful. England was plunged into civil war.

This was a desperate hour for Edward, and he demonstrated willing to do anything to defend his and Gaveston's positions. So willing was Edward that in early 1312 he attempted to enter negotiations with Robert Bruce, allegedly offering to recognize Robert's kingship in exchange for his support against his rebelling barons and for his protection of Gaveston in Scotland. The monumental nature of this cannot be understated: Edward II of England was willing to recognize Robert Bruce as King of Scots if it ensured his own survival – and indeed that of Gaveston's – of this particularly threatening political episode of his reign. This demonstrates the genuine gravity of the situation for Edward in England, in addition to perhaps his own poor decision making as king, for which he is often criticized.

The attempted negotiations between Robert and Edward in early 1312 can be seen to have potentially been founded by earlier similar contact between the two kings. Robert's letter to Edward from Cumbernauld, likely sent in the summer of 1310, can be interpreted as an antagonistic bait or a genuine expression of peace (to be discussed in greater detail during Elizabeth de Burgh's captivity). Whatever the intention was, it may not have been unfruitful. From the summer of 1310, Edward led an expedition into Scotland, more as an attempt for the English king to escape the political tension and criticism of his own nobility than a genuine intention of reclaiming Scotland. Indeed, Edward was to remain in Scotland or northern England for nearly a year and would have no military confrontation with Robert Bruce – much less any victory – to show for it. However, Edward's decision to winter in Scotland from 1310 into 1311 at Berwick-upon-Tweed did result in attempted negotiations between the royal party and the fledgling King of Scots, Robert Bruce, shortly before Christmas in 1310. While Robert and Edward themselves may not have met at this point, we do know that Gaveston and the Earl of Gloucester did represent the English king in talks with the Bruce party; whether Robert was present or was represented by his envoys, we cannot say. Just as Edward's expedition from 1310 to 1311 did not seem to produce much, these negotiations also do not appear to have achieved a result. That is, until we consider these events in the light of Mary Bruce's captivity.

As has been established, attempts to negotiate for a prisoner exchange involving Mary were made at Roxburgh in March 1310. Mary's whereabouts for the period following this until January 1310 are unaccounted for, so we could assume that she remained at Roxburgh or was moved to Newcastle. However, we know for certain that she was at Newcastle from 29 January 1311 on account of backdated allowances paid for her later that same year in October. Therefore, it could be demonstrated that Mary was transferred from her cage in Roxburgh Castle to Newcastle during the winter of 1310 to 1311, where she would be imprisoned in conditions more suitable for a valuable political prisoner for subsequent negotiations. Mary's move to Newcastle occurring around the same period that Edward II was in Scotland and in communication with Robert Bruce cannot be a coincidence. It should be expected that were any talks to take place between the Bruce party and Edward's envoys that the subject of Bruce's imprisoned family members and allies would be discussed. The change in attitude to Mary as a valuable political prisoner from this point may indicate that her possible release in an exchange was considered and that her transfer to Newcastle was in preparation for such an exchange.

Edward II's desperate attempt to save himself and Gaveston in early 1312 by appealing to Robert Bruce can also be connected to Mary Bruce's ongoing position in Newcastle as a potential subject of a prisoner exchange. On 18 February 1312, one month after Edward restored Gaveston to his estates and titles in rebellion against the Ordinances, Edward commanded that another attempt of exchanging Mary Bruce be made. While at first glance this attempt may seem more like Edward trying to get rid of this prisoner ('if he cannot effect this is to get what ransom he can for her'), the timing may suggest that this was part of Edward's attempt to achieve an agreement with Robert Bruce for his support for Edward and the safety of Gaveston. From late 1310 to early 1312, Mary Bruce appears to be a bargaining chip between Edward II of England and Robert I of Scotland.

Despite the attempts made to use Mary in a prisoner exchange, we have no record of a successful negotiation occurring. However, when the major prisoner exchange after Bannockburn concluded the release of Elizabeth de Burgh, Marjory Bruce and Christina Bruce, it is important to understand that Mary is not included. Isabella MacDuff's exclusion from the exchange suggests that she died in captivity; this is supported by her name never appearing in the written record again after 1313. However, Mary Bruce appears regularly in Scottish records after 1314 through her marriages and the birth of her children. She married Neil Campbell of Lochawe, with whom she had three sons, and then in 1316 after Campbell's death, took as her second husband the Chamberlain of Scotland, Alexander Fraser. Mary had two more sons with Alexander totalling five children, but it could be possible that she had daughters who have not been recorded. This could often be the case in medieval records or chronicles, with the sons being primarily recorded for political and dynastic purposes. Regardless, Mary's activity from 1314 proves that she did not die in captivity in England, despite being excluded from the list of exchanged prisoners in 1314.

Her marriage and the birth of three sons occurred before Neil Campbell's death in 1316, suggesting that she may have even been released earlier than previously understood, thus explaining her absence from the Bannockburn prisoner exchange in 1314. The last record from Newcastle concerning Mary is dated 2 November 1313, and details her allowance from Edward II between June 1311 and June 1312. This record stipulates that this rate of payment would continue until Michaelmas following, but it is unclear whether this refers to Michaelmas (September) of 1312 or of 1313. Either way, this is the last record concerning Mary's captivity in England. The consistent attempts to exchange her from 1310 to 1312, her suggested release from 1313-

1314 and her absence from the Bannockburn exchange surely confirm that Mary was successfully used in prisoner negotiations sometime between late 1312 and June 1314.

Mary died in 1323. It is difficult to assess her age, but she must have been born between her parents' marriage in 1271 and her mother's death in 1292. Her brother, Robert, was the eldest son born in 1274 and was married around 1292 to his first wife. Her sister Isabel's marriage to Eric II of Norway in 1293 suggests that she may have been the eldest daughter for such a prestigious match. The rest of Mary's siblings were either married from 1301-1311 or did not marry due to capture and execution. Coupled with the disruption of Mary's captivity, it is nearly impossible to narrow down the years in which she may have been born. By the time of her death, she could have been aged anywhere between her early thirties and fifties. A premature death would not be surprising considering the conditions of her caged captivity for four years before her imprisonment in Newcastle, followed by the quick succession of having at least five children.

The period of imprisonment experienced by Mary Bruce and Isabella MacDuff was both remarkably similar and altogether different. The brutality with which both women were treated is a shocking indicator of the lack of chivalry or mercy displayed by Edward I and later Edward II of England, pointing to the genuine political threat and influence that medieval elite women could hold, and the consequences of which they could pay. It is devastating that a key political player in the inauguration and rebellion of Robert I simply disappears from the historical record after languishing in particularly harsh imprisonment conditions for seven years. Ultimately, Isabella MacDuff was a martyr of the Bruce cause and should be remembered to the same extent as other notable figures who died for their own political missions during this conflict, for example, William Wallace.

Mary Bruce's brutal captivity suggests she enraged Edward I to a similar extent as Isabella MacDuff. This being followed by a period of high-status imprisonment and haggling for her release points to the significance of female captives during warfare and suggests their political and dynastic influence. All of this is essential, but above all, it is key to understand and remember the suffering and the ultimate price paid by women who supported Robert I of Scotland.

Christina and Marjory: Dynastic Prisoners

> 'Nonetheless fear overtook all of them, and they were all separated from one another and scattered throughout various places.'
>
> Walter Bower, *Scotichronicon*

Mary Bruce was not the only Bruce woman who suffered for her political support or mere relation to Robert Bruce; another sister and a daughter would be captured and imprisoned in 1306. While Christina and Marjory's imprisonment in religious institutions in England suggest a more lenient form of punishment than the cages suffered by Isabella MacDuff and Mary Bruce, they still endured a lengthy and isolated captivity. This is all the worse when we consider that Marjory Bruce was only around ten years old at the time of her capture, and thus would spend the formative ages of ten to eighteen in imprisonment.

Christina Bruce was the other of Robert's sisters who was captured and imprisoned for this damning familial connection. Her fate as a target during the immediate aftermath of Robert's seizing of the throne may have been further sealed by the activity of her husband, Sir Christopher Seton, who was one of Robert's closest allies. Indeed, Christopher was with Robert at the fateful meeting with John Comyn in the Church of the Greyfriars in Dumfries, and actively participated in the violence of the event by striking down one of John's allies. Robert's excommunication in the aftermath of the murder of John Comyn also included three of his companions – Christopher, Sir John Seton and Sir Alexander Lindsay – all marked as murderers. Christopher would go on to fully support Robert's political and military campaigns following the Greyfriars murder, including being present at his inauguration ceremony at Scone in March 1306. While the accuracy of where Christopher participated in military action is a little vague – some accounts claim he fought at the Battle of Methven in June 1306, others claim he defended Loch Doon Castle from the English – he was certainly taken prisoner in summer of 1306. Christopher's particularly close political and marital ties to Robert through his marriage to Christina damned him to execution, in accordance with Edward I's instructions that no mercy was to be shown to Scottish prisoners following Robert's rebellion. Sir Christopher Seton was hanged, drawn and quartered in Dumfries, leaving Christina Bruce a widow. The nature of Christopher's execution and the loss of her first husband after only five years of marriage remained with Christina for the rest of her life. Twenty years after Christopher's death and shortly before her second marriage, she founded a chapel in his memory near Dumfries.

Clearly, Christina had already experienced immense hardship as a result of Robert's usurping of the throne of Scotland in 1306. As with the other Bruce women taken captive at Tain in 1306, Christina was transferred to England where she was imprisoned further south than her sister, Mary, at Roxburgh and Isabella MacDuff at Berwick. Christina was imprisoned in the Priory of Sixhills in Lincolnshire, and she would remain here until her release in 1314. This means that it is difficult to understand where or what she may have experienced, as there is no record of any sort of movement or of the exact conditions of her imprisonment, such as the information that remains for both Mary and Isabella.

Indeed, the first record for Christina's imprisonment which mentions Sixhills comes from March 1307, when the Sheriff of Lincoln was instructed by the crown to pay for Christina's daily expenses and for her dress, 'from the morrow of All Souls last year when she came there.' This backdated payment does inform us that Christina was imprisoned at the Priory of Sixhills from the Morrow of All Souls, a business date within the Michaelmas term of the medieval legal year that fell around early November. The initial orders for the custody of all the female Bruce captives is dated to 7 November 1306, thus correlating accurately with the date of this backdated payment for Christina.

Unfortunately, these are the last records relating to Christina's imprisonment in Sixhills Priory until the order for her transfer to York on 18 July 1314, to be brought before Edward II. On 2 October of that same year, Christina was transferred to Carlisle Castle with other Scottish prisoners, presumably to await release in the hostage exchange following the Scottish victory at the Battle of Bannockburn. Christina was certainly released from captivity following this transfer to Carlisle, as there is considerable evidence for events which occurred later in her life, both ordinarily domestic as the sister of the king, but also in direct relation to continued Anglo-Scottish warfare, to be discussed in greater detail.

Among the Bruce women taken captive in 1306 was ten-year-old Marjory, the daughter of Robert Bruce. Marjory was born around 1296 to Robert and his first wife, Isabella of Mar, the daughter of the Earl of Mar. Robert and Isabella's marriage symbolized the close connection between the Bruce Earls of Carrick and the Earls of Mar, alongside a marriage that supposedly occurred between one of Robert's sisters and Isabella's brother, Gartnait. However, the identity of this Bruce sister is unknown and often incorrectly attributed to Christina Bruce. Nevertheless, the possibility of a double union between the two families is evident of their political and personal closeness, a useful factor during a time of immense political instability in Scotland in the wake of Edward I's attempted conquest in 1296. The political concerns of 1296 were doubled for Robert with the death of Isabella while delivering their only child, Marjory.

By the time of Robert's usurping of the Scottish throne in spring 1306, Marjory remained his only legitimate child and thus his heir presumptive. Although Robert did have siblings, in 1306 Marjory was the only potential of a Bruce dynasty directly from Robert. At a time where the very legitimacy of his position as king was under immense pressure and question, Marjory's own position as his heiress was of the utmost symbolic significance. It is for this reason that her capture in 1306, alongside Elizabeth de Burgh, was a devastating blow to Robert and a crucial political victory for his Scottish and English opponents. The impact of their capture was twofold: Robert had no hope of producing more legitimate children with his queen's capture, and his only child was in English captivity. This was both a political and personal disaster for Robert Bruce.

Marjory's initial imprisonment was harsh and symbolic of the brutality with which Edward I approached punishing and removing key political figures of the fledgling Bruce regime. Orders for Marjory's custody instructed that she was to be imprisoned in the Tower of London in the same conditions as the women before her: Isabella MacDuff and Mary Bruce. This meant that ten-year-old Marjory was to be imprisoned in a cage inside the Tower of London. As with Isabella and Mary, this cage would have been constructed especially for her imprisonment with slats and bars, and she was to remain at all times under close guard. While the cage itself would have been large enough to be a bedchamber and protected from the external elements, this does not take away from the barbarism of the punishment. Marjory would have had little to no company or privacy. Indeed, orders for her imprisonment included that she was forbidden to converse with anyone, with the exception of the man chosen by the Constable of the Tower to guard her. The punishment endured by Isabella and Mary was shockingly harsh, but the implementation of such conditions on a child was abominable.

It is possible that Edward I did face pushback on the conditions of Marjory's captivity, or even reconsidered her imprisonment himself, as by March 1307 she had been removed from the Tower and was confined to a priory. On 15 March 1307, the Sheriff of York was commanded to distribute an allowance for Marjory's keep at Watton Priory, backdated 'from the morrow of All Souls last year, when she came there.' This order was made around the same time as orders for Christina Bruce's allowance at Sixhills Priory, suggested to be in early November near the business date of the Morrow of All Souls in the Michaelmas term of the medieval legal year. This suggests that there was a remarkably quick change in approach to Marjory's capture, as the initial orders for the custody of the captive Bruce women is dated to 7 November 1306. Indeed, in the further orders for her imprisonment, the entry outlining Marjory's captivity in the Tower of London is immediately followed by updated orders for her to be placed into the custody of Henry Percy, who was to ensure that she was watched carefully alongside her aunt, Christina, in the same manner. The remainder of Marjory's punishment was therefore parallel to Christina Bruce: she was confined to Watton Priory near York until her release in 1314. The rapid change in the conditions for Marjory's imprisonment speaks to the mercy Edward I was willing to display, or the pressure he was under in the handling of this ten-year-old political captive.

Christina and Marjory were not the only female political prisoners to be confined to a religious institution. Indeed, Christina was not the only woman in her position at Sixhills Priory. Gladys ferch [Welsh for 'daughter of'] Daffyd, daughter to the last native Prince of Wales, had been confined at Sixhills since the brutal execution of her father in late 1283. This Welsh princess would remain at the priory until her death in 1336; an imprisonment of over fifty years. Although Gladys' year of birth is not known, it could only have occurred around or after the marriage of her father, Daffyd ap

[Welsh for 'son of'] Gruffyd, to her mother, Elizabeth Ferrers, in 1265, and before their capture in 1283. While this is generally a fairly wide period of time, it does mean that Gladys could only have been as old as seventeen or eighteen at the time of her confinement to Sixhills, but may have been younger. Life in Sixhills Priory might very well have been all this princess ever knew. The memories of her family and life in Wales may have haunted her through her long stay at the priory.

Indeed, a life confined to a Lincolnshire priory was all that another Welsh princess had ever known. Gwenllian ferch Llewelyn – Gladys' cousin – was the only legitimate child of Llewelyn ap Gruffyd, also known as Llewelyn the Last. Llewelyn had been Daffyd's older brother and Prince of Wales, meaning that Gladys and Gwenllian were cousins and daughters of kings. Unlike the vagueness over Gladys' year of birth, it is known that Gwenllian was born in 1282 and so was only an infant at her capture in 1283 and her imprisonment in Sempringham Priory in Lincolnshire, some 35 miles from Gladys at Sixhills. Gwenllian did take the veil, and so life as a nun in a priory was indeed all that she knew. She would have had no memory of her native homeland, family or language. Indeed, she may not have even known how to properly pronounce her own name, as documents record her name as 'Wencilian' or 'Wentliane'. She remained imprisoned in Sempringham until her death in 1337, only a year after her cousin, Gladys ferch Daffyd. Gladys and Gwenllian's horrifyingly long imprisonments are the ultimate symbol of conquest and the destruction of opposition to Plantagenet authority in Wales.

Despite being children, these cousins posed a future threat to the Plantagenet conquest of Wales. If left to freedom, they could go on to become central political figures in any movement against the English occupation of Wales. If they were to marry or carry on their royal lineage through children, particularly sons, this would certainly open claims to the Welsh principality and thus undo Edward I's firm efforts at subjugating Wales. By imprisoning these female political and dynastic figures in religious institutions, Edward removed them from politics and wealth whilst maintaining a sense of chivalry through a merciful form of punishment for women. Comparatively, Gladys' two brothers, Llewelyn and Owain, were imprisoned in Bristol Castle in harsh conditions that saw their deaths far earlier than Gladys. Through a penal measure devoid of violence and employing religious institutions, Edward was able to detain his female political opponents and prevent any future problems through them.

The intention behind the imprisonment of Gladys and Gwenllian was surely the exact method for the imprisonment of the Bruce women, with particularly strong parallels to Christina and Marjory Bruce. By removing them from the kingdom in which their political influence lay and confining them to religious institutions, these women were consciously separated from any sense of agency, whether through wealth and ownership, or through personal relationships and autonomy. It demonstrated their ultimate significance as political threats to English hopes for continued overlordship of Scotland.

Christina and Marjory's eight-year confinement at Watton Priory and Sixhills Priory is especially comparable to the fates of Gladys and Gwenllian. Christina shared space and perhaps even interacted with the former, a fellow princess imprisoned for the very same reason she was: the crime of being of royal blood and related to a prominent male political opponent of Edward I of England. In the end, Christina and Marjory would be fortunate and released from Sixhills and Watton in 1314 after eight years of confinement. Gladys would remain there until her death in 1336, and Gwenllian in Sempringham until her own passing in 1337. Despite their different fates, the imprisoned Welsh princesses shared common ground with the imprisoned Bruce women and symbolized the potential influence that should have been wielded by royal women of fourteenth-century Scotland and Wales in the face of conquest.

Elizabeth de Burgh: The Captured Queen

> 'And thus all who left the king's side that year were either put to death or captured or committed to prisons.'
>
> Walter Bower, *Scotichronicon*

Elizabeth de Burgh found herself in a position unique from her fellow captives: she was both the wife of a high-status rebel and the daughter of one of Edward I's closest allies. Richard de Burgh, second Earl of

Ulster, was a magnate whom Edward '[relie[d] on… more than any other man in the land', as stated by the king in a letter in 1301. The close loyalty enjoyed by Edward from Richard was crucial in maintaining the authority of the English Crown in Ireland, which had been gradually conquered and acquired by Anglo-Norman invasion from the late twelfth century. The initial invaders of Ireland included Richard de Burgh's great-grandfather, William de Burgh, with Richard inheriting the Earldom of Ulster from his father in the 1270s. In addition to being a major political and military ally to Edward in Ireland, Richard also lent significant military aid to Edward's wars in Scotland; his significance is evident in that he was the highest paid earl to participate in English activity in Scotland.

As a political heavyweight, Richard de Burgh surely prevented Elizabeth from suffering an imprisonment as brutal as her stepdaughter, sisters-in-law and ally in Isabella MacDuff. Indeed, this is particularly obvious when we consider the extent of the punishment placed upon Isabella MacDuff and Mary Bruce in being kept in cages in castles, or the lengthy religious confinement endured by Christina Bruce and Marjory Bruce in their respective priories. Similar fates may have awaited Elizabeth had she not been Richard de Burgh's daughter. Her position as Robert's queen was damning – explicitly treasonous, in fact – but saw her receive a very different imprisonment period from the other female captives taken in 1306.

The orders for the custody of 'the countess of Carrick' provide significant detail as to the intended nature of Elizabeth's captivity in England. After meeting with Edward I himself, Elizabeth was to be sent to Burstwick Manor, a key English royal residence near the Humber estuary and within close distance to York, a crucial royal centre frequented by the Crown. The records and surviving remnants of Burstwick Manor indicate that this was a proper residence rather than a prison, made up of various halls and chambers with at least two chapels. It had extensive grounds, with ponds, gardens and two parks, with the primary buildings surrounded by a moat. This was a secure location, but without the grimness of the towers of Roxburgh and Berwick Castles.

This description of Burstwick certainly matches with the orders given for Elizabeth's captivity, she was to have unlimited access to the gardens and parks and to make use of the private hunting grounds, in addition to residing in the most beautiful part of the manor. Elizabeth was to have three hounds as her companions for her outdoor pursuits and was to be exceptionally well provided for in terms of food and dress. Specific foods are even listed in her imprisonment details, including fish and venison. This kind of imprisonment was not unusual during the medieval period for high-status prisoners, particularly those of royalty. David II of Scotland's eleven-year captivity in England from 1346 to 1357 and James I of Scotland's imprisonment in the early fifteenth century, saw both of their respective incarcerations in relative luxury and their involvement in courtly and political events.

Elizabeth was also assigned household servants. Two women were to attend her – a chambermaid and an unnamed lady-in-waiting – in addition to two valets and a serving boy. With these details of Elizabeth's company and access around the manor, she seems to have been given a comfortable and relatively pleasant stay at Burstwick Manor. However, further orders are provided for the conduct of the members of the household assigned to her. Her two female attendants and valets were to be older than her and not of a cheerful disposition, while her serving boy was to attend to whatever it was she needed, but in a sober manner. Despite the positive details of her custody, the instructions to her household are a reminder that Elizabeth was indeed a prisoner, and at seventeen years old and separated from her natal and marital families, she was to experience isolation as her punishment.

A final addition to Elizabeth's household is evidence for why her captivity in England was to be so much more comfortable than that of Mary Bruce, Isabella MacDuff, Christina Bruce and Marjory Bruce. A valet by the name of John Bentley was assigned to her in 1306, and records for Elizabeth's imprisonment until 1313 demonstrate that John remained with her for most of her captivity. Importantly, the orders for Elizabeth's custody note that she must be attended by a valet of the Earl of Ulster, John Bentley. Therefore, Elizabeth had a key member of her father's household join her for her imprisonment. This, in addition to Edward I of England's relationship with Ulster, ultimately demonstrates that Elizabeth's father had certainly intervened in the event of her capture and imprisonment. This surely explains why Elizabeth experienced a more comfortable imprisonment than her fellow captives and had more freedom within her captive location. Edward I must have been under an immense level of pressure from his crucial ally in Ireland to have issued such imprisonment conditions to the wife of a Scottish rebel. This pressure is perhaps also alluded to in the repeated instructions in Elizabeth's custody order to remember who she is and who she is connected to – the King of England and the Earl of Ulster. Her custody orders offer steady and firm reminders to her prison warden to be mindful of providing her with suitable and correct treatment. The opening year of Elizabeth de Burgh's imprisonment was surely a tense period between the Crown and Ulster.

By June 1308, Elizabeth was still confined to Burstwick Manor. However, the political landscape beyond this corner of England had changed dramatically. Nearly a year previous, on 7 July 1307, Edward I had died at Burgh-on-Sands near the Anglo-Scottish border en route to tackle Robert Bruce's rebellion himself. The old 'Hammer of the Scots' never did make it to Scotland in spite of his fierce determination to no doubt brutally remove Robert from power. Prince Edward – now Edward II – was not with his father at the time of his death, hastily travelling to Burgh-on-Sands in response to the news. Edward was proclaimed King of England and its territories at Carlisle Cathedral on 20 July 1307, three days before his late father's funeral procession departed south. By the end of July, the new King of England also departed from northern England, but at the head of his father's army to march north into Scotland. However, this expedition only lasted around a month and was more a fruitless monitoring of southern Scotland than any real attempt at tackling the Bruce party. By the end of August, Edward II returned to England.

A tale states that upon nearing his death, Edward I ordered the flesh to be boiled from his bones and carried to Scotland. His son and successor, Edward II, has long been criticized for ignoring this rather gruesome request and returning south to see to his father's funeral and his own coronation. Even if this tale were true Edward II was unlikely to follow this order. He had inherited from his father a kingdom on the brink of turmoil: dire financial conditions from decades of warfare and conquest, growing tension with France and unhappy nobility. The new King of England's decision to forgo any real attempt to challenge Robert Bruce was a result of Edward's inherited legacy. He now needed to set up his own government and see to the planning of his coronation and upcoming marriage to Isabella of France. Essentially, Edward had his own domestic issues to tackle in addition to ensuring a smooth ascension to power, issues of greater importance in 1307 than another expensive expedition into Scotland. However, it would be three years before Edward returned to Scotland to re-establish English occupation of the kingdom, providing Robert Bruce with an unprecedented and badly needed window of opportunity to tackle his opponents in Scotland.

The disastrous events of 1306 for Robert Bruce following his seizing of the throne in March of that year cannot be understated. By the winter of 1306-07, he had been forced into hiding after two devastating defeats in battle against both English and Scottish opponents, the deaths of a considerable number of key supporters, including his brother, and the capture of his wife, daughter, sisters and other significant political allies. There are various arguments for where exactly Robert went that winter to hide and lick his wounds. While it could be suggested that he fled to Ireland to seek support and reconnaissance from his connections there – his later activity in Ireland in the years following Bannockburn may support this – it's very likely that his primary base over the winter of 1306-07 was in the Western Isles. From 1307, Robert struck a close alliance with the powerful MacDonalds, whose territory included much of the Scottish west coast and islands. Moreover, Robert also took advantage of a familial connection to the MacRuaris, another family of northwest Scotland, which is particularly evident through his alliance with the leading figure of that family, Christina MacRuari.

Christina MacRuari's military support for Robert Bruce from this turbulent period is a striking example of the reality of female involvement in military and political activity, and ability to assign military resources and establish alliances. Christina was the daughter of Ailéan MacRuarí, Lord of Kintyre and widespread territories that encapsulated significant portions of Scotland's western seaboard and the Hebrides. She was the only legitimate child of that lord alongside two illegitimate brothers. While Christina's brothers' own political and military activities suggest that they did inherit a degree of their father's authority and land, Christina certainly appears to be the primary heir and formal holder of the MacRuarí estates, as evident through the resignation of these lands after 1318, specifically by her. These estates and this regional influence were factors that Robert sought to utilize in his cause. This is very similar to his alliance with the MacDonalds from 1306-07, but while this was based upon a mutual opposition to the MacDougalls, Robert looked to take advantage of his familial connection to Christina MacRuarí.

There are two possible family connections between them. Christina was married within the Mar kindred to Donnchadh of Mar, who was possibly a brother or son to Donald Earl of Mar. As Robert's first wife was Isabella of Mar, a daughter of Donald, this means that he and Christina were essentially of the same kin and potentially brother- and sister-in-law. The Bruce family's long-standing connection to the Earls of Mar made these bonds particularly prominent, and so Christina and Robert certainly knew one another prior to 1306 as family. Moreover, it may be possible that the two were further related through the Carrick kindred by their mothers. The family identity of Christina's mother is unfortunately unclear – she is only referred to as Isabella. It is known that Isabella was widowed by Christina's father between 1286 and 1293, and that she was remarried by 1293 to Ingram de Umfraville, a cross-border landholding noble who made regular defections during the Scottish Wars of Independence. Isabella and Ingram's marriage is perhaps marked in February 1293 by the 40 merks of land assigned to them from Carrick as part of Isabella's tocher (dowry) from her previous marriage to Ailéan MacRuarí. These 40 merks from Carrick perhaps suggest that she was originally from this earldom prior to her first marriage and thus may have been connected to the Bruce Earls of Carrick. This sum of forty recurs twice in Robert's reign: Barbour's *The Bruce* mentions an unnamed female family member lending Robert forty men from Carrick in 1307, while in 1328 Robert assigned an allowance of forty shillings to a Christina of Carrick. Such evidence may point to a wholly separate Christina of Carrick who was connected to the Bruce earls and supported Robert's fledgling kingship, or indeed may all point to Christina MacRuarí. If this were the case, her Carrick connection to Robert in addition to her certain relationship to him by marriage through the Mar kindred, made her a very important familial figure for Robert to turn to for refuge and support over the winter of 1306 to 1307. Christina certainly seems to have done so, lending refuge, men, galleys and monetary support to this outlawed king as part of

Robert's forming of a western coalition that may have included Irish families. Indeed, Robert's later military activity from 1315 in Ireland was perhaps founded by his targeting of western and Irish families for support from 1306 to 1307.

The winter of 1306/07 was spent reflecting and training on a new approach Robert would take to furthering his position as king: guerrilla warfare. With the support of the MacDonalds, the MacRuaris and their respective adherents, Robert returned to mainland Scotland in February 1307 to finally begin his comeback campaign against both his England and Scottish opponents.

Initially, this began poorly with the defeat, capture, and execution of two more of Robert's brothers – Thomas and Alexander – after their failed attempt to revive Robert's rebellion in the very south of Scotland. Robert, accompanied by his last surviving brother, Edward, had more success in their return to the mainland and reinitiating rebellion in the Bruce family heartlands of Carrick and Annandale. Utilising the new military approach of guerrilla warfare – a direct contradiction of the chivalric warfare both brothers were raised to practise – the Bruce party entered a new phase of the war wherein they began to achieve victory. This success became evidently a genuine threat to the English and Scottish opposition to Robert's kingship after his victory in two battles against English-led forces: Glen Trool in April 1307 and a resounding victory at Loudon Hill in May 1307 against Edward I's primary lieutenant in Scotland, Aymer de Valence. Valence's humiliating defeat unlocked Robert's access to his kingdom. While Edward Bruce and James Douglas continued to tackle opposition to the Bruce kingship in the southwest, Robert moved north to directly challenge his greatest Scottish opponents: the Comyns.

It was this growing momentum behind Robert Bruce which triggered Edward I's decision to lead yet another expedition to Scotland in the summer of 1307 to remove the new King of Scots once and for all. Therefore, Edward I's death and Edward II's return south did not interrupt the string of successes and growing support for the Bruce king, but rather improved them. From August 1307, Robert was faced with the unique opportunity to tackle the limited and unsupported English presence in Scotland whilst turning his focus to root out the Scottish nobility who remained staunchly opposed to his controversial kingship.

Robert's northern activity in 1307 saw his destruction of key centres in the Great Glen, including Inverlochy and Urquhart Castles, before taking Inverness and Nairn. Seizing this area of Scotland was a significant tactical advantage as the natural geography of the Great Glen connected western Scotland to the Moray coast. Although Robert failed to take the trade and religious epicentre of Elgin, he remained in the northeast for the remainder of 1307 and into 1308. After suffering a serious illness, 1308 saw Robert continue to strengthen his hold of northern Scotland, skimming the edges of the Comyn heartlands of Buchan and Badenoch. This tension finally came to a head at the Battle of Inverurie in May 1308, in which Robert defeated his primary Scottish opponent, John Comyn, Earl of Buchan. Buchan's defeat was a watershed moment for the Bruce party and was arguably Robert's most important military success to date in securing his position as King of Scots. Moreover, this event marked the beginning of other Scottish nobility transferring political allegiance to Robert. This included William, Earl of Ross, the very magnate who saw to the capture of Elizabeth de Burgh, Isabella MacDuff and Robert's daughter and sisters. The writing was on the wall, and it read that Robert Bruce and his claims to the Kingdom of Scotland were becoming a reality.

Within this context, Elizabeth's experience as a prisoner in England changed. On 22 June 1308, Edward II commanded that Elizabeth, with her retinue and baggage, should go with John Bentley, 'where the king has instructed him'. John Bentley is referred to as being the king's valet rather than that of the Earl of Ulster, so it could be suggested that his role as custodian for Elizabeth's imprisonment as an Ulster representative became part of Edward II's household. This order also refers to a previous instruction by Edward to change Elizabeth's residence to Bisham Manor in Berkshire, some 150 miles south of her original confinement at Burstwick Castle.

What drove Edward II to make such a dramatic change to the location of Elizabeth's imprisonment? It is very likely that concerns were raised regarding Elizabeth's security in the context of the substantial progress that her husband, Robert Bruce, had made in Scotland. Indeed, his victory over the Comyns in May 1308 was a huge blow to both Scottish and English opposition to the Bruce kingship, as it removed the key leader of this Anglo-Scottish resistance to the new King of Scots. Robert's swift progress in northern Scotland and the continuing efforts in the Scottish southwest may have indicated the potential of the Bruce party to turn their eyes across the border into England. Elizabeth's captivity at Burstwick was by no means close to these borderlands, but to keep her in northern England was a fate that Edward II and his advisors were not willing to tempt. One may have expected that all the female Bruce captives may have been moved further south – particularly Isabella MacDuff and Mary Bruce – but Elizabeth's position as Robert's wife and queen made her an invaluable prisoner and not one to be lost.

However, record evidence from Elizabeth's captivity in Burstwick perhaps indicates a different reason for her removal to Bisham. In an undated letter from Elizabeth to Edward II, she complains about the conditions of her imprisonment and accuses the bailiffs of Holderness of not providing for her in the way in which her custody instructed. This letter must have been sent between Edward's ascension in July 1307 and Elizabeth's departure from Burstwick in June 1308. Her complaints included that 'they neither furnish attire for her person or her head, nor a bed, nor furniture of her chamber, saving only a robe of three garments yearly and for her servants one robe each for everything.' This does appear to be a far cry from custody orders issued in 1306 which instructed her captors to see to her every need and provide for both her and the household members issued to her. For an elite woman – a countess, arguably a queen consort and a daughter of the Earl of Ulster – to only have three garments of clothing and no head covering was not indicative of the conditions she was to be confined under. Her complaint furthermore includes no provision of bedclothes and furniture, nor for the upkeep of her servants.

Compared to the conditions in which Isabella MacDuff and Mary Bruce were kept, these may seem like trivial complaints. However, Elizabeth certainly would have been aware of her own importance as a political prisoner. Furthermore, she would know all too well the power she held in being a daughter of a key ally of the English crown, and the pressure she could wield due to this. With the knowledge of her custody details, Elizabeth would have been well within her right to complain about this being breached. Indeed, if her dress, head coverings and servants were not being properly provided for, then it may well have been that other aspects of her imprisonment also breached her custody orders. Essentially, while Elizabeth's complaints were most likely based on very real difficulties she was facing during her confinement, she may also have hoped to use them to better her own situation and once again incur the involvement of her father, Richard de Burgh, Earl of Ulster.

Edward II's order for Elizabeth's transfer to Bisham Manor therefore may have been a result of Elizabeth's complaints against the bailiffs of Holderness and the influence of her father. The breach of the clearly stated custody order for Elizabeth surely inflicted tension between Edward and his late father's trusted earl. This was an already strained political relationship which Edward could not afford to further damage in the context of his own political difficulties in the opening years of his reign.

From Edward's inheritance of the English throne in July 1307, one issue became clear and pressing: his innate ability to alienate his magnates in favour of his closest advisor, Piers Gaveston. Favouritism would be a recurring curse on Edwards' reign and his most prominent negative trait. Gaveston, a Gascon nobleman who had been a member of Edward's household since before his ascension to kingship, became powerful and wealthy as the sole recipient of Edward's inordinate gift-giving and favouritism. Gaveston's influence over the king and Edward's own reliance on his favourite resulted in immense tension and anger amongst the English nobility, to such an extent that civil war nearly broke out in the spring of 1308 over the issue. At the instigation of his nobility and to avoid civil war, Edward eventually agreed to exile Gaveston in May 1308. However, Edward quickly created a loophole within Gaveston's exile by appointing him as Lord-Lieutenant of Ireland, the highest office for that region which allowed Gaveston to spend his 'exile' in English territory and in service to Edward. However, this appointment was made at the expense of Elizabeth de Burgh's father, who had only the day before Gaveston been appointed that very same role. As Earl of Ulster and a crucial ally for the English Crown who had been close to the late king, Richard de Burgh's position as lord-lieutenant should have been a given. Edward's regranting the position only a day later to Gaveston was surely a terrible affront to the Earl of Ulster.

Edward's reappointing of Ulster's office to Gaveston occurred in June 1308, the very month in which Elizabeth and John Bentley were ordered to leave Burstwick Manor and transfer to Bisham Abbey. The timing of this cannot be a coincidence and may suggest that Elizabeth's move to Bisham, within 30 miles of London, was a response by Edward to assert some form of damage control in his relationship with Richard de Burgh. However, it could also be suggested that by bringing Elizabeth closer to the royal watchful eye, Edward was able to ensure Richard's minimal reaction to Gaveston's reappointment. In confining Elizabeth at Bisham Manor, Edward was able to both neutralize the threat of her position in northern England and the growing influence of Robert Bruce and pacify Richard de Burgh's unhappiness regarding the conditions of her imprisonment and his own political relationship with the English Crown. Edward may have attempted to soften the blow by confirming and attending a de Burgh double marriage in September 1308. Maud de Burgh, Elizabeth's sister, wed Edward's close ally, Gilbert de Clare, Earl of Gloucester, on the same day that her brother, John de Burgh, wed Gloucester's sister. The double wedding of two of Elizabeth's siblings occurred at Waltham Abbey in Essex, only 30 miles from her imprisonment at Bisham Abbey.

By 13 November 1310, Elizabeth was still at Bisham Manor, as recorded by the payment of expenses for her keep to John Bentley, who was now referred to as the keeper of Elizabeth's household, demonstrating that she was still served by a retinue. The ceasing of complaints and correspondence between Elizabeth and Edward II may also indicate that since the transfer from Burstwick, the conditions of her custody order were being met. With these relatively relaxed conditions, Elizabeth's captivity at Bisham Manor was what should have been the case at Burstwick Manor. The manor had only been brought into Edward II's hands in 1307, a year before Elizabeth was transferred there. Bisham Manor had been constructed in about 1260 and was originally an institution belonging to the Knights Templar, a religious military order which rose to wealth and power during the Crusades of the twelfth and thirteenth centuries. The order's fall from grace in the wider European political stage also occurred in England, with Edward II seizing all Templar properties and land from late 1307 into early 1308. This included Bisham Manor, which by June 1308 became the location for Elizabeth de Burgh's ongoing prisoner confinement.

This remained the case until 6 February 1312, when Elizabeth was again ordered to be delivered to a different location for her imprisonment:

Windsor Castle. Elizabeth, described as the wife of Robert Bruce, was to be received by the constable of Windsor Castle, with 'sufficient houses' to be provided to accommodate her and her retinue. Again, John Bentley is ordered to be 'in attendance on her', further suggesting his role in managing her household. The language of this order differs from previous records regarding her imprisonment. Rather than John Bentley being instructed to 'deliver' Elizabeth as a prisoner, the move to Windsor Castle can almost be read as Edward's notifying Windsor's constable of a new guest that was to be 'received'. Moreover, John Bentley is mentioned more as an attendant for Elizabeth than her custodian or manager. This could suggest that Elizabeth and John certainly had a cooperative and positive relationship as a lady and her household manager, as opposed to a long-suffering prisoner and the manager assigned by her father to accompany her. Additionally, Edward's welcoming of Elizabeth to Windsor Castle is interesting. While placing Elizabeth in a primary royal castle may have been an act of further security, this could be an unofficial acknowledgement from Edward of Elizabeth's growing significance as a political figure: a queen.

Why would Edward perhaps be approaching Elizabeth as a different sort of political prisoner at this stage of her captivity? The answer likely lies again within the context of her husband's activities hundreds of miles further north in Scotland. After Robert's success against the Comyns in May 1308, and Elizabeth's subsequent removal from northern England to Berkshire, the increasingly confident King of Scots then defeated his other major Scottish opponents, the MacDougalls. By 1309, Robert controlled Scotland north of the River Tay, an impressive achievement considering his struggles only three years earlier. That same year, Robert was able to call his first Parliament where he was formally recognized by the Scottish Church as King of Scots. This was a momentous and symbolic moment, particularly considering that Robert's murder of John Comyn in 1306 had resulted in his excommunication. Although he had consistently retained the support of key members of the Scottish Church, this formal recognition from the entity as a whole was a huge source of legitimation for his kingship.

From 1310 to 1312, Robert turned his military attention south and began to focus on challenging any remaining English presence in Scotland. Linlithgow fell to the Bruce party in 1310, followed by Dumbarton in 1311 and Perth in 1312. This was timed with the introduction of raids into northern England, a tactic which the Bruce regime would consistently apply for the remainder of his reign as an effort to place growing political pressure on Edward II and his already unhappy northern English nobility. The destruction of towns and agriculture and the seizing of money, livestock and other goods had an appallingly detrimental effect on the north of England and would be a major factor in Edward II's continuing political trials and the eventual peace between Scotland and England. The growing military confidence exuded by Robert was clearly cause for concern for the English Crown, already shown to be demonstrated by the anxious moving of Mary Bruce from Roxburgh Castle to Newcastle in 1310.

In addition to his military successes, from 1309 Robert began attempts to form a royal government. The first three years of reign, marked by both military defeats and successes and all out civil war in Scotland, had prevented him from fully formalising his regime as king. His marked victory in the civil strife in Scotland and formal support from the Scottish Church officially allowed him to reattempt such a crucial step in his kingship, in addition to intermittent ceasefires and truces with Edward II of England. Unfortunately, it is difficult to assess exactly how the Bruce party attempted to recover the administrative and financial state of Scotland at this time due to the lack of surviving Exchequer Rolls from this period of Robert's reign. This is made all the more difficult by the patchy survival of Robert's royal acts. However, clear attempts were made from 1309 by Robert to consciously conduct himself as King of Scots, not just a military outlaw. Robert's domestic activity from 1309 to 1312 centred around his assertion of royal authority through royal duties: travelling to all corners of his kingdom to re-establish his presence, dispense justice, build relationships with various religious institutions and issue charters and grants. He also made formal royal appointments, granting offices to his loyal followers who had supported him from his initial usurpation in 1306, and reforming the shape of Scottish landholding to suit his authority over Scotland and reward those who followed him.

Moreover, in October 1310 Robert made a diplomatic attempt at contact with Edward II of England. In a letter to the English king, written at Kildrum in the parish of Cumbernauld, Robert presses for peace between Scotland and England, 'in order that devastation and the spilling of a neighbour's blood may henceforth stop.' Indeed, Robert's tone in this letter indicates that he is genuinely willing for peace and that he would be open to doing whatever necessary to ensure that peace. The letter from Kildrum was written in the midst of an imminent English invasion led by Edward II, so could be interpreted as a desperate attempt by Robert to continue to avoid meeting the English in pitched battle. However, Robert clearly writes to Edward as one king contacting another, and ultimately looks for Edward to acknowledge him as King of Scots particularly in the context of talks between the two kings from 1310 to 1312, as discussed earlier. At this stage in Robert's reign, this was an unlikely occurrence. Therefore, this letter could be interpreted as Robert baiting Edward, or perhaps flexing the generally positive political and military progress he was making as King of Scots, compared to the growing problems Edward was enduring in his own reign in England. What the letter certainly does show is that Robert, perhaps for the first time, felt confident enough to diplomatically address Edward II and demonstrate his improving position as king.

All of this Scottish context may suggest why Edward II changed Elizabeth's confinement to Windsor Castle in February 1312, either as a method of improved security and for his ability to keep a closer eye on her, or as a subliminal recognition of her own increasing political significance. She would remain at Windsor for around a year, before moving to Shaftesbury Abbey by at least 12 February 1313. In addition to this move, a key change occurred in Elizabeth's captivity: John Bentley's departure from his role as her household manager or attendant. In late January 1313, he appears in the record for the last time, being paid £10 for Elizabeth's expenses. From February 1313, any expenses relating to the upkeep of Elizabeth and her retinue were paid directly to her, rather than a household manager. Furthermore, these expenses are markedly increased. Before 1313, John Bentley intermittently received £10 in expenses for Elizabeth's upkeep; from 12 February 1313, Elizabeth was to be directly paid £20 per week for herself and her retinue at Shaftesbury.

It is evident that a change in attitude occurs after Elizabeth's departure from Windsor. It is likely that she met with Edward II himself during her confinement there. While we cannot know what was discussed between this captive queen and her royal captor, Elizabeth departed Windsor with more money and with more authority in the management of her household. This, in addition to the notable absence of John Bentley, may indicate a conscious separation of Elizabeth from the political and financial support of her father, Richard de Burgh, Earl of Ulster. Whether this was at the disposal of Elizabeth, Richard or Edward, we cannot tell. The change in attitude and growth in Elizabeth's agency may also be a result of her age. When she was taken captive and imprisoned in 1306, she was seventeen years old, an age at which her father may have felt he was able to intervene in her condition and support her. By February 1313, Elizabeth was at least twenty-three years of age and perhaps in a stronger position to negotiate the conditions of her captivity and manage her own household under confinement. The move from Windsor to Shaftesbury seems to be a watershed moment for the captive Elizabeth de Burgh.

Elizabeth remained at Shaftesbury for four or five months, until June or July 1313 when she received expenses for her stay at Shaftesbury in addition for her and her retinue's journey to Barking Abbey. This would be the fourth change of location to a new long-term residence for Elizabeth's confinement period, and notably within only four or five months of her initial transfer to Shaftesbury. Bisham, Shaftesbury and Barking are not exactly within throwing distance of one another. Bisham to Shaftesbury would have been a journey of approximately 75 miles, while Shaftesbury and Barking are around 105 miles apart. In fourteenth-century England, these would not have been travels made in one day, but rather a long and exhausting journey across days with overnight stops. Moreover, it would have taken Elizabeth time to adjust to each new location, with no indication of how long she would be there. Indeed, the threat of exactly how long she would remain a prisoner was surely a constant question in her mind. It is unclear how aware Elizabeth would have been of the increasingly strengthening position of her husband in Scotland, or of the diplomatic contact that had taken place between Robert and Edward from 1310 to 1312. However, she must have understood that her move south from northern England in 1308 and the increasing changes in her imprisonment location heralded a change in the English Crown's attitude towards Robert, and in turn, herself.

Elizabeth's stay at Barking Abbey differed from her previous captive residences as she was within the confines of a royal nunnery, as opposed to royal manor houses. Barking Abbey was arguably one of the most important and powerful nunneries in England, with the Abbess of Barking a higher rank than all other abbesses in the kingdom. The English Crown held the right to choose a new nun for the abbey upon the ascension of a new monarch to the throne, thus presenting royal figures with the opportunity to place politically beneficial women in a highly important nunnery where their elevation to abbess was possible. It was therefore common for women of political significance or connection to become nuns of the abbey. As an institution of significance and closely connected to royalty, placing Elizabeth de Burgh here as a prisoner kept her firmly under the watchful eye of the English Crown.

Elizabeth may have experienced a similar situation to her sister-in-law, Christina Bruce, and her stepdaughter, Marjory Bruce, both imprisoned through penal cloistering from 1306 in priories in Lincolnshire. It has been demonstrated that imprisoning political female prisoners in religious institutions was a method consistently employed by Edward of England, with evidence also pointing to this being a common approach to captive noblewomen across medieval Europe. Edward II clearly continued this practice with Marjory and Christina and the Welsh prisoners, and now with Elizabeth de Burgh at Barking Abbey. Indeed, this would occur again during his reign in 1322, when another Elizabeth de Burgh was imprisoned in Barking Abbey for her involvement in a rebellion against Edward. This coincidence indeed demonstrated the continuing use of religious institutions to control and isolate elite women of potential political influence.

On 12 March 1314, Elizabeth was moved to her final place of imprisonment: Rochester Castle. Again, this location was considerably different from the royal manor houses and abbeys she had been confined to. Rochester was a twelfth-century fortress constructed in 1127 during the reign of Henry I of England. It had been a mighty and imposing structure of solid stone built to command the River Medway and the southeast coast of the Kingdom of England. However, two brutal sieges in 1215 and 1268 had resulted in considerable damage and destruction to the castle, including the loss of residential areas in the bailey. As a result, the central military keep of the castle became the primary residential block until the castle was repaired during the reign of Edward III later in the fourteenth century. Elizabeth's final location of long-term captivity must have been a far cry from the quiet manor houses or grand royal abbeys of the previous seven years.

However, this did not mean that Edward had again changed his attitude towards Elizabeth. Indeed, her conditions as a prisoner seem to have improved while she was at Rochester Castle. The constable of the castle was commanded to provide her with a sufficient chamber and continue her weekly payment of £20. Additionally, Elizabeth was to be allowed to exercise within the castle and to visit the Priory of St Andrews at nearby Rochester Cathedral, whilst 'under sure guard'. This cautious allowance of movement again suggests Elizabeth's increasingly important role as a prisoner, in addition to alluding to the positive working relationship she had clearly developed with Edward II since their meeting at Windsor Castle in February 1313. This is further supported by the addition of four more members of her retinue from 23 April 1314: Elena Edgar, John Claydon, Samuel Lynford and William Preston. Clearly, the household and retinue which Elizabeth now managed had changed considerably from the initial terms of her custody, which had included two valets, a serving boy and two female attendants – all to be older than her and sober in manner. The order for the addition of Elena, John, Samuel and William to Elizabeth's retinue does not specify their roles or attitudes. It should very well be considered that these were individuals who Elizabeth had petitioned to Edward II to allow to join her retinue. The spring of 1314 at Rochester Castle may have heralded a more freeing time for Elizabeth, allowed to physically and spiritually exercise and have more company possibly of her choosing.

Why was there such a considerable change to Elizabeth's experience as a prisoner from 1313 to 1314? Again, it is important to relate the conditions of her confinement to the political context, and specifically the actions of her husband, Robert Bruce. After all, Elizabeth's position as a political prisoner in England was due to her marriage and role as a controversial king's queen. Through the changing nature of Elizabeth's imprisonment, we can identify how Edward II's regime were receiving and processing news on Robert's movement. This can additionally be seen with Mary Bruce, who was moved to a more secure location of captivity from 1310 and presented as a key figure in hostage exchanges between Scotland and England.

From Robert's capture of Perth in 1312, the seizing back of Scottish castles from Edward II's administration only continued. Additionally,

Robert persisted with adopting a method of attack against England rather than defence, with raids into northern England intensifying to the extent that the Scots reached Carlisle. In June 1313, the Bruce regime made a significant move against England by invading the Isle of Man and capturing Castle Rushen. The Isle of Man's position between the northwest of England, the east coast of Ireland, and the southwest coast of Scotland, made it an invaluable strategic post for the English in extending authority and resources. In seizing control of the Isle of Man, Robert delivered a devastating blow to Edward II that affected England's interests in both Scotland and Ireland. This was a major strategic event in Robert's reign that was surely felt in Edward's court and council.

The capture of the Isle of Man had likely triggered renewed talks of an English invasion to Scotland, the first attempt to do so in three years. This would have been supported by the achieving of an eventual peace between Edward II and his nobility. Edward had spent the summer of 1313 in France at the court of his father-in-law, Philip IV, and had returned with significantly improved relations between the two kingdoms. Moreover, his regime's financial situation had been greatly boosted by a parliamentary agreed raise in taxation, a personal loan from Pope Clement V and approved revenues from Philip IV. The domestic political settlement and financial improvement placed Edward in a position to gather a major English invasion of Scotland and tackle the problem of Robert Bruce as a certainty.

The looming prospect of an English invasion of Scotland was solidified by the capture of two major castles from the English occupation in early 1314. February 1314 saw Roxburgh Castle fall to the infamous hands of James Douglas, one of Robert's closest retainers. Roxburgh's position close to the Anglo-Scottish border made this a significant and bold move by the Bruce regime. Additionally, Roxburgh Castle had been the location of Mary Bruce's brutal imprisonment in a cage prior to her transfer to Newcastle in 1310. Seizing Roxburgh was both a strategic and symbolic action. Less than a month later, another of Robert's lieutenants, his nephew, Thomas Randolph, seized Edinburgh Castle in a daring night attack. Again, this was a strategically significant castle for the Bruce regime to take back from English hands, done so with the same guerilla warfare that had achieved Robert so much success since

1307. The captures of Edinburgh and Roxburgh left one final major stronghold in English hands: the mighty Stirling Castle.

Stirling Castle was invaluable as a strategic location. Situated at the lowest crossing point of the River Forth, Stirling was both the lock and key to controlling Scotland. Its command of the bridge over the river gave it control of a key route from southern to northern Scotland, and the trade, communication and movement this provided. Stirling Castle's position atop the rock gave it unparalleled views across the Forth Valley; to the south was Scotland's central belt between Edinburgh and Glasgow; to the north was the Trossachs, Perth and beyond. This made the castle of unequivocal tactical value: to control Stirling was to control Scotland. Resultantly, the castle had already been at the centre of a number of military events during the Scottish Wars of Independence, including the Battle of Stirling Bridge in 1297 and the Siege of Stirling Castle of 1304. The English had held Stirling Castle since the 1304 siege; its fall to the Scots would be both a military and symbolic disaster for Edward II of England.

In the wake of Roxburgh and Edinburgh's captures, the anticipated Bruce siege of Stirling Castle likely began in March 1314, led by Robert's brother and heir apparent, Edward Bruce. By this point, plans were already long in motion for an English expedition into Scotland, as on 26 December 1313, Edward II had summoned his nobility to muster at Berwick by 10 June 1314. Barbour's *The Bruce* credits Edward Bruce with triggering the summoning of this significant English army, by beginning the Siege of Stirling Castle in June 1313 and offering the constable of the castle an ultimatum: if the castle was not relieved within a year, it must be surrendered to the Bruce party. However, this has been reconsidered by historians and it is far more likely that Edward II's military summoning in December 1313 was in response to a different ultimatum. In October 1313 at one of his most significantly attended parliaments in Dundee, Robert Bruce issued an ultimatum to his remaining opponents with land and title in Scotland, that they were to support his position as king within a year or be forfeited of all their Scottish landholding. This was a deadline and a threat that affected both English and Scottish nobility, whose cross-border landholding made them susceptible to the Bruce king's genuine intentions to forfeit those who did not pay homage to him. It was this ultimatum set by Robert that triggered Edward II's call to arms and invasion of Scotland in the summer of 1314.

It was within this context of Robert's military achievements and threats, and Edward II's imminent invasion of her husband's kingdom, that Elizabeth was transferred from Barking Abbey to Rochester Castle on 12 March 1314. Her stay at Rochester was not necessarily unpleasant, as she still retained her own expenses and managed her increasingly growing household, in addition to being given the freedom to exercise and visit Rochester Cathedral. However, her transfer from an abbey to a twelfth-century fortress can certainly be explained as a move to deliberately increase her security in the wake of her husband's growing power and in advance of a confrontation between him and her captor, Edward II.

This confrontation finally occurred on 23 and 24 June 1314 at the Battle of Bannockburn. The battle took place within miles of Stirling Castle and was a defeat of utter humiliation and devastation for Edward II of England. His grand army was soundly defeated by Robert Bruce in yet another display of tactical genius by the King of Scots, who utilized the natural landscape and military tactics to his advantage to win the day. The battle was carnage for the English, who were pinned between the raging waters of the Bannock Burn and the schiltron formations of the Scots. Edward II himself was nearly taken captive – his shield and royal seal were seized by the Scots and one of his primary guards was killed defending him. The English king had to be dragged from the battlefield and was forced to flee to Dunbar in the southeast of Scotland to catch a boat to England. He was tailed all the way by James Douglas, who very nearly saw to the capture of the King of England. Other key members of Edward's aristocracy were killed or taken prisoner in the wake of the battle. Although Edward himself escaped, the Scots were still able to imprison a selection of prestigious English elite men. After nearly eight years, Robert finally had the leverage to negotiate a hostage exchange with Edward II. Stirling Castle also finally fell to the Scots. Bannockburn was nothing short of a disaster for the King of England.

Within a month of his humiliating defeat at Bannockburn, Edward II had summoned the Bruce female hostages, in addition to other key Scottish prisoners, to York. On 18 July 1314, Edward II 'order[ed] that Robert Bishop of Glasgow, Elizabeth wife of Robert de Brus, Donald de Mar, and other Scots in England, be brought to him at York.' This included an additional order to Sixhills Priory 'to deliver Cristiana the sister of Robert de Brus, widow of Christopher Seton, to the Sheriff of Lincoln to be brought to him at York.' Marjory Bruce, Mary Bruce and Isabella MacDuff were not included in this command. While it has been previously demonstrated that Mary Bruce had likely been exchanged in the months previous to Bannockburn and that Isabella MacDuff had died in captivity, Marjory Bruce was included in the release of the hostages later in 1314. It may be that a record to Watton Priory ordering for her delivery to York, similarly to that for Christina Bruce, had not survived, or that Marjory was only delivered as a hostage for the release period and not brought before Edward II first. Edward's command for Elizabeth, Christina and other key imprisoned Scots to be brought to him at York was certainly a pre-emptive measure in anticipation of negotiations for a prisoner exchange with the Scots. Edward would have been licking his wounds at York; it is interesting to consider what this meeting between the king and his valuable Scottish prisoners would have been like.

On 2 October 1314, Elizabeth de Burgh, Christina Bruce and Marjory Bruce, were sent from Edward to Carlisle Castle, 'to be taken thence to a place arranged by the Earl of Essex and Hereford and sheriff.' Joining them were other prominent Scottish prisoners, including the elderly Robert Wishart, Bishop of Glasgow, a long-time political ally to Robert Bruce and opponent to the Plantagenet aspirations of conquering the Scottish Kingdom. Wishart had been captured in 1306 and imprisoned in England, branded a 'traitor and rebel' by Edward I of England. A likely combination of Wishart's age and eight years of imprisonment had resulted in him becoming blind by the time of his removal to Carlisle in October 1314 and his death less than two years later. Another key Scottish prisoner ordered to Carlisle was Donald, Earl of Mar, who had also been taken captive as an infant in 1306. Donald's captivity in England had been assuredly different to the likes of Wishart and the Bruce women. Although he was sent to Carlisle for a prisoner exchange, Donald chose to remain in England until 1327.

It is difficult to understand what the reunion of these Scottish prisoners would have been like: particularly for Elizabeth, Christina and Marjory. Whether they were reunited at Carlisle in October 1314, or earlier at York in the aftermath of Bannockburn, these were three very changed individuals from their flight and captivity in 1306. Marjory Bruce had been around ten years old when she was initially imprisoned in a cage in the Tower of London in 1306; she was now around eighteen years of age and had been confined to a priory for almost all of her teenage years. Marjory's imprisonment at such a young age and across incredibly formative years surely had a major impact on her. She may have been well treated and lived in relative comfort at Watton Priory, but the significant isolation from her immediate and extended family would have inflicted a degree of childhood trauma upon this young captive.

Christina Bruce had similarly experienced personal trauma from 1306 to 1314. Again, her isolation from family and friends for her eight years of confinement at Sixhills Priory would have been challenging enough, but Christina also had to bear and process the death of her husband in 1306. Christopher Seton had been hanged, drawn, and quartered in the summer of 1306 for his close support for Robert Bruce's kingship; he and Christina had only been married for five years. Her grief for her late husband was reflected twenty years later when she established a chapel in his honour near Dumfries in 1326, the location of his execution. As a young woman in solitary confinement, the immediate years from 1306 must have been exceptionally difficult.

For Elizabeth de Burgh, reuniting with her sister-in-law and her stepdaughter must have been a conflicting experience. Elizabeth had only been around seventeen years old when she was taken captive in 1306 and placed under imprisonment conditions made more lenient by her father's influence. As her imprisonment progressed, her movement further south and regular changes made to her location indicates that she was a politically important prisoner who required further security through these regularly changing locations. The lenient nature of her imprisonment conditions indicates her political value as attached to her natal family. The more that these conditions improved for Elizabeth and the removal of her father's valet from 1313 suggests that her period under house arrest still allowed her to hold a growing sense of agency over managing her own small household and finances. However, Elizabeth surely learned either during her imprisonment or upon reuniting with her marital family about the nature of the imprisonment of the other Bruce women: ten-year-old Marjory in a cage in the Tower of London, before penal cloistering similarly to Christina Bruce. Elizabeth's natal family connections spared her from the isolation of her sister-in-law and stepdaughter's imprisonment conditions, but there may have been a guilt which came hand-in-hand with this. Any sense of guilt was surely intensified by her knowledge of the suffering of Isabella MacDuff and her other sister-in-law, Mary Bruce.

Elizabeth also found herself in a peculiar personal situation by October 1314 that must have affected her understanding of where her loyalties were supposed to lie. While we know that her father had intervened in her captivity in 1306, placing enough pressure on Edward I that Elizabeth's custody order included extensive details for the nature of her house arrest, there are no other surviving records which indicate her natal family's involvement in her eight years as a prisoner. The continuing presence of her father's valet, John Bentley, until 1313, perhaps indicates an ongoing vested interest and influence from her father in ensuring Elizabeth's comfort and safety. Elizabeth also appeared to have a relatively positive relationship with Edward II, who responded to her complaints in 1308 with an improved situation for her house arrest, and who from 1313 saw to her own personal allowance, increased access for exercise and religious practice, and increased the number of individuals in her household. Elizabeth's own position as the daughter of the Earl of Ulster – not a stranger to the Plantagenet royal court – may have meant that by October 1314, she was wrestling with her own political allegiances. Release and return to Scotland presented Elizabeth with the anxiety-inducing reality of reuniting with a husband she had not seen or presumably communicated with for eight years. At their separation in 1306, Robert had been thirty-two to Elizabeth's seventeen years. October 1314 saw the prospect of forty-year-old Robert and twenty-five-year-old Elizabeth reuniting, both very different people from 1306 who had undergone considerably difficult experiences. As the wife and queen to a king who was in desperate need of a male heir, Elizabeth would also have been all too aware of the expectations that would be placed on her – whether by Robert or the wider political community – upon returning to Scotland to provide for the future of the Bruce royal dynasty. Donald of Mar chose to remain in England after October 1314; did Elizabeth de Burgh have any moments of hesitation about returning to Scotland?

From 2 October 1314, the Scottish prisoners – Elizabeth, Marjory, Christina and Robert Wishart – were stationed at Carlisle in anticipation of their imminent exchange. It is unclear how long that they remained there before this exchange occurred, but expenses paid in October to Edward II's receiver at Carlisle Castle, Stephen Blount, included two casks of wine for 'the Lady Brus'. It may well be that the prisoners remained at Carlisle through October. Indeed, talks for a prisoner exchange continued into November. A brutal raid by the Scots, led by Robert Bruce himself, into Tynedale in November may have been another attempt to amplify the pressure on Edward II to engage in an exchange of his Scottish prisoners for Robert's post-Bannockburn captives. Edward was no doubt facing personal pressure from his sister to see to the release of her husband from Scotland: Humphrey de Bohun, Earl of Hereford and Essex.

While there is no surviving record of a date, Hereford was eventually exchanged for the Scottish prisoners. This was an extraordinary event which saw a high-status earl be exchanged for a queen, an heiress, a bishop, a king's sister and several other Scottish prisoners of noble status. This demonstrates the significance of this earl, but notably the fine political line that Edward II was struggling to balance in his kingdom. For his own sake, it was imperative that he regain Hereford, even if it meant losing key prisoners as bargaining chips who he had held for eight years. For Robert Bruce, he was losing one very valuable prisoner, but in exchange for his family, close allies and the very possible future of his dynasty.

Conclusion

This section began by examining the circumstances of 1306 which led to the capture of five female figures connected to Robert Bruce: his queen, Elizabeth de Burgh; his daughter, Marjory Bruce; his sisters, Christina and Mary Bruce; and his political ally, Isabella MacDuff, Countess of Buchan. Robert's actions in murdering John Comyn in the Church of the Greyfriars before usurping the throne of Scotland in direct rebellion against English claims of overlordship of Scotland sealed his own fate as a fledgling king forced to fight for his own kingship. However, it also damned the women and child closest to him to the wrath of Edward I of England. These women spent eight years in varying degrees of captivity. From the irregular house arrests of Elizabeth and the penal cloistering of Marjory and Christina Bruce, to the brutal captivity in cages experienced by Mary Bruce and Isabella MacDuff, these women suffered for their personal and political connections to a man who defied Plantagenet overlordship, for ill or for good. Isabella MacDuff paid the ultimate price, presumably dying as a captive with no record of her being alive after 1313.

Rather than centring on the losses and struggles of Robert Bruce in grappling for his kingship from 1306 to 1314, this chapter has sought to focus on the experiences and sacrifices of Elizabeth de Burgh, Marjory Bruce, Christina Bruce, Mary Bruce and Isabella MacDuff during their long and gruelling eight years in English captivity. When we remember martyrs and catalytic individuals of this warfare, these women should be included.

Chapter 3

Women in Warfare

In 1997, the skeletal remains of ten individuals were discovered during excavations at Stirling Castle. These were found in an area of the castle previously thought to be the location of an earlier residential area. However, it quite quickly became clear that this was in fact the site of a long-lost medieval chapel. Such a chapel was not a surprising find; the earliest written record indicating a royal castle at Stirling in 1110 includes the confirmation of a grant to a chapel at Stirling by King Alexander I.

Reanalysis of the excavations was conducted in 2010 by Dr Jo Buckberry of the University of Bradford, confirming that of the ten individuals, eight dated to the medieval period, specifically to the late thirteenth and early fourteenth centuries. This means that the radiocarbon dating of the remains demonstrates that these individuals lived and died around the conflict of the Scottish Wars of Independence. Of the eight, five displayed evidence of injuries caused by brutal violence that certainly contributed to their deaths. The skull of one showed fractures caused by severe head injuries, including both blunt force trauma and the use of a sharpened weapon. At the top of their skull, two penetrating injuries with defined edges and evidence of a weapon being removed could be identified, in addition to two separate groups of fractures related to blunt force trauma. This was an individual who had suffered immense physical trauma in an act of deliberate violence. This individual was a woman.

The presence of a single female individual (and an infant) amongst four young adult males rules out the possibility of their burials being that of a monastery or a military cemetery. Moreover, their orderly burials within the chapel of a royal castle are highly unusual; this period favoured burials in religious institutions or parish churches. It could be likely that this group were victims of siege warfare and thus burial within the castle grounds was required. This would not be surprising. Stirling Castle changed hands an impressive eight times across the period of the wars, with the castle being besieged and garrisoned by both Scottish and English forces.

Whilst the burials within the castle chapel indicate that the individuals were surely of relatively high status, their location is further evidence in proving that these were people closely involved in the warfare of the Scottish Wars of Independence. The extent of the injuries suffered by the woman and her companions is testament to the brutality of this period in Scottish history. Her presence and fatal injuries are also evidence that during the Scottish Wars of Independence, women were viewed as acceptable targets of military violence.

Such a view becomes evident in the opening sequence of this conflict with Edward I of England's sacking of Berwick in 1296. The destruction of this prominent Scottish coastal burgh was in response to the forming of the Auld Alliance, a Franco-Scottish alliance which acted against the overlordship of Scotland by Edward I of England. An invasion of Scotland was the suitable response from a king such as Edward, and the vivacity of the initial start of this invasion somewhat set the tone for the brutality of what would be a very long and very violent era of Scottish history to the detriment of men and women alike.

Edward's sacking of Berwick in 1296 has become synonymous with this English king's methods of attempted conquest in Scotland. Contemporary writers' accounts provide a range of casualties, from 4,000 to 17,000, but what is evident is that the targeted victims were ordinary townsfolk 'of both sexes'. Burgesses, merchants and other townspeople were not spared from Edward's brutal destruction of this thriving burgh. Chronicles vary in their depiction of the extent of Edward's merciless treatment.

John of Fordun's Chronicle of the Scottish Nation

> 'On this wise, therefore, was the town taken, and all were swept down; and, *sparing neither sex nor age,* the aforementioned king of England, in his tyrannous rage, bade them put to the sword 7,500 souls *of both sexes*; so that, for two days, streams flowed from the bodies of the slain.'

Walter Bower, Scotichronicon

> 'When the town had been taken in this way and its citizens submitted, Edward spared no one, *whatever the age or sex,* and for two days streams of blood flowed from the bodies of the slain, for in his tyrannous rage he ordered 7,500 souls *of both sexes* to be massacred … So that the mills could be turned round by the flow of their blood.'

An old tale – probably more reliable as rumour than certain fact – notes that Edward was only moved to stop the bloodshed upon witnessing English soldiers slaughter a pregnant woman. While this account may act more as a symbolic description of Edward's invasion of Scotland, the targeting of townsfolk 'sparing neither sex nor age' certainly indicates the merciless nature of the example that was being made of Berwick at this stage of the Scottish Wars of Independence. Indeed, this is a sentiment echoed over twenty years later in the Declaration of Arbroath of 1320, a letter sent to Pope John XXII asserting Scotland's sovereignty as a kingdom and Robert I's claim to kingship. Although engineered by Robert's regime and thus bias to the Scottish perspective of the ongoing Anglo-Scottish conflict, the Declaration does take great pains to highlight specific acts of war committed against the Scots by the English regardless of sex: 'The deeds of cruelty, massacre, violence, pillage, arson, imprisoning prelates, burning down monasteries, *robbing and killing monks and nuns* and yet other outrages without number which he committed against our people, *sparing neither age nor sex*, religion nor rank, no-one could describe nor fully imagine unless he had seen them with his own eyes.'

The Declaration's description of 'deeds of cruelty' committed against both men and women – including men and women of religious orders – is somewhat symbolic of a conflict in which women were clearly viewed as targets just as much as their male counterparts. The remains of a female victim of warfare at Stirling Castle is only one physical example in a singular location from a war which saw conflict occur across vast swathes of the Scottish mainland and northern England. It is not difficult to understand that Berwick's treatment and the casualties noted at Stirling Castle was surely commonplace during this period of intense political instability and violence.

However, the involvement of women in the warfare of the Scottish Wars of Independence went beyond the role of victim. Throughout the conflict, the direct involvement of women in military events can be identified. This involvement often came as a result of the woman being deliberately targeted as a military tactic, demonstrating that with the acceptance of women being targeted, came the expectation of female involvement in military decisions.

Improving the understanding of medieval women in a military context and beyond is a growing field of historiographical study across the Middle Ages and various geographical locations. This is examined by the historian Heather J. Tanner, who reassesses the nature of female power and agency amongst noblewomen and presents the case for 'unexceptionalism'. Essentially, she argues that medieval noblewomen in positions of political, and sometimes military leadership, were not extraordinary but fulfilling an expected duty.

An example of the growing comprehension of women in medieval warfare that includes Tanner's 'unexceptionalism' is Katrin E. Sjursen's work on the roles and responsibilities of noblewomen at the heart of the Breton Civil War. This has been revelatory in the improved understanding of female roles, especially within the context of conflict. Unlike popular assumptions of medieval women, Sjursen does not contain female roles to the 'private sphere' of the home and family. Instead, she takes this crucial sphere and places it hand-in-hand with the space taken up by women in the 'public sphere', such as politics, community and military contexts. Sjursen does not keep these separate; she acknowledges and understands the traditional female and male roles in these medieval sectors, but also argues for their interchangeable nature. Her assessment of the lordship unit being a partnership between lord and lady, husband and wife, man and woman, sees a renewed understanding of the responsibilities that could be undertaken by women in political and militaristic issues. She focuses on three women who over the course of the Breton Civil War undertook leadership roles in warfare and politics in the absence of their husband, to little shock or applause in contemporary evidence. Essentially, the transition of leadership from husband to wife was seamless in nature, proving that elite women undertaking leadership roles in military and political contexts was unsurprising, expected and practised.

Similarly to Sjursen's focus on elite women in the Breton Civil War, the following chapters will focus on four military events of the Scottish

Wars of Independence in which women played a central role. Key comparisons can be made between all four of these events.

Firstly, each event features a strong connection between women and physical property, drawing out a key female duty in protecting and defending the home as well as maintaining it. This is a role more commonly attributed to men, but as previously discussed in relation to the partnership of couples in medieval Europe, these events clearly point to this as a significant female responsibility only heightened by warfare.

Secondly, it is crucial to note that all four of these events occurred within the same decade and stage of the conflict. The 1330s saw the renewed outbreak of Anglo-Scottish warfare with the death of Robert I and the uneasy transition of power to the boy-king David II. Such a transition left the Kingdom of Scotland open once again to both internal and external ambition, and so it is unsurprising that conflict renewed. It is fascinating to see four clear instances of female involvement in warfare during such a short period of time in the Scottish Wars of Independence which lasted approximately sixty years.

Why is there such a concentration of women in warfare during the 1330s, rather than over the entire course of a nearly sixty-year long conflict? If elite women were defending their castles during the 1330s, then it is certain that they must have been doing this in the earlier stages of the conflict. Consider the rebellion of Andrew de Moray in 1297, in which Euphemia Countess of Ross provided troops to defend Urquhart Castle against the rebels. Additionally, consider Edward I's steady stream of invasions in the late 1290s and early 1300s and Robert I's advance through northern Scotland to defeat his Scottish enemies. In all these vast and dramatic events that directly impacted the people of Scotland, it is unlikely that women were never involved in the defence of homes and estates, nor that they never undertook political, military and community-based roles in the absence of male figures during a time of war. What is more likely – and a common and unfortunate tale for medieval Scotland – is that extensive evidence for such events beyond the 1330s simply has not survived.

The general study and understanding of medieval Scotland are afflicted by a common issue: the sporadic survival of primary evidence. Edward I's removal of Scottish records in the late thirteenth century and Oliver Cromwell's similar activity in the seventeenth century guaranteed the destruction and loss of incomprehensible amounts of exchequer records, royal records, church cartularies, private charters and narrative histories. Moreover, the attempted return of Scottish archival records from London in 1660 or 1661 failed miserably with the sinking of the *Elizabeth of Burntisland* on 18 December of that year, the very ship that carried such archival records. These devastating losses are compounded by a lack of ecclesiastical records which do survive for medieval England, such as copies of wills, records of marriages and bishops' notes of births and deaths. Such forms of evidence are extremely useful for understanding the people of medieval England, for instance, and their lack in Scotland for this book's focus on the thirteenth and fourteenth centuries is sorely felt.

It is also key to note that all four of the following chapters focus on events that are recorded respectively by surviving chroniclers: John of Fordun; Walter Bower; Sir Thomas Gray; and Andrew of Wyntoun. It is important to emphasize that these authors often used oral histories, private histories and earlier chroniclers to evidence their own work, written items which are lost to us. How many of these lost written works detailed female involvement in other events of the Scottish Wars of Independence beyond the 1330s? How many other besieged castles saw their defence being organized and led by a woman?

From the island fortress of Lochindorb and the stalwart towers of Kildrummy Castle in the northeast of Scotland, to the contentious border castles at Berwick and Dunbar, elite women can be seen to be involved in the highest levels of warfare. The following chapters will delve into four sieges where, for these women, their families and their political allegiances, the stakes could not have been higher.

Christian Cheyne and the Siege of Berwick, 1333

> 'Thus was that Lady of comfort, when she saw her lord distressed.'
>
> Andrew of Wyntoun,
> *Orygynale Cronykil of Scotland*

Edward III of England's invasion of Scotland in 1333 began with a primary target – the coastal burgh of Berwick, today known as Berwick-upon-Tweed. Berwick was no stranger to the violence of the Scottish Wars of Independence, having suffered at the initial eruption of the wars in 1296 when Edward I of England sacked the burgh.

Berwick was consistently subject to attempts by the Scots to retake the burgh throughout the 1310s. In 1317, King Robert I of Scotland was forced to admit defeat after a failed two-month-long siege of the town and castle. This was partially rectified in 1318 under the leadership of Robert's infamous lieutenant, James 'the Black' Douglas, who seized the town in April of that year. Forces led by Robert arrived to support Douglas' three-month-long siege of Berwick Castle, after which the garrison finally surrendered and Berwick was once again reinstated as a burgh within Scottish territory. For the first time since Edward's relentless sacking in 1296, Berwick was held by the Scots, signifying a monumental solidification of Robert's kingdom.

The symbolism of controlling Berwick was no doubt on the minds of both the attackers and defenders of Edward III's siege in 1333. Edward Balliol's expulsion from Scotland the previous year had given Edward III the excuse to invade Scotland, but it was also perhaps a chance for the English king to rectify what were essentially failures by his Balliol ally. Taking Berwick would be a tactical advantage, but it would also work to tear down the symbolism of the strength of the Bruce dynasty in protecting its territories.

At the time of the siege, Berwick's governor was Alexander Seton who was closely associated with the Bruces, fighting in Ireland under Edward Bruce from 1315 to 1318 and being a signatory of the Declaration of Arbroath in 1320. Notably, Alexander's connection to the Bruces originated before the days of Robert I's kingship with the Setons being close allies of the Bruce Earls of Carrick. It is likely that Alexander was the brother of Christopher Seton, Robert's friend and brother-in-law, who was married to Christina Bruce. Christopher was executed in 1306 for supporting his brother-in-law's seizure of the Scottish throne, an event long grieved by the Bruces.

It was into this tried and tested friendship of Seton and Bruce that Christian Cheyne married. Sporadic evidence makes it very difficult to note exactly when Christian married Alexander, or indeed her family background. It is likely that she was related to the Reginald Cheyne who served as Chamberlain of Scotland in the 1260s, possibly as a daughter of his son – another Reginald Cheyne – who held the offices of Sheriff of

Nairn and Inverness and was financially linked to Edward I of England in 1305. As such, Christian's background would appear to be firmly linked to northern Scotland, particularly around Inverness and the Moray Firth. The younger Reginald Cheyne's receipt of funding from Edward I for the construction of Duffus Castle suggests that he would have initially opposed the rebellion and usurpation of Robert Bruce in 1306. As such, the marriage of Christian Cheyne to a loyal supporter of the Bruces is quite interesting and reflects the changing political allegiances of various families during the Scottish Wars of Independence.

Edward III's siege of Berwick began in late March 1333, initially led by Edward Balliol for a period of nearly two months with English ships preventing access to Berwick by sea. Isolating the burgh was a primary tactic in the opening days of the attack. A scorched-earth policy was implemented in the surrounding area to reduce further resources for the town, whilst communication with external allies was cut-off. When Edward III of England arrived in early May with supplementary forces, construction had already begun on siege engines and weaponry, such as trebuchets and catapults. The English forces were well-supplied and prepared for a long siege and a determined attack.

Over the following weeks, Berwick was relentlessly hammered by the attacking English army. The town's defenders had held out against their opponents since late-March, a testament to the strength of the town and how thoroughly it must have been prepared for the return of attackers to its gates. In late June, a naval assault from the English ships was repelled by the defenders, who set fire to tar-soaked wood which they set adrift, presumably on their own boats. However, this defence method went horribly wrong when Berwick itself caught fire, resulting in the destruction of a significant portion of the town. Consider this disaster and the violence of the attackers in the context of nearly three months of limited supplies and severed communication. This was surely a monumentally unstable period for the people of Berwick, reminiscent of the town's role as a major target of warfare during the first stage of the Scottish Wars of Independence.

It was in the context of these limited supplies and injuries that Alexander Seton requested a short truce from the English forces beyond his town gates. Seton likely saw a town depleted and desperate, and in terrible conditions after months of bombardment and fire. On a more personal note, Seton's son, William, had been killed while defending Berwick from the naval attack which had resulted in the town being set alight. For Seton, this had become incredibly personal and a far graver situation of life or death. It could be possible – particularly considering what happened next – that Christian Cheyne played an advisory role to her husband and supported or suggested the request for a truce. Such a truce would allow Berwick to momentarily recuperate, in addition to giving Christian and her husband a brief moment to begin processing the death of their son. Edward III accepted the requested truce on the condition that if Berwick were not relieved from siege by 11 July, that Seton must surrender. Additionally, Edward requested that he receive twelve hostages to ensure the validity and security of such an arrangement. Seton accepted, and alongside the eleven hostages sent to Edward was another of his and Christian's sons, Thomas.

While the majority of the Scottish forces, led by the Guardian of Scotland, Archibald Douglas, laid waste to the south of Berwick in an effort to distract Edward III, a small group led by Sir William Keith approached the town. Despite Douglas' efforts failing to draw Edward's interests from Berwick, Keith was able to gain access to the burgh, and thus claimed to have relieved the town and castle from siege. However, when Edward was made aware of the Scots' demand for the English to depart upon them fulfilling the relief of Berwick, the English king refused. Instead, Edward declared that since Keith's forces had arrived from England, not Scotland, they had not fulfilled the truce. To make matters worse, Edward argued that in addition to the town not being relieved, it had not surrendered by the required date and thus had breached the agreement of the truce. Berwick's hostages were now in a compromised position.

It is difficult to imagine the utter horror that was surely experienced by Alexander Seton and Christian Cheyne as they watched from the ruinous walls of Berwick as gallows were constructed outside of the burgh. As the son of the leader of Berwick's defence, Thomas Seton was immediately targeted and hanged directly in front of his parents. The building of the gallows before the walls of Berwick and the public execution of Thomas was certainly a deliberately calculated move by Edward. Perhaps the English king had expected that Alexander would relent and surrender Berwick to save his son's life or in the wake of his death. That Alexander did not surrender can be attributed to the crucial and selfless role of Christian Cheyne, according to the chronicler, Andrew Wyntoun.

Wyntoun's account of Thomas' hanging before his 'fadyre and modyre' records that Christian set aside her own grief to comfort her husband by declaring that their son had died defending Berwick for their family's honour. She also reminded Alexander that they were young and could yet have more children: 'Thau sayd the lady, that scho wes yhyng, And hyr lord wes yhowng alsua, Off powere till have barnys ma.' This thought must surely have been at the forefront of the couple's minds when we consider that in the space of one year they had lost three sons in the conflict of the wars: Thomas and William in the Siege of Berwick, and another son, Alexander, in battle with Edward Balliol the previous year. Despite the consistent tragedies that seem to have plagued this couple, Christian urged Alexander not to give up and surrender the town, but to fight on for his country and channel the bravery of his ancestors. Christian perhaps reminded Alexander of the bravery of his brother, Christopher Seton, who was executed for his loyalty to the Bruces.

Essentially, Christian advises Alexander to resist Edward III's threat and position, and to choose the kingdom over the life of their son. This means that this is an event which sees a woman – a noblewomen of her own political opinion, as well as a mother and a wife – stand up to the might of the King of England. The prominence of Christian's comforting influence within chronicle accounts of the siege also demonstrates the magnitude of this event to her contemporaries and chroniclers of medieval Scotland. Her courage in her role as advisor is recorded and celebrated, placing her alongside the active military leadership of her husband, Alexander Seton. Christian Cheyne may not have physically led the defence of Berwick, but her advisory role to her husband temporarily thwarted Edward III's plans and patience in an act of rebellion.

It was after the fateful truce and the hanging of Thomas that leadership of Berwick's defence switched over to William Keith, who had attempted to relieve Seton of the siege. While Keith maintained Seton's refusal to surrender the town and castle, concern for the lives of the remaining hostages resulted in renewed negotiations with Edward III. An updated truce agreed that if Berwick were not relieved, or the English were not defeated in pitched battle, by 19 July, Keith would surrender the town and castle to Edward. This ultimately led to the disastrous Battle of Halidon Hill on 19 July 1333, which saw a far-larger Scottish army decimated by forces under Edward III. Thousands of Scots were killed, taken prisoner or executed, including the Guardian of Scotland, Archibald Douglas, and King David II of Scotland's half-brother, Alexander Bruce, Earl of Carrick. Berwick surrendered the following day.

Christian Cheyne's role in the Siege of Berwick contrasts to the following accounts of the sieges of Kildrummy, Lochindorb and Dunbar. Importantly, Cheyne suffered considerably at Berwick, achieving no victory and losing two sons in the process. Her actions and contribution also differ; she supports and advises, but she does not lead. Some may view this as unimportant or of little impact, but this would be incorrect and may reflect the automatic assumption that only physical acts of war can be deemed as a significant contribution. Christian set aside her own fears and summoned her own courage to support her husband and maintain their rebellion against the forces of Edward III. She is remembered in chronicles for her bravery and for the verbal influence she held. Such bravery is not to be undervalued, and Christian Cheyne deserves her appreciated position among the key contributors and heroes of the Scottish Wars of Independence.

Christina Bruce and the Siege of Kildrummy Castle, 1335

> 'She was a most noble matron.'
>
> Walter Bower, *Scotichronicon*

From the rolling foothills of the mighty Cairngorms to the coastal cliffs dropping into the North Sea, the ancient Earldom of Mar covered a region of Scotland both unique and unpredictable. The earldom's formative years as a *mormaerdom* saw its centre of authority and administration at the Doune of Invernochty in Strathdon. However, by the middle of the thirteenth century, power in Mar had shifted with the construction of Kildrummy Castle.

In the midst of the straths and glens beneath the Cairngorms, Kildrummy was a bastion of northeastern power constructed with both comfort and defence in mind. Positioned above a steep ravine to its north and with sloped approaches to its south, east and west, the castle's defensive position was bolstered by a shield-shaped layout and the presence of multiple impressive towers. At its medieval peak, Kildrummy Castle was one of the most important and largest fortified residences in the Kingdom of Scotland. It can be of no surprise that the Scottish Wars of Independence saw Kildrummy as both a target and a site of major English occupation. In 1335, it became the location of one of the most impressive displays of elite female involvement in warfare in medieval Scotland.

By 1335, the second stage of the Scottish Wars of Independence was in full swing. The death of Robert I in 1329 and the subsequent deaths of Robert's major supporters Thomas Randolph and James Douglas may not have been coincidental with the renewed outbreak of war in 1332. Edward Balliol, son of the deposed and disgraced former Scottish king John Balliol, sought to pursue his family's legitimate claim to the Kingdom of Scotland with the support of the Disinherited. Edward and his Disinherited allies shared a similar vendetta against the Bruce regime; all had been stripped of lands and titles in Scotland for continuing to oppose the kingship of Robert I, and all sought to restore that which they believed was rightfully theirs.

Robert's policy of forfeiture and redistribution of lands and title formerly belonging to his Scottish and English opponents benefited the Bruce regime for a time as he effectively restructured the shape of Scottish landholding to his own advantage. Supporters who had been loyal – or eventually chose to be loyal – to the Bruce king from the early years of his kingship were granted lordships, earldoms and titles which would change the passage of Scottish politics and landholding for centuries. Figures rose to become the most powerful magnates and families of late medieval Scotland, such as the Douglases and the future royal Stewarts, enabled by the patronage of Robert I.

However, Robert did not create a contingency plan for the inevitable backlash of this restructuring. It may be that the first Bruce king did not anticipate a revival of his Disinherited opponents strong enough to restart a war. Far more likely is that by the mid-1320s, growing older and battling with poor health, Robert was all too aware of the growing unhappiness with the fledgling Bruce dynasty, perhaps accepting that such a political and military resurgence would certainly occur during the kingship of his infant heir, David.

Robert's anxieties for his son's future against Edward Balliol and the Disinherited may partly explain how Kildrummy Castle ended up in the hands of the king's sister, Christina Bruce. Christina, an already tried-and-tested loyal supporter of her brother's kingship, was granted by Robert lordship for life of the Garioch, a coveted lordship within the Mar nexus of northeastern Scotland. While the date for this original grant is unfortunately unknown, it had at least occurred by 1326, when the lordship was regranted jointly to Christina and her new husband, Andrew Murray.

Robert's positioning of his sister in the northeast was no coincidence or meaningless gift, particularly when we consider when Christina came into possession of Kildrummy Castle.

The Bruces had long been tied to the Earldom of Mar, with Robert's first marriage being to a daughter of Donald, Earl of Mar, Isabella. Moreover, Donald's son and heir, Gartnait, is noted by Walter Bower to have married the eldest Bruce sister in the 1290s, around the same time that Robert would have married Isabella. With no name being attributed to this Bruce sister and with theories that Christina was Gartnait's wife being criticized by historians, it is possible that Bower has named the incorrect woman. Nevertheless, the Bruce-Mar link is made explicitly clear by Robert's marriage to Isabella and by the continuing Bruce interest in the future of the Earldom of Mar throughout the first stage of the Scottish Wars of Independence. By 1305, Kildrummy Castle was held under the keepership of Robert, most likely as a result of the death of Gartnait by this date and Robert's assumption of guardianship of the new Earl of Mar and his young nephew, Donald. Christina's keepership of Kildrummy by 1335, the same year in which Donald of Mar died, suggests that she was following Robert's example and continuing to exercise Bruce guardianship of Mar in the absence of young heirs to the earldom, in this case, Thomas. While it may be possible that Christina was entrusted with keepership of Kildrummy by her husband, Andrew Murray, who was Guardian of Scotland by 1335, it cannot be coincidental that her tenure at Kildrummy appears to begin the same year in which the earldom again faced a minor as its earl. Robert's positioning of Christina in the Garioch prior to 1326 also suggests that the Bruce king was consciously continuing the Bruce-Mar link and ensuring a capable and loyal Bruce figure was present in the region.

By late-1335, Christina was keeper of Kildrummy Castle when it was targeted by the formidable David Strathbogie, claimant to the ancient Earldom of Atholl. Strathbogie was one of several key Disinherited figures who supported Edward Balliol's English-backed invasion of Scotland in 1332. His father, also named David Strathbogie, had been forfeited of his Earldom of Atholl and office of Constable of Scotland for opposing the kingship of Robert I. These lands were instead redistributed to Neil Campbell of Lochawe, another grateful recipient of Bruce patronage whose family would go on to become one of the most powerful in Scottish history. While the elder Strathbogie did not return to Scotland, instead pursuing a career as Warden of Northumberland and in English military service in Gascony, the younger was determined to take back the Earldom of Atholl and all other lands lost to the Bruce forfeiture.

Strathbogie's close involvement in Balliol's invasion and Edward III's support can be spotted as early as the summer of 1331, when Strathbogie travelled to Picardy to finalize the Balliol-Disinherited pending plans. However, that Strathbogie was accompanied by his father-in-law, Henry de Beaumont, demonstrates the depth of Strathbogie's role in not only Edward Balliol's vision for Scotland, but also that of Edward III of England. As well as being a leading figure amongst the Disinherited movement, Beaumont was also a military veteran of Anglo-Scottish warfare and a powerful political ally to Edward III. It could be said that Balliol's supposed leadership of an Edward-backed invasion of Scotland in 1332 was realistically at Beaumont's design, and that Strathbogie, as a Comyn descendant, could have potentially replaced Balliol's claim to kingship. Regardless of Strathbogie's potential place in the political bigger picture, he appears to pursue his forfeited inheritance with the same relentless vigour as his father-in-law. After taking part in the successful military campaigns of 1332, Strathbogie was granted considerable swathes of land by Balliol and appointed his warden in the north of Scotland.

Despite this, by February 1335 Strathbogie appears to make a brief defection to the Bruce faction and plays an active role in the

Dairsie parliament of April 1335 which nearly concluded in violence. Regardless of his defection, Strathbogie was welcomed back into the arms of Edward III of England by 24 August 1335, and by September had been reappointed as Balliol's lieutenant in northern Scotland. It is from this point that Strathbogie executed an infamously relentless campaign across northeastern Scotland in an effort to extend and confirm his authority in the region.

John of Fordun's Chronicle of the Scottish Nation

> 'The great tyranny and cruelty this Earl practised among the people words cannot bring within the mind's grasp: some he disinherited, others he murdered; and, in the end, he cast in his mind how he might wipe all the freeholders from off the face of the earth.'

This display of intimidation and violence culminated in a siege at Kildrummy Castle, the administrative seat of the Earldom of Mar. Strathbogie's motivations for taking Kildrummy were clear. By seizing Kildrummy, Strathbogie could control a major centre of northeastern power, helping to expand his influence in the region whilst cutting Bruce authority off at the root. Above all, Kildrummy conveniently happened to be under the keepership of Christina Bruce herself, aunt of David II and wife of the Guardian of Scotland, Andrew Murray. By targeting Kildrummy, Strathbogie was directly attacking the Bruce claim to kingship.

Despite Strathbogie's ruthless treatment of the northeast and his persistent ambition, his siege of Kildrummy was ineffective against Christina's leadership. Properties Historian Morvern French, has conducted illuminating research on the responsibilities undertaken by medieval elite women in warfare, particularly in relation to their defence of their homes. French has highlighted the consistent management roles held by elite women; they managed the household, coordinating staff and supplies for the business of life in the medieval home; they were involved in the financial background of managing their households; they undertook the leading role in managing their often-vast estates, and all of the details within such a prominent responsibility. Such roles are especially important when we consider them within the context of a period like the Scottish Wars of Independence, a time fraught with intense warfare and political instability. Within the themes of warfare and the dangerous game of medieval politics, the consistent absence of male family members – to war or to court – means that the crucial roles of household and estate management surely were even more likely to fall to the elite women. In a time of absent husbands, brothers, sons and fathers, it was the wives, sisters, daughters and mothers who maintained the households and estates left behind. Above all, French has highlighted the utter normalcy of such an arrangement. Women managing estates and households was not a shocking result of decades of warfare; it was absolutely expected and unexceptional.

Such unexceptional expectations would have transferred into the realm of warfare, especially when violence came knocking at the doors of the households of elite women. Using Christina as a particular case study of this, French has shown that an elite woman's experience in managing their staff, supplies and finances within their household would allow them to utilize similar skills in managing the defence of the home against a siege. As the leader – or manager – of the household in particular, the elite woman would have known the people physically defending the castle, in addition to coordinating the practical matters of resources during what may be a lengthy siege. Furthermore, the household manager would have been well-aware of the tactical advantages and physical layout of the castle itself; such details would be key in defending against a siege. These were details which Christina would have taken full advantage of in her confrontation with David Strathbogie.

Kildrummy Castle's significance within the Earldom of Mar has already been highlighted, as has the geographical advantages of its position on a slope with a steep ravine to the north. The layout and tactical strengths of the castle itself were bolstered by English engineers during the first Scottish Wars of Independence when it was occupied by an English garrison. A once mighty gatehouse at the south and main entrance of the shield-shaped site would have provided an ample defence that attackers would meet head-on. Several squat towers around the castle's shield mixed luxurious accommodation with military defence, towering over the dry moat which co-functioned with the natural ravine to reinforce the castle's defence system. Christina Bruce may have faced a formidable opponent in David Strathbogie, but she was defending a castle that had been altered for the warfare of the Scottish Wars of Independence.

As explored by French, Christina's experience in managing the household at Kildrummy allowed her to utilize the castle's resources, natural surroundings and carefully designed defensive features to resist Strathbogie's forces. It is difficult to say just how long this siege lasted. Strathbogie was certainly again in opposition to the Bruce faction by 24 August 1335, when he defected back to Edward III and Edward Balliol, and by September he was once again acting as Balliol's main lieutenant in northern Scotland. Commissioned with subduing opposition to Balliol and bringing Scots into the royal claimant's peace, Strathbogie's ravaging of northern Scotland likely began with his renewed position as lieutenant and surely timed with his siege of Kildrummy Castle. Therefore, the siege was at least two months long, with Christina being relieved from siege in late November 1335.

For two months, Christina defended Kildrummy and withstood the ambitions of a man backed by the King of England himself. She was surely plagued by the memories of her own brother's defence of Kildrummy in 1306, an attempt to ensure the safety of both her and her other female family members. Neil Bruce's defence ended in disaster when the castle blacksmith allegedly betrayed the defending garrison to the Prince of Wales. While Christina fled north with her fellow Bruce women, Neil Bruce was taken to Carlisle and hanged, drawn and quartered for his role at Kildrummy. Her brother's sacrifice for her safety must have been prominent in her mind as nearly thirty years later, she sought to defend the same castle in the same war he had died in.

Christina was finally relieved from siege by her husband Andrew Murray, who had been renamed Guardian of Scotland in September 1335, possibly the same month in which Strathbogie began his siege at Kildrummy. Murray had rushed north from Bathgate, Lothian, to challenge Strathbogie and come to his wife's aid. The confrontation between the two men ultimately occurred at the Battle of Culblean, a decisive victory for the Bruce party under Murray's leadership which saw the defeat and death of David Strathbogie on 30 November 1335. This victory was a pivotal moment for the Bruce faction in this stage of the Scottish Wars of Independence. It saw the removal of a powerful

Disinherited earl backed by Edward III and with a pedigree strong enough to make a claim for the Scottish throne himself. Moreover, it was a badly needed victory to boost Bruce morale after significant defeats to Balliol's cause and arguably was the factor which turned the tide against Balliol. Andrew Murray has, of course, been credited with this crucial victory as Guardian of Scotland and leader of the Scots in this particular battle. However, Christina Bruce's remarkable success over Strathbogie's siege was a deciding factor in enabling the confrontation between Murray and Strathbogie to occur. By withstanding Strathbogie's forces for two months, Christina demonstrated the innate ability held by elite women to lead and manage the household whilst also setting the stage for one of the most important Bruce victories of the 1330s.

Katherine de Beaumont and the Siege of Lochindorb, 1335/6

> 'From there, he rode over the mountains, where he rescued the Countess of Atholl, who was besieged at Lochindorb.'
>
> Sir Thomas Gray,
> *Scalachronica*

Christina Bruce's triumphant success in defending Kildrummy Castle allowed her husband, Andrew Murray, to defeat the forces of David Strathbogie, the claimant to the Earl of Atholl, at the Battle of Culblean on 30 November 1335. Strathbogie's death in battle severed one of the leading figureheads of the Disinherited and doubled the successful impact that Culblean had on the position of the Bruce party. In the space of two months, Christina and her husband had turned the tide of this stage of the wars.

While the situation for the pro-Bruce faction was looking considerably more positive, one woman had found herself in the exact opposite position. On 30 November 1335, Katherine de Beaumont, Countess of Atholl, suddenly became a widow when her husband, David Strathbogie, was slain in battle. Worse, she was a widow on the run.

With David's death and the defeat of his army, Katherine was forced to take refuge at the island fortress of Lochindorb Castle, where she would be besieged by Murray's forces for nearly eight long months.

Ironically, Strathbogie's death and Katherine's position as a target were the result of Murray rushing to relieve his own wife from the clutches of the enemy. This situation saw two married couples connected by two sieges at two bastions of northern authority, all dramatically involved in this stage of the Scottish Wars of Independence.

That Katherine was near the site of the Battle of Culblean is not unusual; the medieval period regularly saw queens and elite women accompany their husbands on military campaigns. She may have been with the camp following of her husband's forces or residing close by, ultimately making her a target when the situation did become negative for Strathbogie. Such incidences were not unheard of. Whilst Edward III besieged Berwick in 1333, Archibald Douglas targeted his queen, Philippa of Hainault, who had accompanied her husband north and was residing at Bamburgh Castle. Isabella of France, queen to Edward II, was very nearly captured on two occasions; first by James 'the Black' Douglas in York in 1319 whilst her husband attacked Berwick; and second in 1322 when she and her husband were forced to flee Rielvaux after the Battle of Old Byland. By this stage of the Scottish Wars of Independence, it cannot be surprising to see a woman viewed as an acceptable target of warfare. Indeed, the Battle of Culblean's very occurrence was due to Christina Bruce's defence against Strathbogie, a siege that ironically would place his own wife under very similar circumstances.

Katherine's flight from Andrew Murray and subsequent precarious position in northern Scotland in the wake of her husband's death could be perceived as a foreign English countess fleeing for her safety in an unfamiliar land. However, Katherine was certainly no stranger to the politics and geography of northern Scotland. Her mother was Alice Comyn, the last Comyn heiress to the mighty Earldom of Buchan. As a member of the powerful Comyns family who had dominated Scotland's northeast since the early thirteenth century, Alice would have spent considerable time in northern Scotland. While her marriage to Henry de Beaumont, an English baron closely linked to the English crown, may have brought her further south, Alice most certainly would have maintained the knowledge and connections of the northeast region through the decades-long foundations of Comyn influence. When her uncle, John Comyn, Earl of Buchan, died in 1308 without heirs of his own, Alice should have inherited his earldom. Instead, Buchan went to her younger sister, Margaret, who had married within Scotland and thus was a more acceptable heiress to the Bruce regime than the wife of a major English baron connected to the English throne. By 1321, Alice had inherited the English lands of her sister, presumably meaning that Margaret had passed away and that Buchan was again Alice's to legally claim. It can be seen that from the 1320s, Alice and Henry began to relentlessly pursue her claim to the Earldom of Buchan, a pursuit that ultimately led to the initiation of the second stage of the Scottish Wars of Independence in 1332.

It is in this context of Comyn dynasty, inheritance and disinheritance, that Katherine de Beaumont was raised. Additionally, her marriage to David Strathbogie, another Comyn descendant and equally persistent in pursuing his disinherited Earldom of Atholl, would only encourage Katherine's own sense of her heritage and inheritance in northern Scotland. Through the guidance of her determined parents and the partnership of her ambitious husband, Katherine surely approached Scotland's northeast with familiarity and active family connections. This may further explain why Katherine was present with Strathbogie during his subjugation of the northeast. Indeed, research by Morvern French and Iain A. MacInnes argues that Katherine and David had already settled in northern Scotland to assert their authority in the wake of Anglo-Disinherited success in 1333, and that their son and the future of the Disinherited Comyns may have been born there. Katherine's presence with David in this would have been essential; they were a combined force of Comyn heritage and influence. From 1333, the presence of Katherine's parents has also been identified by French and MacInnes, with their establishing of their authority further northeast in Buchan through her mother's lineage. With her parents, Katherine was perhaps intent on extending the influence of her own natal family in partnership with her husband's ambitions for northern Scotland.

The Battle of Culblean on 30 November 1335 saw Katherine's personal and political situation completely turned on its head. French and MacInnes have presented that Katherine's parents had already departed Scotland after Murray's forces besieged their castle at Dundarg, with her husband's death at Culblean causing a collapse of Strathbogie/Disinherited authority in northern Scotland. Katherine, likely only in her early twenties, was suddenly a widowed mother, politically and personally isolated. Katherine may have already been within the vicinity of her and her husband's territory when news of Culblean reached her, or she may have been forced to flee from Culblean to safety. Katherine's flight to Lochindorb Castle upon the Dava Moor may have been a challenging one beyond the threat of Murray. The guardian's arrival from the south removed that direction as an option for the countess. It is possible that she attempted or at least considered heading east to Aberdeen in order to find safe passage from Scotland via the sea, but it is possible that Murray also had eastern access under his control in the wake of Culblean. Instead, Katherine set out northwest, plunging herself deeper into the Highlands and far from Murray and Christina Bruce's influence in Mar. As the daughter of the last Comyn heiress, northwest was certainly the best option for Katherine, with Comyn links or sympathizers in lordships such as Badenoch potentially able to provide her with support. Nevertheless, the journey from Culblean to her eventual refuge at Lochindorb Castle in the Lordship of Badenoch cannot have been an easy one. It is unlikely that she headed north and then west to avoid the rough terrain of mountains and hills of the Grampians, due to Christina Bruce's position at Kildrummy Castle occupying the north of Culblean. Therefore, it is likely Katherine had to cross the Grampians to reach the safety of Lochindorb Castle.

The Grampians are a major mountain range in Scotland, stretching from the eastern to the western Highlands and encapsulating a number of mountain ranges. Katherine's flight from Culblean would have taken her through the mountain passes and glens of the eastern Grampians, through or close to a range known as the Cairngorms. As impressive as they are huge, the Cairngorms are particularly known for their arctic-like environment, unique to Scotland and generating unpredictable and fast-changing weather events and temperatures. The straths and glens through which the traveller passes are the homes of mighty Caledonian pine forests. We know that travel did occur through the Cairngorms during the medieval period: castles constructed by the Comyns in the thirteenth century were deliberately placed at the wide maws of mountain passes to control passage through these mountains. Edward I himself travelled close to the Cairngorms during his attempted conquest of Scotland in 1296, travelling from Kildrummy to Elgin Cathedral, and again in his invasion of 1303-04 when he resided at Lochindorb Castle for several months. Despite the well-trodden routes through these mountains, it cannot have been an easy feat for Katherine to make the long journey from Culblean to Lochindorb in turbulent and dangerous winter conditions, not to mention whilst being hunted down by her husband's opponent.

Katherine arrived at Lochindorb on St Andrew's Day 1335, the same date as her husband's death at Culblean. Her choice of Lochindorb brought her firmly into the Lordship of Badenoch, once an undisputed homeland of the Comyns and a territory which she and her husband had likely been operating in since 1333. Lochindorb Castle itself is an island fortress, located in the centre of a loch of the same name upon the Dava Moor. While its later history as a prison and connection to the infamous Alexander Stewart, Wolf of Badenoch, has left it with a popular reputation of unease, this castle was probably a comfortable hunting lodge according to its size. Indeed, the castle and surrounding area were enjoyed by Edward I of England for hunting when he stayed at the castle from 1303 to 1304, alluding to the vastness and quiet of the moor. At nearly 1,000 feet above sea level and perched deep in northern Scotland, one can imagine the weather that Katherine endured on her journey to and arrival at the castle in the winter of 1335. If snow did not cover the Dava Moor and its solitary castle, then the mists and the rain surely did. Katherine would have crossed to the castle by boat; archaeological excavations undertaken in the 1990s initially suspected that a causeway linked the island to land, but this was disproved by the loch's depth and the glacial origin of the examined geology. French and MacInnes have argued that Katherine may have had several weeks to prepare for siege, as Murray and his forces were involved in sieges and administrative business elsewhere during December. However, this was surely a terribly anxious and dark time for Katherine as she processed both the death of her husband, her complete isolation from allies and the peril of her situation.

The Siege of Lochindorb probably began in late December or January, according to Edward III's knowledge of the siege by late January when a truce was negotiated. This truce lasted until April, but extended to 12 May, acknowledged that Murray's forces had been besieging Lochindorb and halted this siege until the end of the truce in May. However, Katherine would remain at Lochindorb and be besieged for nearly eight agonising months. This suggests that the terms of the truce were not adhered to, potentially by both or one of the parties involved. However, French and MacInnes have also suggested that a winter of extreme weather – proven by evidence from Ireland during this period – may have prevented Katherine from leaving Lochindorb or properly provisioning the castle, an issue similarly faced by Murray's forces. This 'winter stalemate' was possibly responsible for the dragging out of this siege.

When the siege began again, presumably in May 1336, Katherine would have employed similar methods of defence to those by Christina Bruce at Kildrummy Castle and Agnes Randolph at Dunbar. As the manager of an extensive household, the strong use of resources and the castle's tactical advantages were crucial. The castle itself was strategically very strong. Its water-bound nature held obvious advantages and fourteenth-century upgrades made to the castle during the earlier stages of the wars made it a formidable stronghold. Quadrilateral in shape with tall walls, each corner of the castle featured a round tower. The primary rooms and lean-to buildings were safely housed within the defensive walls and towers of the castle, which would have included a hall block and a chapel. On the eastern side of the castle, an additional curtain wall provided further shielding from attack, as this was the part of the castle closest to the shore. Katherine's base for the next seven months was clearly constructed and upgraded with defence in mind, and it is testament to her prepared ability to endure a siege that she chose this castle to retreat to after the Battle of Culblean.

Lochindorb's defensive qualities can largely be attributed to the improvements made by the English garrison which was stationed there following Edward I's residence of the castle in 1303, meaning that the castle can technically be classed as an 'Edwardian' castle. The construction or upgrading of castles was a method of conquest consistently used by Edward I, and can be particularly seen in the vast network of castles built during his conquest of Wales in the late thirteenth century. Lochindorb shares key features with these Welsh castles, such as stout round towers and thick curtain walls. Edward's castles in Wales were designed in the heart of warfare and conquest, and for the purpose of being the ultimate defence against Welsh resistance and a symbol of Plantagenet authority. Lochindorb's upgrades echoed such powerful context and intention.

While the events of the siege itself are not recorded, archaeological, record and narrative evidence provide an overview of what this seven months siege may have looked like for both Katherine's defenders and Andrew Murray's attackers. During investigations of Lochindorb's island and shoreline, two stone granite balls were discovered. Measuring nearly 30cm in diameter, it has been presented that these were likely ammunition from Murray's siege of the castle, fired from a trebuchet. As no other lengthy siege of the castle is known to have occurred, this is very likely the case and alludes to the forms of violence against which Katherine oversaw her castle's defence. It also testifies to the effectiveness of Edward I's upgrades to the castle, particularly when considering the significant additional curtain wall added to the castle on the side closest to shore.

Narrative evidence allows us to understand that Katherine was not alone as an elite woman during this siege, but that she was surrounded by companions. Andrew Wyntoun's account of the siege describes Katherine's presence at Lochindorb, 'withe othir ladeis, that war lufly' (*with other ladies, that were lovely*). This can be supplemented when we understand that as an elite countess, wife of a key Disinherited leader, and mother of a Disinherited son, Katherine would have had an extensive household which was her duty to manage. This would have taken up a significant amount of her time at Lochindorb in addition to overseeing the defence of the castle against besieging forces. Again, it is important to remember that Katherine was only in her early twenties, but bore an enormous responsibility during a personally difficult period.

In addition to protecting her son, overseeing a siege and managing the survival and operation of a household, Katherine was also forced to defend her inheritancc as a widow. In an undated petition to Edward III of England, Katherine requested the custody of the lands of her late husband, David Strathbogie, the Disinherited Earl of Atholl. She presents this petition with the detail that her husband died in service to Edward and that she is not able to maintain herself as custodian of the successor to her husband's estates. Katherine's language in referring to her husband as late, in addition to the description of his death in the king's service, clearly shows that this undated petition was surely produced and sent during the Siege of Lochindorb. This is further confirmed by a responding grant to Katherine from Edward III on 3 June 1336, of her wardship of her late husband's lands until her son reached his majority. As the Siege of Lochindorb was not lifted until mid-July of

1336, Edward's grant confirms that Katherine was petitioning the king in the direct wake of her husband's death at the Battle of Culblean on 30 November 1335. Katherine clearly wasted no time over the winter and early spring of 1335 and 1336 to lay claim to her late husband's land on the behalf of a son who was too young to hold and manage said lands.

However, with some 200 miles of military hostility separating her from the English lands and estates of her late husband, Katherine was in a difficult position to claim and defend both her son's inheritance and her own dower lands. Moreover, it would be a struggle for her to benefit from these lands, as seen in her response to Edward's grant of wardship. Although Katherine's response is again undated, it was likely sent in the summer of 1336 as it directly corresponds to the instruction in Edward's grant to pay sums from the lands of her wardship to the king. Katherine responds with the request that she be excused from paying these sums as the king has granted them to others before Katherine could receive any of the profits. Evidently, Edward's grant of wardship to Katherine was confirmed six months too late from David Strathbogie's death, with others already seeking to reap the rewards from lands and income out of the control of a minor heir and the widow.

Importantly, these records highlight more than just Katherine's financial concerns. The note that her son is in the hands of the King of England in the wake of David Strathbogie's death hints to a concern over custody of her son for dynastic reasons, but additionally on a surely personal level. That her son was unable to assume control of his inheritance and that Katherine was assigned as ward of this inheritance in June 1336 demonstrates that her son was a child, likely under the age of ten. While there is no recorded date for her marriage to David Strathbogie and thus no firm way to determine the age of this child, the marriage of Katherine's parents occurring in 1310 indicates that by the Lochindorb siege of 1335 Katherine was at most aged twenty-five. It is unlikely that the formality of a marriage between Katherine and David, nor the birth of a child, took place before she was fifteen. This therefore suggests that, depending on Katherine's age and the timing of her marriage to David, this inheriting child cannot have been much older than ten years old. This places a new personal perspective on Katherine's position over the winter of 1335 into 1336. She was in her early twenties and freshly widowed, in addition to being separated from her young son and any other children produced by her and David prior to his death in November 1335. This was certainly a time of utmost adversity for the besieged Countess of Atholl, and perhaps places a greater tone of urgency in her petition to Edward III of England for the security of her late husband's lands and her child's inheritance. Katherine was in a precarious position of perfecting the balance between the accepted and expected point of authority in defending her position and castle in Scotland, and the grieving widow attempting to consolidate custody of her child's inheritance in England.

Edward III's relief of Lochindorb

In the end, Katherine's relief from the Siege of Lochindorb came from the very individual she had been petitioning for custody of David Strathbogie's inheritance: King Edward III of England. Edward's campaign in Scotland in the summer of 1336 is nothing short of extraordinary, despite going under the radar in historiographical interest and not regularly being recognized alongside his many impressive military achievements. Again, the work of historian Iain A. MacInnes is essential in understanding the unique urgency of Edward's journey to Lochindorb in 1336. MacInnes explores this event through the crucial survival of a newsletter from Queen Philippa—Edward III's queen—to John Stratford, Archbishop of Canterbury, who was Edward's chancellor. This newsletter provides details about Edward's movements that summer in a diary format and possibly came from the king himself or another member of his retinue. Various chronicles also account for this event and though these are useful in understanding the events which occurred, MacInnes demonstrates the English newsletter provides a close and unique insight into Edward's activities in Scotland at that time. Crucially, at the heart of this well-documented campaign was Katherine de Beaumont and her defence of the castle at Lochindorb.

In May 1336, the English resurgence into the Scottish Wars of Independence began with three invading forces. Two armies by land were led by Edward Balliol and Henry of Lancaster respectively, while Thomas Roslin led a naval expedition to the northeast of Scotland to regarrison the stronghold of Dunnottar Castle. Edward III himself remained in England. The reason for the immensity of the campaign in

Edward's absence was due to two primary reasons: the need to stamp out the Bruce comeback in northern Scotland; and the threat of an imminent French invasion. Escalating tension between the kings of England and France – bearing in mind that these events occurred only a year before the outbreak of the Hundred Years' War – were increased by the rumour of a Franco-Scottish alliance which would see considerable French military aid arrive in Scotland with the intention to invade England. With a twelve-year-old King David II of Scotland remaining at court in France, the foundations for such a military movement are clear. A French invasion via the north would pin Edward between two enemy kingdoms, and therefore likely explains the major Anglo-Balliol military response in 1336 and Edward's subsequent personal involvement.

Andrew Murray's leadership of Bruce resistance continued with his siege of Lochindorb, regardless of the growing military occupancy of Balliol and English armies in Scotland. It was an embarrassing situation for the Balliol-Scottish occupation, to be in Scotland with considerable military strength and still unable to challenge Murray's success in the northeast. More embarrassing, however, would have been the fall of Lochindorb to Murray. The castle's command over a key route between Badenoch and Nairn ensured the castle's strategic quality to both the Bruce party and their Balliol-English opposition. Within the context of an imminent French invasion of England via Scotland's northeast, the English and Scottish need to hold Lochindorb was heightened.

In addition to the French threat, Andrew Murray's continuing challenge to Anglo-Balliol military opposition was no doubt a key factor in Edward III's decision to join his allies in Perth in June 1336. In what appears to be an extraordinarily last-minute decision, Edward departed Newcastle on 14 June with a small number of household knights and squires, reaching Perth by 18 June. Sir Thomas Gray's *Scalachronica* emphasizes the speed and minimal size of this incredibly fast journey to Perth: '[he] came unexpectedly to the Scottish March with barely more than 50 men-at-arms … and set out in head-strong fashion to go to the town of Perth, having him no more than five score men-at-arms. He came to the town so suddenly, that all were amazed at his arrival, and that he should have dared to consider doing it in this manner.'

This must have been a moment of desperation and perhaps anxiety for the English king, with the source of this surely being related to the very real threat of a French invasion occurring via Scotland. It must also explain the following three weeks, in which Edward remained at Perth, allowing him to make a rapid return journey south if required, while also providing him with crucial and quick access to the more geographically difficult northern Scotland beyond the Mounth. These three weeks must have been frustrating for Edward, as despite his ongoing residence at Perth, Andrew Murray's direct resistance continued obstinately with his siege at Lochindorb.

Although Edward's three-week residence in Perth did not see progress made against Scottish opposition, neither was it a time of waiting in frustration for French movement. MacInnes points out that these three weeks saw minor clashes between the Balliol-English forces and pro-Bruce forces, due to the reported loss of horses in Perthshire belonging to English units. The events following these clashes and Edward's residence at Perth suggests that these were no mere chance altercations between the opposing parties. The surviving English newsletter notes that on 12 July 1336, Edward finally left Perth 'so suddenly that no one was notified to arm himself' to ride north with approximately 800 mounted troops. So began an extraordinarily rapid military expedition, led by the King of England himself, into the heart of northern Scotland to directly challenge Andrew Murray and the French threat. Such a mission is explained by MacInnes as being evidence that the three weeks of Edward's presence at Perth and the loss of horses were part of an effort by the Balliol-English forces to clear military opposition from northern Perthshire to reduce the peril of Edward's journey. Again, it is important for us to remember that this sudden movement was additionally a rescue mission for Katherine de Beaumont, who Walter Bower claims had written to Edward with a plea for help. This is not difficult to believe, as by this stage Katherine had been besieged in Lochindorb Castle for seven months.

MacInnes uses the English newsletter to track Edward's movements on this rescue mission. Edward's retinue covered 12 miles before 'camping in the fields,' with the second day including a 30-mile ride to the castle at Blair Atholl. On 14 July, the third day of Edward's travels, his force travelled 45 miles 'through the highest and most difficult areas of Scotland' into the Lordship of Badenoch. Similarly to Katherine's flight from Culblean to Lochindorb, this route took Edward across the Grampian Mountains, although undoubtedly further west through the Pass of Drumochter. The record's mention of Blair Atholl Castle and Badenoch made Drumochter the clear route for Edward; both locations book-end the pass, with Blair Atholl Castle's construction in the thirteenth century by the Comyns completed to control this historically key route through the mountains. The Pass of Drumochter is isolated, its wide plateau framed by mighty mountains. It is not difficult to imagine the treacherous conditions that travelling through this pass could include, as hinted at by the record. However, a mid-July journey for Edward need not have been as difficult as Katherine's escape from Murray further northeast in December 1335, where the countess had faced winter conditions through another route across the Cairngorms.

On 15 July, the diary notes that English scouts brought intelligence to Edward of Andrew Murray's forces, including his location and the number of his army. Edward subsequently moved further into Badenoch and Strathspey, travelling 24 miles to the Church of Kincardine at Pityoulish. It is likely that Edward had spent the previous night at Ruthven Castle; the castle's location matches well with the detail of the 45-mile journey from Blair Atholl and the 24-mile ride to Pityoulish. The church which Edward had based himself at was only 12 miles from Lochindorb's position upon the Dava Moor, providing the English king with a temporary base before his confrontation with Murray. The stage was set for a showdown between Edward and his ultimate Scottish opponent, the Guardian of Scotland. Moreover, it brought Katherine de Beaumont tantalisingly close to the closing stages of this long, drawn out siege.

However, Edward never would manage to confront Murray. The English newsletter tells us that as soon as Murray and his forces heard word of Edward's coming, they fled northwest to Ross to avoid the wrath of the King of England. This contrasts with Wyntoun's chronicle, which notes that Murr ay was undisturbed by the warning of Edward's proximity and took his time praying, eating and dressing before readying his men for departure from Lochindorb. Wyntoun also writes that Murray's men fled to Forres and were pursued by Edward's army, but were successful in evading their challengers, who subsequently returned to Lochindorb and its besieged countess.

Andrew Murray's departure and the following arrival of the King of England and his retinue must have been a sorely welcome sight for Katherine de Beaumont. It is important to remember that she had been at Lochindorb since early December 1335, enduring an eight-month siege over the winter months in northern Scotland. Moreover, Katherine had been widowed and as seen in petitions to Edward III, separated from her young son who probably remained in England. She had been forced to assert her right to her inheritance as David Strathbogie's widow from hundreds of miles away, with the knowledge that others were taking advantage of her absence and her son's youth. This must have been an extraordinarily trying experience for Katherine and the ladies who endured their long defence of Lochindorb Castle. Indeed, MacInnes highlights that the English diary of Edward's flight north records that Edward and his army were welcomed by the countess, who came ashore from the castle to greet them. She informed Edward 'of the plight of those within the castle', which certainly indicates the dwindling supplies and possible injuries that the castle inhabitants had been struggling with. Edward replenished the castle and stationed a garrison there, before turning his attention northeast to begin a brutal chevauchée of Moray and Aberdeenshire.

It is unclear when Katherine finally managed to leave Lochindorb and turn south, no doubt keen to return to her son and to another type of defence of her property and land. While both Wyntoun and Bower state that Katherine returned south with Edward after his harrying of the northeast, MacInnes points out that the English newsletter records that Katherine departed on 16 July while the king was rampaging through the northeast of Scotland. While the diary does not note where Katherine travelled to, it does report the loss of horses 'in the mountains' belonging to Henry de Beaumont. MacInnes suggests that she was escorted south to Perth by a Beaumont retinue, presumably from or perhaps including her father, with the note of travelling through the mountains indicating a return through the Mounth, possibly via the Pass of Drumochter. A Beaumont presence in Edward's forces and their ability to leave Edward to his chevauchée demonstrates the personal vested interest that Edward had in this mission north. In addition to tackling Murray and the French threat, he was responding to a personal plea for help in conducting a genuine rescue mission of a key ally's daughter. While this point shows the importance of personal relationships in influencing Edward's northern campaign in the summer of 1336, it also reminds us of the significance of medieval elite women as political figures and active participants in warfare. In this particular instance, Katherine de Beaumont's defence of Lochindorb Castle saw her at the centre of a campaign by the King of England himself.

MacInnes presents that Edward III of England had several primary motivations for his journey to the north of Scotland to relieve the Siege of Lochindorb. This included the need to challenge Andrew Murray and reinstate an English military presence in response to rumours of a French invasion via Scotland's northeast. If the castle were to fall to Murray during a period of considerable Anglo-Balliol presence in Perthshire, this would have been a strategically damaging move, particularly in the context of the French threat. In addition, the personal relationships which influenced this campaign have been considered. However, Macinnes also assesses that Katherine's situation at Lochindorb against Andrew Murray presented Edward III with an opportunity to fulfil the English king's conscious development of a romantic image of chivalry and honour. His rapid venture into northern Scotland to come to Katherine's aid is no doubt a 'damsel in distress' cliché that would have boosted his image as a romantic and chivalric king. That this would be the first act of the campaign almost justified his following brutal actions in putting Moray and Aberdeenshire to the torch, even if the real motivations for this had been political. The chronicle renditions of a good and knightly king rescuing a countess and slaughtering her assailants would certainly have been in Edward's mind. Finally, MacInnes identifies that this act of gallantry also inadvertently challenged Murray, whose own rush to defend his wife at Kildrummy Castle from David Strathbogie certainly captured the attention of chroniclers like Wyntoun and Bower. Edward would have known of this event, and the opportunity to essentially overshadow Murray's actions and reinforce his own public image and qualities would have been of interest to a king who was certainly conscious of the careful development of his legacy and image. The importance of Edward's decision to relieve Katherine from siege as part of his northern campaign is obviously understood. However, I would argue that the true heroines of the Lochindorb event were the countess and her female companions who defended the castle for seven months and prevented a humiliating loss for the Anglo-Balliol party in Scotland.

A Widow

Many of the women studied in this book remained in Scotland meaning that record evidence of their lives and careers is incredibly sparse. However, this is not the case for Katherine de Beaumont, who returned to England after the events at Lochindorb and therefore has a greater presence in the stronger surviving evidence from fourteenth-century England. This presence is further strengthened by the fact that Katherine faced a number of considerably challenging issues to her land, finances and dower property. The various instances of legal action or petitions to Edward III of England means that she has left her mark in record evidence for her life following the Siege of Lochindorb.

To summarize, Katherine's position after her husband's death and her return to England does not appear to have been particularly smooth. For the next thirteen years after Lochindorb, she was consistently in contact with Edward III over issues regarding money and the security of her dower lands and properties, in addition to being involved in legal action related to her ownership of dower properties. The most prominent of the latter issue can be seen in October 1345, when Edward commanded his justices to proceed with a lawsuit by Katherine against Sir Edmund Cornwall and his wife Isabella. Edmund and Isabella had previously challenged the inheritance of Collingbourne Valence Manor by Katherine's son, David. This challenge had been upheld and had caused 'no small loss and injury' to Katherine, who held the manor as her young son's guardian. While the outcome of this lawsuit is not apparent, this stands as an example of the kinds of legal challenges that elite widows such as Katherine had to defend themselves against. In a century which saw complaints by younger noblemen in England about the long tenures of 'rich old ladies' (see Rowena E. Archer and recommended reading list for more), Katherine's involvement in legalities is not surprising. This is all the more unsurprising considering that she had to battle for her dower and her son's inheritance while besieged at Lochindorb.

When Katherine's dower lands and wardship of her son's lands were legally confirmed, they were not physically secure. On 30 May 1337, Edward III was made aware of one of Katherine's dower manors being prevented from delivery to her by an armed force led by Robert Atholl. Brabourne Manor, in Kent, had only been confirmed by Edward to Katherine in December 1336 in lieu of other property in Northumberland. This suggests that Brabourne was not initially supposed to be part of Katherine's dower, and that this amendment by Edward had directly impacted Robert Atholl's claim to the manor. Nevertheless, Atholl's use of force to 'physically' prevent Brabourne from being confirmed as

Katherine's is evidence of the issues she faced with the security of her dower properties. This is further emphasized by an incident in December 1341 when Katherine complained to Edward about ten of her properties being compromised by a group of twenty-seven attackers, in addition to the assault of one of her servants and the thievery of her belongings. Moreover, Katherine had to be financially compensated by Edward in 1342 and 1349, after her dower lands in Northumberland were 'wasted by the Scots.'

Katherine appears to be financially reliant upon Edward III from 1336 until around 1349, when Edward saw to her compensation of her lands in Northumberland damaged by ongoing Anglo-Scottish warfare. Records indicate that Katherine was paid an annual sum of 100 marks; in May 1341 Edward sourced forty marks of this from Horton Priory, near her property in Kent. One year later, she was granted an additional fifty marks in compensation for damage to her lands in Northumberland. That same year, Edward arranged the marriage of her son David to Elizabeth Ferrars, the daughter of Henry Ferrars, a former retainer of Katherine's father. As David was still in his minority years, upon his marriage his custody transferred from Katherine to Edward, and then to Henry Ferrars. As a result of her son's marriage and transfer of custody, Katherine was informed that she would no longer be due the 100 marks for herself and David's upkeep. However, this was a relatively fruitless decision, as Edward conceded to still pay Katherine 100 marks annually in recognition of the damage to her dower lands as a result of warfare. This sum indicates the devastation wrought upon the northern English territories during the Anglo-Scottish warfare of the fourteenth century.

Nevertheless, Edward's financial support of Katherine did contain one caveat: she must remain unmarried. This surely placed Katherine somewhat between a rock and a hard place. The damage inflicted to her lands and the physical threat from thieves and competitors for inheritance must have led her to consider a second marriage. In particular, Katherine may have considered sourcing a husband with a significant military following. Indeed, there are several examples of elite women in Scotland in the fourteenth century deliberately choosing men with strong military followings as their second or third husbands, even if they were not of strong dynastic prestige. However, if she were to remarry, she would lose a considerable source of income that she was clearly reliant upon. Indeed, in November 1346 there is another record of her 100 marks in annuity during her widowhood. Furthermore, in 1348 Katherine presented the dire straits of her financial situation to Edward III, including reference to the monetary damage of her seven-month defence of Lochindorb Castle. She claimed that Edward's payments to her were in arrears, that she had received no profit from the manors that he had granted her and that she had been forced to maintain her son herself. Katherine requested more manors to make up for the missing 100 mark sum, and that Edward recovered those losses. This seems quite a tall order for Katherine to continually expect from Edward, but it should be remembered that her husband had died in service to Edward and that she had been instrumental in retaining hold of a key fortress in Scotland's northeast. Moreover, her time at Lochindorb had prevented her from swiftly recovering her son's inheritance and her dower lands. Katherine surely felt entitled to Edward's financial support and to make sure that he paid in full what he had promised.

The record evidence for Katherine goes quiet through the 1350s and 1360s, except for her brief nomination of two attorneys in 1352 in which she is still described as a widow. Edward also granted a special licence to her son David in 1356, which would allow him to grant land from Katherine's dower. This was presumably done with Katherine's permission, as she does not seem to dispute it.

On 13 November 1368, the first of two inquisitions into Katherine's landholdings and heirs occurred, meaning that she had died by this date. Sadly, a similar inquisition would be held only one year later when her son David also died. Despite the financial difficulties and physical threats that Katherine seems to have endured through the 1340s, we can hope that the quietened record until her death means that the final decades of her life were spent in the peace and security which she surely deserved after being posed with such difficulties during the Scottish Wars of Independence. Indeed, Katherine's premature widowhood in 1336 and defence of Lochindorb heralded the end of her family's interest in Scotland, as her father Henry de Beaumont would never return to the kingdom in which he had so relentlessly pursued his wife's inheritance of the Earldom of Buchan. The death of Katherine's mother in 1349 was the death of the last Comyn heiress of that earldom.

Katherine's defence of Lochindorb was more than a military success for her king; it was the final mark that her natal family would leave on northern Scotland.

Agnes Randolph and the Siege of Dunbar, 1338

'That brawling, boisterous Scottish wench.'

Andrew of Wyntoun,
Orygynale Cronykil of Scotland

Agnes Randolph is probably one of the more well-known women of the Scottish Wars of Independence. Her defence of Dunbar Castle in 1338 has been immortalized in historical writing, and a somewhat stereotypical caricature of what one might expect a heroine of this warfare to look and act like has emerged. Indeed, Agnes' ambiguous nickname of 'Blak Agnes' and her supposed confident and antagonistic attitude to her attackers is in some measure comparable to her male contemporaries. Consider James 'the Black' Douglas, a revered heroic figure and spearhead of Robert Bruce's regime; cannot comparisons be drawn between him and Agnes, both in nickname and in confident military action? This perhaps explains why Agnes is generally the woman of the Scottish Wars of Independence who receives more popular recognition than others who were remarkably similar to her, like Katherine de Beaumont and Christina Bruce. This chapter will seek to explore the life and career of Agnes Randolph, in addition to telling the story of her intrepid leadership in her infamous defence of Dunbar Castle.

It is impossible to provide an exact and definite date for Agnes' year of birth, but we can attempt to make a general deduction of this based on the life timelines of herself and other family members. Dates for marriages and the births of children are particularly helpful in this regard. Beginning with Agnes, she received a papal dispensation to wed her husband Patrick, Earl of March, in February 1324. It is crucial to note that this dispensation was not confirmation of a new marriage, but rather permission for Agnes and Patrick 'to remain in the marriage they have contracted, declaring their past and future offspring legitimate.' This does not necessarily confirm that Agnes and Patrick had produced any children before 1324 – the inclusion of this in the dispensation was standard practice for marriages contracted prior to receipt of a papal dispensation. However, it does indicate that Agnes had married for the first time by February 1324. This provides a general idea for her age, with elite wives entering marriage contracts for the first time usually during their teenage years, narrowing the year of her birth to the early 1300s. Her parents, Thomas Randolph, 1st Earl of Moray, and Isabella Stewart of Bonkyll, were certainly married at some point during 1300-1310, on account of Agnes' age for her marriage by 1324. Additionally, Thomas and Isabella's two sons, Thomas and John, succeeded to the Earldom of Moray in 1332 without their succession being challenged based on being minors upon the death of their father in July 1332 (Thomas the younger would be killed less than a month later, with John succeeding). The younger Thomas died unmarried and without children in 1332, with John not marrying until around 1343, which may suggest that both brothers, while not minors, were young at the time of their father's death and resultantly unmarried.

The life events for Thomas and John, in addition to Agnes, might possibly mean that Thomas and Isabella were married closer to 1310. Indeed, there are factors which may support this. Thomas Randolph was knighted in the spring of 1306, possibly at the inauguration ceremony of his uncle, Robert Bruce, in March of that year. By the time Thomas was captured at the Battle of Methven in June 1306 and imprisoned in England, he was described as 'a newly made knight'. Young men were generally knighted between the ages of sixteen and twenty-one during this period, highlighting that Thomas was perhaps still a bachelor in 1306. He then briefly defected to the English, before reconciling with his uncle in 1308 after being captured by James Douglas. Indeed, from his resubmission to Robert in 1308, Thomas appears to have been thoroughly welcomed back into the Bruce party and quickly rose through the ranks to become one of Robert's closest lieutenants. It could be suggested that as a reward or celebration for his support for Robert, Thomas' marriage to Isabella Stewart of Bonkyll was arranged around this time. Issuing 'rewards' to his supporters was a method which Robert continually employed, and therefore could be a plausible reasoning for Thomas and Isabella's marriage to have occurred somewhere between 1308 and 1310. This would provide a general idea of a year of birth for

Agnes Randolph, in time for her marriage to Patrick, Earl of March, before 1324.

To fully appreciate Agnes' success at the Siege of Dunbar, it would be beneficial to first understand the weight of the family legacy that she held. Agnes was the daughter of one of the most important leading figures of the Scottish Wars of Independence: Thomas Randolph, Earl of Moray. His loyal support for Robert Bruce throughout his reign could be attributed to the two men's blood relation – Randolph's mother was Robert's half-sister – but his brief capture and defection to the English from 1306 to 1308 undermines this. While family ties no doubt did play a part in Randolph's decision to fully commit himself to the Bruce regime from 1308, he must have been a trustworthy and capable character in addition to being a loyal half-nephew. His military accomplishments were many: the capture of the impenetrable Edinburgh Castle in 1314; the command of one division of the Scottish army at the Battle of Bannockburn in June 1314 (the other two commanded by Bruce himself and his brother, Edward Bruce); accompanying Edward Bruce on the Bruce campaign in Ireland from 1315 to 1318; capturing the hotly-contested border burgh of Berwick in 1318; leading numerous raids into northern England; and co-commanding victories on English soil at the Battle of Myton in 1319, the Battle of Old Byland in 1322 and the Battle of Stanhope Park in 1327 alongside Sir James 'the Black' Douglas.

Randolph's obvious military prowess had carved his place amongst the heroes of the Bruce dynasty, but his iconic role was only to be compounded by his political and diplomatic achievements. Arguably, this was a role in which none other of Robert Bruce's loyal lieutenants excelled to the extent which Randolph did. The Declaration of Arbroath, one of three letters written to Pope John XXII advocating for Robert's kingship and Scotland's position as a sovereign kingdom, heralded a new wave of European diplomatic efforts by the Scots, predominantly represented by Randolph. Indeed, the Declaration appears to have set up Randolph's incoming role as a diplomat, as his name follows that of the King of Scots in the document. In 1323, alongside the Bishop of St Andrews, William Lamberton, Randolph was a leading representative of the Scots in negotiations for peace with the English, which resulted in the agreement of a thirteen-year truce between the two kingdoms. A year later, Randolph represented the King of Scots in a meeting in

Avignon with the Pope himself. This papal mission was successful to an unprecedented extent; Randolph managed to convince the Pope to recognize Robert Bruce as King of Scots after nearly twenty years of papal opposition to the Bruce regime, in exchange for the Scots pushing for peace with England. Randolph's success in this and evidence of the same trustworthy and confident character as the early years can be seen in a personal letter to him from Pope John XXII in 1325, in which the Pope both re-emphasized his hope that Randolph would sue for peace and granted permission for Randolph to go on pilgrimage to the Holy Sepulchre in Jerusalem. That same year, Randolph was again on a diplomatic mission, this time to successfully persuade Charles IV of France to sign a renewal of the Auld Alliance between Scotland and France, known as the Treaty of Corbeil.

The capabilities which saw Randolph become a prominent military and diplomatic figure were surely the same that secured his rapid rise to land and title as a key lieutenant to Robert I of Scotland. His monumental elevation to the rank of earl in 1312 is early evidence of this, with Robert creating the Earldom of Moray specifically for his half-nephew to replace the power vacuum left behind by the decimated Comyns. Randolph's popularity as a key figure of the Bruce regime also resulted in him becoming Prince Regent upon the death of Robert I in 1329, tasked with governing the kingdom during the minority of Robert's son and heir, David. A role which may have been taken advantage of as a grasp for the throne, especially considering that Robert and Thomas did share blood, Randolph instead appears to have governed well and genuinely in representation of an absent monarch. His sudden death in Musselburgh in July 1332, while probably of natural causes, was evidently viewed as a disaster by the Scots as rumours of him being poisoned by Bruce enemies soon spread. Ultimately, Randolph was one of the most influential and powerful political individuals of fourteenth-century Scotland. While his inheritance passed to his sons, his monumental legacy was carried by all of his children in their actions and own capability of character. And so we come to Agnes Randolph.

The heroic and skilled military leadership enacted by Agnes in her valiant defence of Dunbar would not be the only piece of her father's legacy she would display. On 17 October 1346, a Scottish army led by King David II of Scotland, successor to Robert I, was disastrously defeated by a smaller English army headed by Lord Ralph Neville and the Archbishop of York, William de la Zouche. This key event of the second stage of the Scottish Wars of Independence was catastrophic for the stability of the Bruce regime as it resulted in the captivity of David in England for the following eleven years, in addition to the deaths and capture of the majority of David's household and close supporters. This included the death of John Randolph, the third and final Randolph Earl of Moray and brother of Agnes Randolph. In the absence of the monarch and under the *laissez-faire* guardianship of David's nephew, Robert Stewart, Scottish magnates were able to capitalize on the power vacuum left behind as a result of Neville's Cross. This included Agnes Randolph and her husband Patrick, Earl of March. Only Agnes and her sister, Isabella, remained of the four children of Thomas Randolph. Agnes was clearly the elder sister – this is consistent with the earlier assessment of her potential year of birth – as in the wake of her brother's death she and Patrick assumed control of the Moray estates. This not only included the Earldom of Moray, but also the Isle of Man and swathes of baronies across lordships in southern Scotland, from Berwickshire in the southeast to Galloway, Ayrshire and Clydesdale in the west. These southern lands would especially suit Patrick's interest; he was earl of the southeast Earldom of March and a prominent border military leader. Essentially, Agnes Randolph became her father's heiress and one of the most influential female elite figures in Scotland. She had more than proved her place amongst the Randolph legacy through her actions in defending Dunbar; now she had the inheritance to reaffirm her position. Indeed, Agnes' personal seal displayed the heraldry of Dunbar and Moray alongside her title: Agnes, Countess of March and Moray.

However, it does remain curious that even upon the return of David II to Scotland in 1357, with a whopping ransom of 100,000 marks to contend with, Agnes and Patrick remained in authority of the Earldom of Moray. Upon death of this countess and earl by 1368 without heirs, David ensured the smooth inheritance of the Earldom of March by Agnes' nephew by her sister, George Dunbar, but made no such contingencies for Moray and took the earldom into crown hands. The reason for this was based on the explicit legalities of the initial creation of the Earldom of Moray in 1312, when Robert Bruce elevated his loyal nephew, Thomas Randolph, to the status of earl. This earldom was held by a male entail, meaning that if Thomas, or his successors, failed to produce a male heir, the earldom would revert to the crown and become part of royal territory. Following Agnes and Patrick's deaths, the Earldom of Moray remained in crown authority until 1372, when Robert II saw to its inheritance by John Dunbar, another of Agnes' nephews by her sister. With the male entail in mind, it is interesting to consider why Agnes and Patrick were so able to take smooth control of the Moray inheritance following the death of John Randolph without a male heir. The chaos in the wake of Neville's Cross and uninvolved governance of Robert Stewart may be the reason, but even upon David's return to Scotland in 1357 he does not appear to attempt to correct this legal contrast with the male entail under which the earldom was created. Agnes and her husband clearly had no hesitation over what they believed was their right to inherit the estates of Thomas Randolph. Her death without heirs saw her father's earldom and legacy pass to her nephews through her younger sister, Isabella. All four of the children of Thomas Randolph, a leading hero of the Scottish Wars of Independence, held the inheritance of Moray; Agnes held it the longest, while Isabella saw to its future.

Context

The Siege of Dunbar lasted for approximately five months, with Agnes' defence against William Montagu, Earl of Salisbury, beginning in January 1338 and closing in June of that same year. Unlike the other three sieges primarily defended by women that we have already examined Berwick, Kildrummy, and Lochindorb – this siege generally occurred under different circumstances for the attacking army. The Anglo-Balliol siege of Berwick in 1333 was an opening act for Edward III's invasion of Scotland. Christina Bruce's defence of Kildrummy in 1335 was against a Disinherited earl in the wake of another English invasion earlier that year. Andrew Murray's siege of Lochindorb, defended by Katherine de Beaumont, was a key event of resurgence for the Bruce party in Scotland following Murray's victory at the Battle of Culblean in November 1335. By contrast, the Anglo-Balliol opponents of the Bruce party were not in the midst of a momentum of success when they besieged Dunbar Castle in January 1338.

Edward III's invasion of Scotland in the summer of 1336 to both relieve Katherine de Beaumont from Lochindorb and to tackle a potential French invasion can be initially viewed as a success. His brutal herschips (hardships) of northeastern Scotland cannot be understated. However, despite his efforts in subjugating this region of Scotland to his rule, this was difficult territory for Edward to retain long-term authority over at this stage of the wars. Andrew Murray's effective and singular leadership as Guardian of Scotland meant that no sooner had Edward withdrawn from the north and returned to England, Murray's pro-Bruce forces quickly began to deconstruct Anglo-Balliol authority in this area. The effect of Edward III's absence from Scotland was soon compounded by the opening stages of one of the most defining periods of warfare in Anglo-French history: The Hundred Years' War. April 1337 saw Edward's attention turn in primary focus to France; the following month saw the all-out beginning of war between the Kingdoms of France and England.

While the outbreak of the Hundred Years' War distracted any French military assistance from arriving in Scotland, the same effect occurred for the English. The majority of English military strength, including a vast number of English Disinherited lords, went to France, rather than north to Scotland. This left an ageing Edward Balliol, the long-term and would-be King of Scots in Edward III's plans, with limited military support from the King of England. Under Murray's guardianship, the Bruce Scots took advantage of this moment of isolation and weakness for the Anglo-Balliol occupation in Scotland. Much like when Robert Bruce focused on his Scottish opponents in Edward II's absence from 1307 to 1310, the Bruce Scots began a consistent tackling of Anglo-Balliol opposition in Scotland. Invasions into Fife and the Balliol heartland of Galloway saw key strongholds fall, while the kingdom north of the Forth became fully under control of the Bruce administration. Edinburgh Castle was besieged as other remaining English garrisons fell, with raids into northern England taking place.

The year 1337 also saw an attempted siege of the hotly-contested coastal burgh of Berwick, previously within Scottish territory, which had suffered significantly during the Scottish Wars of Independence. From 1296, the burgh became a regular target as both English and Scottish opponents sought to retain control of it for its strategic location and valuable trade connections to the continent. An attempt to besiege the burgh and its castle by William Douglas was threatening enough to finally spur the English into action after months of limited military response to the Bruce Scots' progress. This resulted in an English force, led by William Montagu, Earl of Salisbury, entering Scotland in January 1338 and commencing a siege of another coastal stronghold only 25miles north of Berwick: Dunbar. Like Berwick, Dunbar's position on the east coast of Scotland granted it advantageous access to the North Sea and the continental trade connections which lay across that water. A further factor which may have caused this peculiarly-timed English invasion was possibly the ongoing threat of a French military force arriving in Scotland to support the Bruce Scots. It could be considered that just as there were concerns about northeastern Scotland being a potential landing point for a French army in 1336, the southeastern coast of the kingdom was now viewed in a similar light. By attacking Dunbar, Montagu was both responding to threats to English control of Berwick and re-establishing English presence on this vulnerable coastline. Furthermore, Dunbar was the southernmost Bruce stronghold; seizing it would be a blow to the Bruce party's recent progress.

Coverage and Evidence

Agnes' defence of Dunbar is far more known than the likes of Christina Bruce, Katherine de Beaumont and Christian Cheyne, because it is more significantly documented. The two primary accounts of the Siege of Dunbar in 1338 come from Walter Bower's *Scotichronicon* and Andrew of Wyntoun's *Orygynale Cronykil of Scotland.* These two authors and their most famous works share various similarities: both chronicles are histories of Scotland; both were written in the first half of the fifteenth century; and both authors were Scottish churchmen. Bower's career in the Scottish church saw him study at the University of St Andrews, before going on to become Abbot of Inchcolm Abbey, an island religious site in the Firth of Forth. Andrew of Wyntoun was a canon and prior of St Serf's, in addition to being a canon of St Andrews Cathedral. It could be possible that these two iconic chroniclers of late medieval Scotland knew each other, and that Bower, writing twenty years later than Wyntoun, was aware of or perhaps inspired by Wyntoun's chronicle.

Importantly, these two chronicles are crucial for covering the Scottish Wars of Independence from a Scottish perspective and are therefore invaluable evidence for understanding this period of Scottish history. However, as with all forms of primary evidence, both *Scotichronicon* and the *Orygynale Cronykil* must be approached with caution. Neither author was alive during the events which took place at Dunbar in 1338, meaning that they cannot give firsthand accounts of individuals or occurrences, which leaves room for inaccuracies. Their sources for this event, and indeed the entire conflict, must have come from other written or oral histories of the period that are lost to us. The very written coverage of much of the fourteenth century may have been penned by different unnamed authors altogether and collated by Bower and Wyntoun. The likelihood of this is possible, with scholarship regarding Bower's *Scotichronicon* as a compilation of several works by different authors, with his comments and later account of the late fourteenth and early fifteenth century being appended to earlier original works. These original works include John of Fordun's *Chronica Gentis Scotorum*, an account written in the fourteenth century which covers up until the death of King David I in 1153. The portion following, book-ended by Fordun and Bower, is known as *Gesta Annalia I* and *Gesta Annalia II*, which cover the events of the Scottish Wars of Independence and are written by an anonymous author. This rather confusing jumble of chronicles utilized and edited by Bower is exemplary of the issues of consistency and accuracy in medieval chronicles. Earlier sources used by Bower and Wyntoun may have had their own errors and biases, before being extended and interpreted by Bower and Wyntoun with their own perspectives in mind. For example, Bower's prominent role within the reign of King James I of Scotland means that his interpretations of earlier events and characters can often be seen as direct symbolism or lessons from the past for the present, but not necessarily historically accurate.

The conflicting nuances of medieval chronicles and their authors should be kept in mind when using them to understand events in history. However, in the case of Agnes' defence of Dunbar, Wyntoun and Bower's extensive accounts of this siege are joined by commentary from other late medieval chroniclers from beyond the Scottish border. Additionally, the fact that Agnes' actions at Dunbar are so much more well-known than similar actions by other contemporary women alludes to this iconic event in Scottish history being remembered over the centuries in verse and song, propelled on by Bower and Wyntoun. There should be no doubt over whether her valiant defence occurred or not; this was a woman who left an undeniable mark on Scottish history and stands as evidence of the military involvement and vibrant character of women living in fourteenth-century Scotland.

The Siege

In response to the progress of the Bruce Scots in expelling Anglo-Balliol presence in Scotland and threatening the northern English marches, the Siege of Dunbar began on 13 January 1338. According to Bower, this siege was led by William Montague, Earl of Salisbury, accompanied by the Earl of Arundel. Montague's role in leading the siege is backed up by various chronicles, including Wyntoun, but the presence of other prominent English commanders is also verified by English sources. Sir Thomas Gray, a fourteenth-century English knight and author of the secular *Scalacronica*, claims that the Earls of Arundel and Gloucester joined Montague, in addition to Barons Percy and Neville. This is confirmed by the *Lanercost Chronicle*, a chronicle from the northern English Lanercost Priory which covers the thirteenth century until the mid-fourteenth century. This priory, hammered by the Anglo-Scottish warfare of the Scottish Wars of Independence, provides a crucial English perspective of this conflict and attitudes towards key figures which impacted the state and survival of Lanercost. In addition to English commanders mentioned by Bower and Gray, this chronicle also claims that the Earls of Derby and Redesdale and the Baron Stafford were present at Dunbar under Montague. If Gray and the *Lanercost Chronicle* are correct, then this means that Montague arrived at Dunbar in January 1338 with a sizable force.

William Montague, Earl of Salisbury, was an important figure to be reckoned with and Wyntoun's 'lord off gret bownté'. He was a key ally to King Edward III of England, having grown up in the royal household alongside Edward before serving the king's late father, Edward II. This background between Montagu and Edward made him an obviously genuine friend to the King of England, supporting Edward from his sudden ascension to the throne in 1327 and being part of an exclusive group who plotted with Edward for the coup against Roger Mortimer in 1330. Montagu continued to serve his king in military operations in

Scotland, and reward for his loyalty came in 1337 in the form of the creation of the Earldom of Salisbury. Such a reward could be compared to Robert Bruce's creation of the Earldom of Moray for his nephew, Thomas Randolph. Montagu was quite the enemy to contend with; he was the king's friend and a newly appointed earl, allegedly flanked by other key English nobles. However, his opponent was the unshakeable Agnes Randolph, Countess of March.

According to Wyntoun, Dunbar was targeted for siege by the English army in the absence of its earl and Agnes' husband, Patrick, Earl of March. As seen from the Sieges of Kildrummy and Lochindorb, elite women in fourteenth-century Scotland were more than capable and qualified in the sole management and defence of a castle household. Additionally, it has been pointed out that the defending women of Kildrummy and Lochindorb were deliberately targeted by their attackers for both the strategic advantages of the castle and for the political person of the female defender: Christina Bruce was the aunt of the King of Scots; and Katherine de Beaumont was the new widow of the invading David Strathbogie. This could arguably be the case for Agnes at Dunbar, as the *Lanercost Chronicle* claims Dunbar Castle was chosen to besiege as 'it was irksome and oppressive to the whole district of Lothian' and describes Earl Patrick as 'traitor alike to himself and the kingdom.' As Patrick's wife and countess of the 'oppressive' Dunbar Castle, not to mention daughter of Thomas Randolph, Agnes was likely viewed as acceptable a target as the castle itself. Indeed, *Lanercost* makes note that 'the Countess of Dunbar … was in chief command of the castle.'

The siege began. *Lanercost* describes that the castle was surrounded by a trench, before wooden outbuildings were constructed in front of the castle gate and pavilions erected as lodgings for the commanders of the army. Wyntoun and Bower both agree that Montague's first course of attack was using large siege engines to throw missiles at the castle, strong enough to make 'the towers tremble'. Despite such an undoubtedly terrifying action to endure, Agnes responded by sending a young woman out onto the castle battlements, 'adorned like a bride for her husband', to simply dust off the walls where the missiles had struck. Wyntoun notes that this was done deliberately within sight of Montague to anger the commander of the besieging forces, providing us with a clear insight into the character of Agnes Randolph.

Wyntoun writes that following this failed barrage, Montague and his companions were arguing about the next stage of attack when arrow fire from Dunbar struck the man beside Montague in a fatal blow. Montague replied by describing the arrow as one of Agnes' hair pins, and that 'her love shafts go straight to [his] heart' (translated). This seems to be quite a theatrical creative licence on Wyntoun's part, but Bower's account matches with the idea of there being a verbal jousting match between Montague and Agnes. Bower does not include the incident of the arrows, but instead describes Montague's next mode of attack following the failed missile bombardment. Montague 'renewed the attack with vigour' (Agnes' mocking dusting of the ramparts had clearly hit its mark) by using a 'sow' siege machine to attack the castle. Bower describes this as a wooden screen with wheels; this may have been a form of siege tower, battering ram or a mobile shelter for the English forces to get closer to the castle. Agnes responded to this threat with wit and violence, shouting out: 'Montague, Montague, beware, for your sow will farrow!' Her reference to a sow producing a litter of piglets must have become horrifyingly obvious to Montague with Dunbar's defence against this new siege attempt: 'With that, she caused an ingenious machine inside the castle to be drawn back for charging a missile, and a large heavy stone, almost like a millstone, came down from a high trajectory, struck the sow fiercely like lightning, and dashed the heads of many inside to pieces.'

The jeering conversation between Montagu and Agnes seems dramatic, but it is interesting that this bold and confident behaviour, particularly on Agnes' part, is recorded by both Bower and Wytoun, two separate authors of separate works. When we consider the earlier written and oral histories that both authors must have accessed to formulate their chronicles, it would not be surprising to suggest that an earlier account or infamous tales and songs of this siege perhaps included the clever verbal barbs of Agnes Randolph. Bower's introductory description of the countess and her actions at Dunbar sound more fact than dramatic retelling: 'The countess, who was commonly called "Black Agnes", defended this castle courageously. It is said that she was very active and cautious, showing manly feelings as she zealously incited her people to defend [the castle], and even ridiculed the invaders wittily with gestures and words.'

Bower correlates traits such as courage and zealous military encouragement with masculinity. He repeatedly accounted for this behaviour in key male military figures of the Scottish Wars of Independence who he portrayed as heroes, alongside other chroniclers of the period. Agnes' confidence is something that Bower could easily criticize for its perceived lack of medieval femininity; indeed, he does not hesitate to criticize other key elite women of fourteenth-century Scotland for political and personal ambition or assertiveness. However, his lauding of Agnes' courage and zealousness could mean two things: she was already a popularly celebrated heroine by the time of Bower's writing; and female assertiveness and bravery was accepted and expected in military situations, particularly in the defence of the home. Agnes' famous 'masculine' traits may also explain why her role in the defence of Dunbar Castle is so much more well-known than the likes of Christina Bruce and Katherine de Beaumont, whose roles are recorded but not quite in the same detail as Agnes Randolph. Her recorded behaviour sets her beside iconic figures such as Robert Bruce and James Douglas: she is viewed as a heroine of the Scottish Wars of Independence in the same light as its most famous heroes.

While Wyntoun and Bower's accounts briefly separate over arrows and sows, they realign again for the next two stages of the siege, albeit told in different order. Both authors describe Montague's next mode of attack: bribing one of the gatekeepers of Dunbar Castle to open the gates of the castle at an agreed time. This craftier method of warfare is understandable, as Montague had no doubt grown frustrated with the lack of progress in his costly siege of Dunbar, including the human cost of this military expedition. He surely saw light on the horizon when the gatekeeper accepted the bribe. However, unbeknownst to Montague, the gatekeeper was far craftier than the English earl and reported Montague's plans to his countess, who in turn formed her own plans for Montague's clever attempt.

When Montague's forces arrived at the gates of Dunbar, the English earl led at the front in expectation of the gate opening, as agreed with the supposedly treacherous gatekeeper. The gate opened as agreed and Montague and his force moved forward. However, a squire in the English army named John de Coupland (the same man who would capture King David II at the Battle of Neville's Cross in 1346 at the expense of two front teeth) was said to have sensed danger and thrown

Montague behind him. At this moment, the Dunbar garrison suddenly dropped the portcullis and trapped Coupland inside the castle instead of their intended target: William Montague. As Montague and his forces retreated, Bower records that Agnes 'shouted at him mockingly and said: "Adieu, Monsieur, Adieu!"'

Both Wyntoun and Bower describe that Montague also conducted a naval blockade of the coastal castle to prevent communication and resources from entering. After what was by this point weeks of siege, Agnes and her garrison were surely struggling physically and mentally. The toll of being trapped inside the castle with dwindling supplies must have been excruciatingly difficult, no matter how self-assured and unbothered an attitude Agnes presented to her attackers beyond her castle walls. However, the garrison was to experience a brief moment of hope. Both authors describe that Alexander Ramsay of Dalhousie, a prominent figure among the Bruce Scots, stepped in to assist Agnes' garrison against Montague's siege by sneaking past the naval blockade during the night in a small ship to Dunbar Castle. Entering the castle through the postern gate and providing much-needed supplies for the struggling garrison, Wyntoun is surely correct in his claim that Alexander's arrival brought great comfort to Agnes and her people. His presence must have been all the more comforting when in the morning he broke out of the castle with his supporters to attack Montague's besieging forces. The result of this attack is not recorded and may have only been a brief skirmish, but it no doubt wounded the already frustrated and strained morale of Montague and his army after months of siege.

These are the final stages of the siege accounted by Bower and Wyntoun. However, the *Lanercost Chronicle* includes another attempt by Montague to seize the castle. In 1335, Agnes' brother, John Randolph, Earl of Moray, had been captured by the English and imprisoned in the Tower of London. *Lanercost* claims that Montague had John brought to the siege at Dunbar and displayed him to Agnes in an attempt to pressure her to surrender the castle. Agnes' reply was 'that the castle belonged to her lord and had been committed to her custody, nor would she surrender it except at his command.' In response to her continuing stubbornness, the English besiegers threatened to kill John. Again, Agnes responded in total self-assuredness: 'If ye do that, then I shall be heir to the earldom of Moray.' This version of events may be testament to Agnes' commitment to defending Dunbar at any cost, but it is likely that this is a fabricated, or at least augmented, event promoted by the author of the *Lanercost Chronicle* to paint Agnes as a cold-hearted and ambitious woman willing to sacrifice her own brother for her political gain. Indeed, this event is strikingly similar to Christian Cheyne's experience at the Siege of Berwick in 1333, when her son was used as a bargaining chip by the besieging Anglo-Balliol army. Christian Cheyne's resoluteness ultimately cost the life of her son. John Randolph, however, would remain in English custody until 1340, when he was freed and returned to Scotland.

All chronicle accounts of the Siege of Dunbar in 1338 – English and Scottish – agree on the same factor which caused the end of the siege: Edward III of England. In June 1338, Edward ordered Montague and his commanders to call off the Siege of Dunbar and return south to support him in his war with France. The spring of 1337 had seen the outbreak of the Hundred Years' War, with Philip VI of France confiscating the Duchy of Gascony from Edward, who subsequently challenged Philip's right to the French throne. Although this was the defining moment to begin this conflict, serious military action between the two kings did not truly begin until Edward's invasion of France in 1340. Therefore, it is curious why Edward chose to recall Montague's forces and end the Siege of Dunbar in 1338. The *Lanercost Chronicle* states that Edward did not wish to go to war with France without Montague, and offered a truce to Agnes' garrison on the condition that they did not refortify the castle or remove the English outbuildings (the author notes that these conditions were not observed). Sir Thomas Gray's *Scalachronica* casts a more sinister tone to Edward's orders, claiming that there were rumours that any English nobles preventing his planned expedition to France would be seen as traitors. His account sees Montague understandably rush southward at this rumour, abandoning the siege, but claiming that the garrison was close to surrendering. Bower and Wyntoun both follow a similar claim; Edward so keenly required Montague's counsel that he refused to take no action unless he was with him to advise. As far as can be seen, the remainder of 1338 saw no serious military action taken by Edward against France. The rushed end to the Siege of Dunbar may suggest that there was a planned invasion that did not occur, or that Edward was focusing on preparation for his invasion in 1340. Although twenty-six years old, Edward may have simply required the advice and guidance of his old friend, William Montague, during a heightened time of war and political tension.

Whatever the reasoning behind Edward's order to recall the Siege of Dunbar, 16 June 1338 saw the abandonment of the siege. This had been a long and costly five months for Montague, with no result to show for his efforts. In Bower's words, William Montague, Earl of Salisbury, 'dishonourably returned to his own land.' Wyntoun, of course, sees Montague leave with a vow and a defeated lament:

> "I vow to God, scho beris hir weill,
> That Scottish wenche with hir ploddeil [band of thieves],
> For come I early, come I late,
> I find ay Annes at the yait [gate]."

Conclusion

It is difficult to understand where and what Agnes did next in her life and career. As has been shown, pinpointing the movement and activity of medieval elite women in Scotland is nearly impossible when they are not involved in specific events or with certain people. Despite her monumental role in successfully defending Dunbar Castle against one of the closest allies and friends of Edward III of England, there is little record of the rest of her life. As discussed earlier, she and her husband Patrick inherited the Earldom of Moray upon the death of her brother, John Randolph, at the Battle of Neville's Cross in 1346. It appears that she and Patrick did not produce children, as upon the earl's death in the late 1360s, the Earldoms of March and Moray passed to his and Agnes' nephews by her sister, Isabella; George inherited March, and John inherited Moray.

It is deeply frustrating, and somewhat an injustice, that we do not have the evidence to understand what occurred over the next thirty years in the life and career of this incredible countess. However, this is the unfortunate nature of studying women in medieval Scotland. Instead, we must focus on and celebrate the evidence that we do have and ensure that the impactful actions of women like Agnes Randolph are remembered. This was a woman who defied her enemy in unapologetically stoic and confident fashion. This was Agnes Randolph, Countess of March, and her iconic defence of Dunbar Castle.

Afterword

Women were drastically affected by the Scottish Wars of Independence. This book has sought to explore and prove this to readers who may be new to this period or to understanding the lives of women in the thirteenth and fourteenth centuries. Women lost a great deal in this war or gained from it. Women witnessed their families plummet from the highest position in the kingdom to being virtually wiped out, while some witnessed their family's own rise to power. Women were viewed as acceptable targets of warfare, from the victims of Edward I's sack of Berwick in March 1296 and Siege of Stirling Castle in 1304, to the Anglo-Balliol-Bruce sieges against women in the 1330s. Women were at the centre of the recurring crises of dynasty and succession that plagued this period. Essentially, this book has demonstrated that without accounting for the contribution of women, we completely limit our understanding of the Scottish Wars of Independence.

The research for this book took time and patience due to the sporadic nature of primary evidence that considerably impacts our understanding of women across the wars. However, while conducting original research and learning from the invaluable work achieved by other historians on this topic, I have been taught that there is evidence to formulate a greater understanding of the female experience of this conflict. Women have left their mark in different forms of sources, from chronicle accounts to government records, and more. I have done my utmost to use this evidence within the wider context to explore the lives and careers of women in the Scottish Wars of Independence.

That being said, this book could have been longer. There are broader thematic approaches that could be explored to a greater depth that would bring in evidence to analyse women of all social classes and backgrounds. Instead, I have chosen to focus on elite women for this book, telling the stories of the royal women of the Bruce dynasty and the noblewomen who fought politically and militarily for their survival. I have explored the female experience of hardship and triumph, from captives in cages in English prisons to victorious defenders of castles. What I hope to have achieved is to show that whether negative or positive, dramatic or calm, women were massively impacted by the Scottish Wars of Independence and played a crucial role in different areas throughout. I look forward to this one day being expanded to include more women of more diverse backgrounds.

It was an honour to research the experiences of the women of this book and to tell their stories. We stand separated by seven centuries, societal differences, social backgrounds and context. But there is a connection to women of the past, who lived, triumphed and suffered in the same land and whose stories have been forgotten by history. It is our duty to remember them.

Acknowledgements

This book was a labour of love. The writing of it would have been impossible without the support of many, many people.

Firstly, thank you to Kerrin Wilkinson and everyone at Pen & Sword for your guidance and support (and patience!).

I would like to acknowledge the assistance that I received at the National Records of Scotland (Edinburgh) and the National Library of Scotland (Edinburgh). I must also thank the incredible staff at Newcastle Castle who welcomed me to their site and provided me with further information about Mary Bruce's time there. The efforts of the heritage site staff are priceless, and I am very grateful.

Several primary sources for this book, particularly for Women in Captivity, were written in French and I am indebted to Océane Lopez and Dr Lindsay Randall for their help with translating these. Your time and help provided me with a deeper understanding of what these captive women endured: thank you.

To Alyth Allen, Clara Chamberlain, and Hannah Crooks for their assistance in hunting down certain materials across the United Kingdom: I am so appreciative.

I would also like to thank Christopher Riley for providing thought-provoking discussions about the reign of Edward III of England, especially regarding the outbreak of the Hundred Years' War and its impact on events in Scotland. Your knowledge of this was incredibly helpful.

I have been fortunate enough to be taught and supervised about the Scottish Wars of Independence by several incredible educators, from my time at Cumbernauld Academy to my undergraduate and postgraduate degrees at the University of Stirling. Their passion for the subject and their encouragement of my research and quest to tell more people about the women of the wars and the wider period have been instrumental in allowing me to be where I am today. I will always be grateful to them for inspiring the younger Beth who first fell head-over-heels for medieval Scotland.

I would like to thank the wonderful online community of supporters that I am so blessed to have on Instagram and Substack. Unfortunately, you are far too many to name individually, but every message and comment of support or chat about Scottish history has brought me so much joy. This book is because of you.

Finally, there are countless friends who have supported me through the journey of writing this book – too many to name here – and I am beyond thankful for their love. I must also try to express my gratitude to my family, but I am not sure I will ever have the words to do justice to their unconditional love, kindness and encouragement. To my parents, Pete and Helen, for raising me with faith in my dreams and for always being there. To my sister, Louise, for the endless voice notes, pep-talks, and excitement in my achievements. To my husband, Dan, for being my greatest cheerleader and most patient advisor: I am so grateful for everything.

Bibliography

For any readers interested in diving into certain themes, events, or individuals that have been covered in this book, the following bibliography notes in full of the primary and secondary sources consulted.

As a starting point, the *Oxford Dictionary of National Biography* is a helpful online resource for researching the lives of key figures from this period. *People of Medieval Scotland 1093–1371* is another particularly useful resource as an online database for people of Scotland mentioned in documents from 1093 to 1371. Another invaluable online database is *Records of the Parliaments of Scotland,* which views the parliamentary and council proceedings during the reigns of kings and queens of Scots. Finally, *Canmore* is an online collection of Scotland's built heritage, and was a crucial resource for researching certain castles covered in this book.

There are a number of key general texts that are essential reading for covering the Scottish Wars of Independence, including the reigns of Robert I and David II of Scotland, and Edward I, Edward II, and Edward III of England. The following works provided historical context throughout this book:

Barrell, A. D. M., *Medieval Scotland,* (Cambridge: Cambridge University Press, 2000).

Barrow, G. W. S., *Robert the Bruce and the Community of the Realm of Scotland,* (Edinburgh: Edinburgh University Press, 1988).

Beam, Amanda, *The Balliol Dynasty, 1210–1364*, (Edinburgh: John Donald, 2008).

Brown, Michael, *The Black Douglases: War and Lordship in Late Medieval Scotland, 1300–1455* (East Linton: Tuckwell Press, 1998).

Brown, Michael, *The Wars of Scotland, 1214–1371,* (Edinburgh: Edinburgh University Press, 2002).

Duncan, A. A. M, *The Kingship of the Scots, 842–1292: Succession and Independence,* (Edinburgh: Edinburgh University Press, 2002).

MacInnes, Iain A., *Scotland's Second War of Independence, 1332–1357,* (Boydell Press, 2016).

McNamee, Colm, *The Wars of the Bruces: Scotland, England and Ireland 1306–1328* (Edinburgh: Birlinn Ltd, 2022).

Morris, Marc, *A Great and Terrible King: Edward I and the Forging of Britain* (London: Windmill Books, 2009).

Penman, Michael, *David II, 1329–71,* (East Linton: Tuckwell Press, 2004).

Penman, Michael, *Robert the Bruce: King of the Scots,* (London: Yale University Press, 2014).

Warner, Kathryn, *Edward II: The Unconventional King,* (Stroud: Amberley Publishing, 2015).

In general, the study of medieval women is an ever-expanding field, and there are a number of texts which have been incredibly informative throughout this book for understanding what the lives, careers, responsibilities, and agency of thirteenth to fourteenth century noblewomen looked like in different contexts:

Archer, Rowena E. 'Rich Old Ladies: The Problem of Late Medieval Dowagers'. In *Property and Politics: Essays in Later Medieval English History*, edited by A. J. Pollard, (New York: St Martins, 1985).

Archer, Rowena E. 'How Ladies … Who Live on Their Manor's Ought to Manage Their Households and Estates'. In *Woman is a Worthy Wight: Women in English Society, 1200–1500,* edited by P. J. P. Goldberg, (Stroud: Sutton, 1997).

Castor, Helen, *She-Wolves: The Women Who Ruled England Before Elizabeth,* (London: Bloomsbury House, 2015).

Coss, Peter, *The Lady in Medieval England,* (Stroud: Sutton, 2000).

Earenfight, Theresa, *Women and Wealth in Late Medieval Europe,* (New York: Palgrave Macmillan, 2010).

Goldberg, P. J. P, *Woman is a Worthy Wight: Women in English Society, 1200–1500,* (Stroud: Sutton, 1992).
Mate, Mavis E, *Women in Medieval English Society,* (Cambridge: Cambridge University Press, 2008).
Mitchell, Linda E, *Joan de Valence: the Life and Influence of a Thirteenth Century Noblewoman*, (New York: Palgrave MacMillan, 2016).
Sheridan Walker, Sue, *Wife and Widow in Medieval England* (Michigan: The University of Michigan Press, 1997).
Sjursen, Katrin E. 'The War of the Two Jeannes: Rulership in the Fourteenth Century'. *Medieval Feminist Forum* 51 (2015): 4–40.
Sjursen, Katrin E. 'Pirate, Traitor, Wife: Jean of Belleville and the Categories of Fourteenth Century French Noblewomen'. In *Medieval Elite Women and the Exercise of Power, 1100–1400: Moving beyond the Execeptionalist Debate*, edited by Heather J. Tanner, (New York: Palgrave Macmillan, 2020).
Tanner, Heather J, *Medieval Elite Women and the Exercise of Power, 1100–1400: Moving Beyond the Exceptionalist Debate,* (New York: Palgrave Macmillan, 2020).
Ward, Jennifer. 'Noblewomen, Family and Identity in Later Medieval Europe'. In *Nobles and Nobility*, edited by Anne Duggan, (Suffolk: Boydell and Brewer, 2002).
Ward, Jennifer, *Women in England in the Middle Ages,* (New York: Hambledon Continuum, 2006).
Ward, Jennifer, *Elizabeth de Burgh, Lady of Clare (1295-1360): Household and Other Records,* (Woodbridge: The Boydell Press, 2014).

The study of medieval women in Scotland has not progressed as much when compared with England and wider European kingdoms, which can be largely explained by the difficulties with primary evidence for this period in Scottish history. However, there are invaluable works which have shed much light on understanding women of thirteenth and fourteenth-century Scotland. Some key texts are below, alongside recent research papers and unpublished doctoral theses which focus on specific women within certain themes:

Bennett, S., Byatt, M., Main, J., Oliver, A., Trythall, J. *Women of Moray* (Edinburgh: Luath Press Ltd, 2012).

Boardman, Stephen. 'Lords and Women, Women as Lords: The Career of Margaret Stewart, Countess of Angus'. In *Kings, Lords and Men in Scotland and Britain: 1300–1625*, edited by Boardman, Stephen, and Goodare Julian, (Edinburgh: Edinburgh University Press, 2014).

Cochran-Yu, David Kyle. 'A keystone of contention: The Earldom of Ross, 1215–1517'. (Unpublished doctoral thesis, University of Glasgow, 2016).

Ewan, Elizabeth, and Meikle, Maureen M., eds., *Women in Scotland, c.1100–c.1750,* (East Linton, Tuckwell Press, 1999).

Ewan, Elizabeth *et al* eds., *The New Biographical Dictionary of Scottish Women,* (Edinburgh: Edinburgh University Press, 2018).

Jack, Katy. 'Decline and Fall: The earls and earldom of Mar c.1281–1513'. (Unpublished doctoral thesis, University of Stirling, 2016).

Marshall, Rosalind, *Virgins and Viragos: A History of Women in Scotland from 1080–1980,* (Chicago: Academy Chicago Ltd., 1980).

Marshall, Rosalind, *Scottish Queens, 1034–1714,* (East Linton: Tuckwell Press, 2003).

Sutherland, Elizabeth, *Five Euphemias: Women in Medieval Scotland, 1200–1420,* (London: Constable and Company Limited, 1999).

Women in the Scottish Wars of Independence have not gone unnoticed in historiography, and there are several works which were informative for specific events covered in this book, particularly in relation to warfare. There are a number of works which focus on how women involved in warfare during this period have been represented in literature covering the conflict, while recent years have seen greater research attention given to the actual military events including women. Any readers specifically interested in the events or literature that the following texts cover should read these for more in-depth analysis and information:

Boorsman, Rebecca. 'Women of Independence in Barbour's Bruce and Blind Harry's Wallace'. In *A History of Everyday Life in Medieval Scotland* edited by Edward J. Cowan and Lizianne Henderson, (Edinburgh: Edinburgh University Press, 2011).

Dunnigan, Sarah M., Harker, C. Marie, and Newlyn, Evelyn, eds., *Woman and the Feminine in Medieval and Early Modern Scottish Writing,* (Basingstoke: Palgrave Macmillan, 2004).

Ewan, Elizabeth, 'A Realm of One's Own? The Place of Medieval and Early Modern Women in Scottish History'. In *Gendering Scottish History: An International Approach*, ed. Brotherstone, Terry, Simonton, Deborah, and Walsh, Oonagh, (Glasgow: Cruithne Press, 1999).
French, Morvern. 'Christina Bruce and Her Defence of Kildrummy Castle'. *Royal Studies Journal* (2020).
French, Morvern and MacInnes, Iain. 'Katherine de Beaumont, Countess of Atholl, and the Second Scottish War of Independence'. In *The Scottish Historical Review*, Volume 102 Issue 3 (2023).
Goldstein, James R. 'The Women of the Wars of Independence in Literature and History'. In *Studies in Scottish Literature* 26:1 (1991).
Royan, Nicola. 'Some Conspicuous Women in the Original Chronicle, Scotichronicon and Scotorum Historia'. In *The Innes Review* 59:2.

Primary evidence formed the backbone of this book. The bibliographies below detail exactly which printed documents or archival materials were used for each chapter of this book. However, I feel it is important to highlight some key resources that were consistently illuminating for various themes and chapters.

For a period of Scottish history that is so blighted by sporadic primary evidence, chronicles are crucial in our understanding of events. These should be approached with caution in case of author or commissioning biases, and we should not rely too much on them for absolute accuracy. Moreover, too many women are missing from chronicle accounts of the Scottish Wars of Independence. However, accounts of female contributions during this conflict can be found and can be incredibly useful. From women leading sieges and being taken captive to leading conspiracies and acting as bargaining chips, these are the key chronicles which were consulted throughout this book:

Barbour, John. *The Bruce*, A. A. M. Duncan ed. (Edinburgh: Canongate, 1997).
Gray, Sir Thomas. *Scalachronica: The Reigns of Edward I, Edward II and Edward III*, Andy King ed. and trans. (Suffolk: Boydell Press, 2005).
Skene, W. F., ed. *Johannis de Fordun, Chronica gentis Scotorum,* 2 vols. Edinburgh: 1871–2.
Watt, D. E. R., ed. *Walter Bower, Scotichronicon,* 9 vols. Aberdeen, 1987–99.

Wyntoun, Andrew of, *The Orygynale Cronykil of Scotland*, D. Laing ed., 3 vols (Edinburgh, 1872–9)

Wyntoun, Andrew of, *The Original Chronicle of Andrew of Wyntoun*, A. Amours, ed., Scottish Text Society, 6 vols (Edinburgh, 1903–14).

In addition to accessing archival materials through the National Archives and National Records of Scotland (details below for specific chapters), printed primary sources have been essential during the research and writing of this book. Below are key sources that were consistently used throughout to identify the whereabouts, finances, property, and marriages of women in Scotland, in addition to the experiences of women captive in England:

Bain, Joseph, ed. *Calendar of Documents Relating to Scotland Vol. 3, 1307–1357* (Edinburgh: HM General Register House, 1887).

Balfour Paul, James. *Scots Peerage,* 9 vols. (Edinburgh, 1904–14).

Burnett, George, ed. *The Exchequer Rolls of Scotland,* 23 vols. (Edinburgh: 1880).

Duncan, A. A. M., ed. *Regesta Regum Scottorum: The Acts of Robert I*, (Edinburgh: 1984).

Palgrave, Francis, ed. *Documents and Records Illustrating the History of Scotland,* Vol I (London, 1837).

Webster, Bruce, ed. *Regesta Regum Scottorum: The Acts of David II* (Edinburgh, 1982).

Women in Politics

Secondary

Barrow, Lorna G. 'Fourteenth-Century Scottish Royal Women, 1306–1371: Pawns, Players and Prisoners'. *Journal of the Sydney Society for Scottish History* 13 (2010): 2–20.

Everett Green, Mary Ann, *Lives of the Princesses of England from the Norman Conquest,* Vol III (London: Longman, Brown, Green, & Roberts, 1867).

Hayes, Amy, 'The Late Medieval Scottish Queen, c.1371–c.1513'. (Unpublished doctoral thesis, University of Aberdeen, 2016).

Neville, Cynthia J. 'Widows of War: Edward I and the Women of Scotland during the War of Independence', in *Wife and Widow in Medieval England* edited by Sue Sheridan Walker, (Michigan: The University of Michigan Press, 1997).

Neville, Cynthia J. *Native Lordship in Medieval Scotland: The Earldoms of Strathearn and Lennox, c.1140–1365,* (Dublin: Four Courts, 2005).

Neville, Cynthia J. 'Women, Charters and Land Ownership in Scotland, 1150-1350'. *Journal of Legal History* 26:1 (2005): 25–54.

Turpie, Tom, *The Declaration of Arbroath,* (Edinburgh: Luath Press Ltd, 2020).

Warner, Kathryn, *Edward II: The Unconventional King,* (Stroud: Amberley Publishing, 2015).

Weir, Alison, *Isabella: She-Wolf*, (London: Random House, 2005).

Primary

The National Records of Scotland: *GD42, Viscount Cowdray (Dunecht papers), specifically GD42/1; GD90, Yule Collection, specifically GD90/1/24 and GD90/1/25*

Bain, Joseph, ed. *Calendar of Documents Relating to Scotland Vol. 3, 1307–1357* (Edinburgh: HM General Register House, 1887).

Barbour, John. *The Bruce*, A.A.M. Duncan ed. (Edinburgh: Canongate, 1997).

Bliss, W. H., ed. *Calendar of Entries in the Papal Registers relating to Great Britain and Ireland: Papal Letters,* 20 vols. (London, 1893).

Bliss, W.H, ed. *Calendar of Entries in the Papal Registers relating to Great Britain and Ireland: Petitions to the Pope*, Vol I (London, 1896).

Brown, K.M., *et al. Records of the Parliaments of Scotland to 1707*, (University of St Andrews, 2007–2024), https://www.rps.ac.uk.

Burnett, George, ed. *The Exchequer Rolls of Scotland,* 23 vols. (Edinburgh: 1880).

Duncan, A. A. M., ed. *Regesta Regum Scottorum: The Acts of Robert I*, (Edinburgh: 1984).

Gray, Sir Thomas. *Scalachronica: The Reigns of Edward I, Edward II and Edward III*. Andy King ed. and trans. (Suffolk: Boydell Press, 2005).

Macpherson, D. *et al*, eds. *Rotuli Scotiae in Turri Londinensi et in Domo Capitulari Westmonasteriensi Asservati* (1814–19).
Palgrave, Francis, ed. *Documents and Records Illustrating the History of Scotland,* Vol I (London, 1837).
Skene, F. J. H, ed. *Liber Pluscardensis*, (Edinburgh, 1877–80).
Skene, W. F., ed. *Johannis de Fordun, Chronica gentis Scotorum,* 2 vols. (Edinburgh: 1871–2).
Theiner, A., ed. *Vetera Monumenta Hibernorum et Scotorum Historiam Illustrantia.* (Rome, 1864).
Watt, D. E. R., ed. *Walter Bower, Scotichronicon,* 9 vols. (Aberdeen, 1987–99).
Webster, Bruce, ed. *Regesta Regum Scottorum: The Acts of David II* (Edinburgh, 1982).

Women in Captivity

Secondary

Barrow, Lorna G. 'Fourteenth-Century Scottish Royal Women, 1306–1371: Pawns, Players and Prisoners'. *Journal of the Sydney Society for Scottish History* 13 (2010): 2–20.
Dean, Lucinda. 'Projecting Dynastic Majesty: State Ceremony in the Reign of Robert the Bruce', *International Review of Scottish Studies* 40 (2015).
Geltner, Guy. 'A Cell of Their Own: The Incarceration of Women in Late Medieval Italy'. *Women, Gender and Prison: National and Global Perspectives* (2013).

Primary

The National Archives: Ancient Correspondence, especially SC 1/15/135 (petition to the king by Elizabeth de Burgh)
Bain, Joseph, ed. *Calendar of Documents Relating to Scotland Vol. 3, 1307–1357* (Edinburgh: HM General Register House, 1887).
Barbour, John. *The Bruce*, A. A. M. Duncan ed. (Edinburgh: Canongate, 1997).

Brown, K. M., *et al*, *Records of the Parliaments of Scotland to 1707*, (University of St Andrews, 2007–2024), https://www.rps.ac.uk.

Burnett, George, ed. *The Exchequer Rolls of Scotland,* 23 vols. (Edinburgh: 1880).

Calendar of the Patent Rolls, 11 vols, 1272–1334 (London: HMSO, 1891-1903).

Calendar of the Close Rolls, 11 vols, 1272–1333 (London: HMSO, 1898-1906).

Duncan, A. A. M., ed. *Regesta Regum Scottorum: The Acts of Robert I*, (Edinburgh: 1984).

Gray, Sir Thomas. *Scalachronica: The Reigns of Edward I, Edward II and Edward III.* Andy King ed. and trans. (Suffolk: Boydell Press, 2005).

Luard, H. R, ed. *Flores Historiarum*, Vol III (London: Eyre and Spottiswoode, 1975).

Palgrave, Francis, ed. *Documents and Records Illustrating the History of Scotland,* Vol I (London, 1837).

Skene, W. F., ed. *Johannis de Fordun, Chronica gentis Scotorum,* 2 vols. (Edinburgh: 1871–2).

Watt, D. E. R., ed. *Walter Bower, Scotichronicon,* 9 vols (Aberdeen, 1987–99).

Women in Warfare

Secondary

Barrow, G. W. S. 'The Wood of Stronkalter: A Note on the Relief of Lochindorb Castle by Edward III in 1336', *Scottish Historical Review* 46 (1967)

Brown, Michael, *Scottish Baronial Castles 1250–1450*, (Bloomsbury Publishing, 2012).

Dunnigan, Sarah M., Harker, C. Marie, and Newlyn, Evelyn, eds., *Woman and the Feminine in Medieval and Early Modern Scottish Writing,* (Basingstoke: Palgrave Macmillan, 2004).

Ewan, Elizabeth. 'The Dangers of Manly Women: Late Medieval Perceptions of Female Heroism in Scotland's Second War of Independence'. In *Woman and the Feminine in Medieval and Early*

Modern Scottish Writing, edited by Sarah M. Dunnigan, C. Marie Harker, and Evelyn Newlyn, (Basingstoke: Palgrave Macmillan, 2004).

French, Morvern. 'Christina Bruce and Her Defence of Kildrummy Castle'. *Royal Studies Journal* (2020).

French, Morvern and MacInnes, Iain. 'Katherine de Beaumont, Countess of Atholl, and the Second Scottish War of Independence'. *The Scottish Historical Review*, Volume 102 Issue 3 (2023).

MacInnes, Iain A. 'To subject the north of the country to his rule: Edward III and the Lochindorb Chevauchee of 1336', *Northern Scotland* 3 (2012).

Ranald Nicholson, 'The Siege of Berwick 1333', *The Scottish Historical Review* 40:129 (1961)

Sjursen, Katrin E. 'The War of the Two Jeannes: Rulership in the Fourteenth Century'. *Medieval Feminist Forum* 51 (2015): 4–40.

Sjursen, Katrin E. 'Pirate, Traitor, Wife: Jean of Belleville and the Categories of Fourteenth Century French Noblewomen'. In *Medieval Elite Women and the Exercise of Power, 1100–1400: Moving beyond the Execeptionalist Debate*, edited by Heather J. Tanner, (New York: Palgrave Macmillan, 2020).

Primary

The National Archives: Ancient Petitions, especially SC8/226/11294, SC8/13/611 and SC8/73/3604 (petitions to the king by Katherine de Beaumont).

Bain, Joseph, ed. *Calendar of Documents Relating to Scotland Vol. 3, 1307–1357* (Edinburgh: HM General Register House, 1887).

Barbour, John. *The Bruce*, A. A. M. Duncan ed. (Edinburgh: Canongate, 1997).

Bliss, W. H., ed. *Calendar of Entries in the Papal Registers relating to Great Britain and Ireland: Papal Letters,* 20 vols. (London, 1893).

Calendar of the Patent Rolls, 11 vols, 1272–1334 (London: HMSO, 1891–1903).

Gray, Sir Thomas. *Scalachronica: The Reigns of Edward I, Edward II and Edward III.* Andy King ed. and trans. (Suffolk: Boydell Press, 2005).

Maitland, Richard, ed. *The History of the House of Seytoun* (Glasgow, 1829).

Maxwell, Herbert, ed. *The Chronicle of Lanercost 1272-1346* (Glasgow: James Maclehose and Sons, 1913).

Skene, W.F., ed. *Johannis de Fordun, Chronica gentis Scotorum,* 2 vols (Edinburgh: 1871–2).

Theiner, A., ed. *Vetera Monumenta Hibernorum et Scotorum Historiam Illustrantia* (Rome, 1864).

Thomson, J. M. *et al,* eds. *Registrum Magni Sigilli Regum Scottorum – The Register of the Great Seal, 1306–1688*, 11 vols (Edinburgh, 1882-1914).

Watt, D. E. R., ed. *Walter Bower, Scotichronicon,* 9 vols. Aberdeen, 1987–99.

Wyntoun, Andrew of, *The Orygynale Cronykil of Scotland*, ed. D. Laing, 3 vols (Edinburgh, 1872–9)

Wyntoun, Andrew of, *The Original Chronicle of Andrew of Wyntoun*, ed. A. Amours, Scottish Text Society, 6 vols (Edinburgh, 1903–14).

Index